# Daring Wives

# Daring Wives

INSIGHT INTO
WOMEN'S DESIRES FOR EXTRAMARITAL AFFAIRS

FRANCES COHEN PRAVER

PRAEGER

Westport, Connecticut
London

**Library of Congress Cataloging-in-Publication Data**

Praver, Frances Cohen, 1937–
   Daring wives : insight into women's desires for extramarital affairs / Frances Cohen
Praver.
     p. cm.
   Includes bibliographical references and index.
   ISBN 0–275–98813–9 (alk. paper)
   1. Adultery—United States.   2. Wives—United States—Sexual behavior.
3. Married women—United States—Psychology.   I. Title.
HQ806.P74   2006
306.73'6—dc22     2005034802

British Library Cataloguing in Publication Data is available.

Library of Congress Catalog Card Number: 2005034802
ISBN: 0–275–98813–9

First published in 2006

Praeger Publishers, 88 Post Road West, Westport, CT 06881
An imprint of Greenwood Publishing Group, Inc.
www.praeger.com

Printed in the United States of America

The paper used in this book complies with the
Permanent Paper Standard issued by the National
Information Standards Organization (Z39.48–1984).

10   9   8   7   6   5   4   3   2   1

*To all of the wives who dare to err,*
*repair, and create change*

# Contents

# Acknowledgments

The diverse influences on the writing of this book are multiple, stemming from various directions—personal, sociopolitical, and professional. The first influence began before I was born. As youngsters, my parents, Bessie, and Sam fled the Nazis in Eastern Europe for the promise of freedom in Canada. They were daring, indeed.

The sociopolitical climate of the sixties—the era of change and Second Wave Feminism—had a profound influence on my sensibilities. I am indebted to so many daring women who spearheaded the movement and changed the consciousness of a world. I stand on the shoulders of these daring women.

In a very early phase of our relationship, my husband Bob had faith in me. He dared to support my quest for higher learning and intellectual thought. My son Leland has supported my creative and loving sides, just as he dares to be true to his own creative and loving sides. I am fortunate to be the sister of Dorothy—a woman who dares to challenge herself to grow daily. I have also been supported and loved by my women friends—all daring, unique women with diverse voices.

My psychoanalyst, Dr. Roberta Jelineck, has seen me through many a trying time, encouraging me to dare to have my own voice. Debbie Carvalko, my editor, not only dared to give me a green light to say it like it is, but has supported my work with enthusiasm and zeal. Dr. Lew Aron has generously shared his vast insights into relational psychoanalysis and the human condition of love. I am honored to have him support my work.

Most important, I want to thank all the daring wives in my practice who dared to share their stories with me. It is not easy. My hat goes off to their daring and often painful efforts to gain insight for repair of themselves and their relationships.

# Introduction

*Most people would like to be delivered from temptation but would like to keep in touch.*
—Robert Orben[1]

*The universe is made of stories, not atoms.*
—Muriel Rukeyser[2]

Day turned into night in a matter of minutes. Turning on the lights, I checked my watch. It read 2:00 PM. An impending storm howled through the windows, catching me off guard. I had been lulled into thinking the unseasonably mild, almost balmy December days would go on and on. Spring in winter, a tantalizing treat, turned out to be merely a hiatus. My reverie suddenly came to an abrupt halt as reality set in. Julie had arrived. Usually composed and dignified, but now utterly devastated, she bolted into the therapy room.

"It's over," she wailed.

"Over? What's over?" I was thunderstruck by her disheveled appearance. She had been looking spiffy lately—svelte, coifed, and confident—a more empowered, sexy woman.

"My life's over," she shouted between sobs.

*Just when I thought we had turned a corner. Julie had come alive lately—more than alive—radiant, animated, even exuberant! Our work together seemed to be giving her a new lease on life—or so I thought. Julie and I were on a journey to access and express her true self, her authentic self, her innermost desires. She seemed to be making great headway.*

"What happened?" I was bewildered.

"He's leaving me." She collected herself somewhat at this point.
"Your husband's leaving you?" I inquired.

*Was her new expressiveness too much for him? Was she threatening him with her emerging desires?*

"No, it's not my husband; he's not leaving me. It's Hank, my handsome hunk; my delicious lover's leaving me. How could he?" Her eyes welled up again, and the tears poured relentlessly down her silk blouse. While I felt her abject despair, other thoughts came to mind.

*So, the lifting of her mood from despair to delirious joy over the last six months was not about the work, not about a turn of events in her marriage. What hubris to think that I had something to do with it! Her good spirits were related to an extramarital affair with Hank. Julie had not only found a new loving part of herself but also a new partner in love.*

Julie, in the above snippet of a clinical case story, is just one of many married women in my practice. She not only desired an extramarital affair, but she dared to go for it. She found herself in a quandary. In the following pages you will meet other daring wives with different stories, desires, dilemmas, and denouements. I hope by relating to some aspects of these wives, you will gain insight into your self, your marriage, and your relationships.

Daring wives choose to act on their despair by engaging in extramarital affairs. Rather than remaining inert in dead or frictional marriages and existing in quiet desperation, discord, and emotional anguish, daring wives choose to live more fully by engaging in extramarital affairs. Indeed, a rich life with love, even if it means temporary pain, is a far better option than a life not lived.

Marital strife and dissatisfaction are the most common reasons women engage in extramarital affairs. Many wives feel helpless and hopeless prior to an affair. Like Julie, they have not been getting their desires for attunement, mutual power, understanding, recognition, and sensitivity met in the marriage, so they seek fulfillment elsewhere. Nothing else seemed to work.

While an extramarital affair may not necessarily be the most prudent choice, it may act as a catalyst for change in the marriage and/or the self. People often stay in unsatisfactory marriages for the sake of their children. Parents in miserable marriages, however, only make for miserable children. The legacies for these children are blighted models of marital relationships. A daring change may thus be best for both children and parents.

Not only is the act of engaging in an extramarital affair daring, but the act of engaging in therapy is equally daring. It takes courage to enter a course of deep analytic therapy where you face your inner demons, your role in the flagging marriage, and your painful past. With insight, daring wives unravel tangled feelings of excitement and fear, joy and despair, lust and love, so that they feel empowered to take new paths for life changes.

I, too, have lusted and longed, loved and lost, despaired and dared to make changes. I am often plagued with the moral question of whether infidelity is a good or bad thing. I believe that there is no one truth about the morality of extramarital affairs, no cut-and-dry, right or wrong truth—but rather a relative truth. That said, most wives, however, feel their affairs empowered them to get on with their lives, so for them, they were a good thing. That does not mean that affairs are a slippery slope to moral decay.

As a society we need moral judgment, but not any moral judgment. We need fair, informed, flexible moral judgment; not arbitrary, rigid, prejudiced moral judgment. In my practice, before placing judgment my patients and I try to turn their infidelity inside out and derive meaning from it. Our hope is to gain insight and garner the courage to create fresh experience.

Infidelity depends on the circumstances and the individuals involved. I neither condone nor condemn it. Sure, some women resist their feelings, work on their problems, and find better solutions. But, not all women are the same; some act before they really ponder the problems thoroughly.

As we all know, we humans make plans, and God laughs. Things do not always work out as we have planned. We cannot control all the chess pieces on the board. The other players may have moves of their own that will affect us. Women's infidelity, in some cases, wreaks havoc in marriages and may end in divorce and/or violence. It is a risk.

There is a lot to consider. When we are caught up in the passions and pleasures of erotic desire, thinking beyond the moment of ecstasy does not always enter our consciousness. Indeed, we are merely human, with great possibilities and weaknesses. A famous aphorism by Harry Stack Sullivan comes to mind: "Everyone is simply much more human than otherwise."[3] So, as diverse as we are, we are inextricably bound by our common humanity.

Diversity, multiple meaning systems and values, tolerance for differences rather than dualities, arbitrary single-mindedness, and prejudice are themes that reverberate throughout this book. Wives engaged in extramarital affairs are lightning rods for discrimination and can readily be sullied with derogatory terms like slut, sinner, or cheat. When you read about these daring wives, you will no doubt see them in a different light. Each daring wife is a unique, multifaceted person.

Just as we cannot paint all daring wives engaged in extramarital affairs with one single brushstroke, neither can we paint a group of people of diverse colors, races, religions, ethnicities, or sexual orientations with one single brushstroke of prejudicial paint. Within our common humanity, we are all different, with diverse backgrounds, personalities, and proclivities. By grouping people into discrete groups of opposites, we fail to recognize individual differences and run the risk of making prejudicial judgments.

I have traveled a multitude of roads to hear the many voices of daring wives, to mine the multiple meanings of wives' sexual experience, and to gain insight into their diverse desires for extramarital affairs. To enrich the journey, I have drawn on disparate disciplines that are in dynamic dialogue with each other—psychoanalysis, feminism, postmodern philosophy, history, and pop culture. Lived experience is still one of the best guides, and so I have illustrated these theories with vivid case studies of daring wives in therapy with me.

As the daring wives disclose their most intimate thoughts, feelings, and desires in the case studies, not only will you learn what makes them tick but you will also learn a little of what makes me tick. As a contemporary, relational psychoanalyst, I will disclose my intimate thoughts, feelings, and desires as well. So you will be privy to the secret lives of daring wives and one of their psychoanalysts.

To protect the confidentiality of these women, who have courageously shared their most innermost secrets and fantasies with me, I have disguised their identities. The case studies are composites of the interactions between my patients and me: their relationships with others, my reactions to them, and their reactions to me.

No matter the analytic training that emphasizes staying with the psychic reality of patients, my own subjectivity, inevitably, enters into the analytic dialogue. Many of the women I see are wracked with inner conflicts between pleasurable self-indulgence—going for it—and repugnant morality, shame, or guilt. Together these torn women and I go from side to side seeking a balance, a way of tolerating the ambiguity, the contradictory feelings. Walking a tightrope with another person is not an easy feat. One false step, and one of us falls. I carry with me a marginal balancing bar of theory, analytic training, research, and clinical and personal experience.

Yet, I, too, may grope for a clearing in the fog of uncertainty. It is unnerving to desire concrete solutions backed by certainty in the wake of ambiguity and uncertainty—a paradox no less. We cannot, however, avoid paradox. Paradox surrounds us, infiltrating desire, love, and human experience. The ability to tolerate ambiguity and uncertainty strengthens the balancing bar.

Note that I use the term "desire" not only as sexual desire but mainly to signify a psychic self with will and agency. Desire and desperate need differ. Desperate need enslaves and diminishes. Desire, on the other hand, can be a liberating and life-expanding force. There are many times, however, that we are desperately in need. At other times, we have the luxury to desire. At still other times, need and desire coexist.

Many of us have had the desire for an affair. We may have harbored the fantasy of a fling. Some women, like Julie in the above case study, have dared to act on their desires. Other wives have not. Our desires may not be overt; they may be secret desires. Or we may harbor unconscious desires of which we are ashamed, so we disavow them. Like ladies-in-waiting, disavowed desires do not really disappear; they remain out of awareness, waiting on the sidelines ready to serve us later. Only by bringing hidden desires and lust in our hearts into awareness and gaining insight can we make informed choices.

Many a wife has lust in her heart for the half-naked body of that sexy film or television star. Male heartthrobs like Jude Law or Denzel Washington are baring their brawny chests in films, much the same as women have bared their bosoms. It seems the tables are turning. Formerly sex objects to men, women have come into their own.

Women are expressing their erotic desires more openly. Just look at the popularity of the Golden Globe award-winning television show *Desperate Housewives*. The racy show has struck a chord with American viewers as they identify with the dilemmas, desires, and actions of the sexy female stars. Recent films like *Unfaithful, Closer,* and *We Don't Live Here Anymore* also speak to the issue of women—not only men—engaging in extramarital affairs.

More and more wives are taking lovers outside of marriage, much like many men have done in the past. Women are catching up with men. Estimates indicate that approximately 40 percent of women compared to 60 percent of men have engaged in an extramarital affair. The fair sex has come out of the closet!

Women's sexuality has shifted with the sands of time, as have their choices. The changing roles of women have evolved over a rich historical and political landscape. The sociopolitical constructions of oppressive eras, double standards, artificial ideals, and unrealistic, rigid moralities lend insight into women's changing sexual desires.

Not so long ago, in the sexually repressive nineteenth century, the vibrator was developed for male doctors to use to induce orgasm in female patients. I wonder who benefited the most—the women or their doctors! You will read about the draconian double standard and the detrimental consequences for women's psyches and bodies, and for society at large.

In the twentieth century, second wave feminism—a formidable force—arrived on the scene. The movement awakened women's consciousness of their inner selves, allowing them agency and the will to make choices for change. A curtain opened to a stage of female actors, diverse yet united in their desires for recognition, autonomy, equal power, and the right to express their sexual desires. Feminism heralded the inextricable relationship between the personal and the political, an entwinement of individual psychic selves with sociopolitical and cultural constructions.

Scores of married women have stepped up to the plate of economic realities and gone back to work. You will meet working wives who shoulder the brunt of family responsibilities in addition to their careers. You will also meet other women who have left exciting careers to be stay-at-home wives, often resenting their husbands and feeling unfulfilled. Within the ranks of full-time working wives, part-time working wives, and non-working wives, diverse voices speak out. Some are strident, some are poignant, and some are otherwise.

Then there are younger women, older women, and women that overlap and fall between the age lines. You will read about younger women who define themselves as third wave feminists and their sisters steeped in traditional moral values. Despite differences, these young wives share some similarities. One of these similarities is the desire for personal and marital satisfaction. Failing to achieve happiness in marriage, these wives may desire extramarital affairs. Not only young feminists, but even conventional, religious young wives may engage in extramarital affairs.

You will encounter older wives, influenced by second wave feminism. These daring wives feel freer today to express their sexuality in new ways. One of these new—and not so new—ways is by taking a younger lover. Now, as we all well know, older men who enjoy younger women lovers are par for the course. Times are a-changing. By taking a younger lover, an older wife may be a daring trendsetter who deals a deathly blow to the double standard.

Among the various wives you will meet are wives who have remarried. They find themselves bogged down with excess baggage, stepfamilies, and chaotic emotions. Attachments to former spouses, problems with stepchildren, and financial concerns stir the boiling pot to overflowing. Along comes an attentive, younger man, unencumbered, foot-loose, and fancy-free— and bingo!

In one chapter I explore wives who take lovers of the same sex. A wife having an affair with another woman may bear a sexual identity as bisexual or lesbian, or she may define herself as heterosexual; it all depends on the meaning and significance she places on her same-sex affair. Indeed, the very definition of sexual identity varies from woman to woman.

Some wives choose variations of sexuality in which to explore their authentic selves outside of marriage, and you will meet two of these wives. These variations are only two of several unusual ways to express sexual desires. The women's behavior may seem outrageous, but if you can withhold judgment, I will unravel the poignant childhood trauma that spawned the behavior. These wives are neither good nor bad, saints nor sinners, beautiful nor ugly. They are all those things.

There are no black-and-white realities, no right or wrong answers. Each of us is unique, and we all interpret sexual desires differently. Internal psychic presences interact with ongoing experiences. In this book, I examine these interacting forces—the multiplicity of experience—to glean insight into women's desires for extramarital affairs. My examination is written in multiple voices: that of a clinician, a scholar, a raconteur, and a woman sharing her personal musings and meanings.

This book is for all those wives who are thinking about having an affair, who are having one, or who have had one or more affairs. My guess is, that list pretty well covers most of us wives. The book is also for husbands. Every man to whom I mentioned the topic is eagerly awaiting a copy. Husbands want to know why wives have extramarital affairs, where daring wives are coming from, what happens to their spouses, and what they—as husbands—can do to prevent wives from taking lovers other than themselves.

Much like the book that features women with men as their accomplices, I trust that women readers will also find male participants. Through a better understanding of their wives, husbands will gain insight into their wives' desires and inner lives. Men can also get a glimpse of the role other husbands played in the betrayal by wives. With this book, men will better understand what women want and need for intimacy. Regardless of gender, I believe we all would like to feel intimate with someone and to know that we have the ability to satisfy the intimate needs of another.

The meaning of intimacy cannot be reduced to sex. Indeed, it is so much more. Intimacy begins with mutual understanding and recognition of each other. I hope husbands and wives share their insights derived from this book and together are inspired to seek honest, open, and new resolutions to old conflicts.

I believe the book opens more questions than it answers. It may get you thinking, questioning your desires and actions and looking for answers from your own experiences. It is my hope that you will feel inspired to seek creative solutions that will bring you some measure of peace of mind, love, and fulfillment.

# 1

# Out of the Closet

## THE FAIR SEX AND INFIDELITY

*We cannot change anything unless we accept it. Condemnation does not liberate, it oppresses.*
—Carl Gustav Jung[1]

Shedding light on women's infidelity, historically a closeted and taboo topic, has swung into high gear. Once shameful and secreted, female indiscretions have come out of the closet. What has happened to our demure damsels—the fair sex? It seems wives are leading not-so-secret lives. The unspeakable is now a hot topic of public discourse. People are talking not only about husbands, but also wives who dare to act on their desires for extramarital affairs.

In my practice, wives are increasingly discussing their extramarital affairs. Of course, some wives are in therapy because of their husbands' dalliances. Husbands often are in therapy with problems related to their wives' infidelity. Although I have worked with numerous men having affairs, lately I see more and more women having them, too.

Is the gap between men and women narrowing? What about societal attitudes toward women having extramarital affairs? A look at pop culture may give us some clues.

## POP CULTURE IN THE NEW "MORAL" MILLENNIUM

Pop culture reflects the trends I see in my practice. The topic of women's infidelity sells national magazines, television talk shows, television series, and movies. The cover story of the July 12, 2004, *Newsweek* reads "The New Infidelity: From Office Affairs to Internet Hookups, More Wives Are

Cheating Too." The stars of the hit television show *Desperate Housewives*, launched in 2004, have made the rounds of national talk shows. Eva Longoria (who plays Gabrielle in the show) graced the cover of the February 2005 issue of *Self* magazine. The five stars of *Desperate Housewives* strutted their stuff on the cover of the December 29, 2004, *Newsweek*. The caption on the cover was "Mad about 'Housewives': Behind TV's Guilty-Pleasure Hit: Has Pop Culture Gone Too Far?" My clinical experience leads me to believe that pop culture may not have gone far enough. Indeed, people are hungry to hear and talk about daring wives who enact their desires for extramarital affairs.

The December 5, 2004, cover of the *New York Times*, Long Island section, reads "High Infidelity." The story is about infidelity of "real" suburban wives whose identities have been disguised. The cable "reality show" *Diary of an Affair*, which launched in 2004, features the torrid tales of "real" people. Unlike the *New York Times* story, in *Diary of an Affair* people's identities are not disguised. The participants are not just men; women are also coming forth with their stories of infidelity.

In two award-winning television series, *Desperate Housewives* and *The Sopranos*, the female lead characters engage in extramarital affairs. Gabrielle (played by Eva Longoria) of *Desperate Housewives* is dissatisfied with her marriage. A trophy wife, Gabrielle plays a showy accessory to her high-powered husband. He is too busy getting ahead to get into her. Feeling ignored and exploited, Gabrielle exploits someone else to gratify her. She dares to act on her desires and takes up with a high school hunk who services her lawn—not to mention her sexual desires. As an extra treat, women viewers at home get to lust over the buff body of John, Gabrielle's lover. Well, Gabrielle does not really get off so easily; indeed, she meets with retribution. Her husband is hauled off to jail for illegal dealings, the free flow of money stops, and her lavish lifestyle comes to an abrupt halt. She has been dealt a deadly blow. Alas, poor Gabrielle must go back to work.

Bree (played by Marcia Cross), an uptight and obsessive-compulsive woman, has shed her inhibitions and is reaching outside of the marriage to her pharmacist. Bree's motivation for her choice of another man is retaliation at her philandering husband. In a similar vein, in *The Sopranos*, Carmela (played by Edie Falco) dares to engage in an extramarital affair out of revenge at her husband, Tony (played by James Gandolfini). Indeed, Tony has engaged in numerous affairs, some one-night stands, and other more serious involvements. In all three cases, women's infidelity is related to misery in the marriage. These women are feeling justified, without a morsel of guilt. They are getting something out of their affairs—attention, romance, revenge, sex, and empowerment.

Recent films have tried to flesh out the desires of fictional women who dare to take lovers outside of marriage. Whereas the television characters react to troubled marriages, in film, infidelity by women may occur even in good marriages. In the 2002 film *Unfaithful*, Connie Sumner (played by Diane Lane) has it all—a handsome, successful husband in Edward Sumner (played by Richard Gere) and a beautiful home in an affluent suburb. To top it off, she is happily married. Indeed, the opening scene shows Connie and Edward in bed together, in a loving embrace, enjoying the pleasures of marital sex.

Despite all of her bounties, Connie is smitten by Paul Martel (played by Olivier Martinez). She simply cannot resist his seductive charms. She acts on her desires in chancy corners like a narrow hallway in a restaurant frequented by her friends. So the affair of the forbidden takes on yet another thrilling dimension. Extramarital sex is inherently risky. To top it off, the affair is played out in dangerous, dicey places.

Without justification for an affair, Connie ends up paying a hefty price for her lusty self-indulgence. Her guilty conscience devastates her, and her husband finds out about the affair. Unlike nineteenth-century heroines Anna Karenina[2] and Emma Bovary,[3] who dared to have extramarital affairs and killed themselves, Connie does not die. Her lover does. Perhaps her failing marriage and her internal pain and guilt are punishment enough. Even here, in the year 2002, there is a sense of moral justice.

In contrast to *Unfaithful*, where dysfunctional marriage is not the motivation for female infidelity, in the 2003 film *We Don't Live Here Anymore*, it decidedly is the case. The marriages here are in deep trouble—the impetus for wives having affairs. Terry Linden (played by Laura Dern) is married to Jack Linden (played by Mark Ruffalo). Edith Evans (played by Naomi Watts) is married to Hank Evans (played by Peter Krause). The two couples exchange partners. The affairs act as catalysts for change. Terry's critical husband demoralizes her. Even though he coerces her into an affair, she is devastated with remorse. Terry uses her affair as a signal for a marriage overhaul.

Edith's husband has casual affairs and ignores her. In turn, Edith has an affair with her husband's best friend. Rather than remorse, she feels empowered by the affair and decides to leave the painful marriage. The extramarital affairs for both women were born out of flagging relationships, and not undertaken just for fun.

The disturbing, sad, and salacious 2004 film *Closer* takes a different slant on women's infidelity. Here the relationships of two couples are not flawed; instead, it is the characters who are flawed and so very vulnerable. Anne (played by Julia Roberts) marries Larry (played by Clive Owen) and reengages in an affair with the sexy Dan (played by Jude Law). Unconscious, disavowed sadistic and masochistic traits are enacted in cruel and painful ways. Often, the sadistic and masochistic enactments are conscious and intentional.

Larry is a crude, superficial character who functions at a primitive, caveman level. Interestingly, he is cast as a dermatologist, where his work is only skin-deep. Anne subjugates herself to his animalistic power. I see similar attractions by many women in my practice. Are women still disavowing their animalistic, powerful parts? Do gentle, kind women desire rough, ruthless men in order to vicariously live through their power? Some do.

Alice (played by Natalie Portman) is a stripper, and she strips men of their power. She beguiles men and renders them her powerless slaves, placing her in the one-up, powerful master role. At other times, she reverses the roles with a man; she becomes the slave and he becomes the master. Her sadistic and masochistic sides are always split off from each other, and they alternate. Does any of this strike a familiar chord? Have you been on either or both sides of a power struggle for dominance?

In the above examples, the characters and the motivations for daring to act on their desires vary from situation to situation. Either the marriages are unraveling or the partners themselves are unraveling. Extramarital affairs are not undertaken merely as an expulsion of sexual drives. It seems our pop culture does not portray wives having affairs simply to express their sexuality— motivations are far deeper. Another telling aspect of pop culture's take on infidelity is that women taking lovers are right up there with men. So, in the media the double standard is beginning to wane. Indeed, in television and films the fair sex has come out of the closet!

While current pop culture shows women's desires for extramarital affairs stemming from inner problems or interpersonal problems, a glimpse of pop culture in the sixties and seventies tells a different story. Sociopolitical forces have always influenced women's sexuality, but never quite so radically as in the sixties and seventies.

## POP CULTURE IN THE SEXY SIXTIES AND SEVENTIES

Three decades ago, a sexual revelation swept the nation. At the height of the women's liberation movement, many women engaged in extramarital sex, not necessarily as a statement of marital dissatisfaction or of internal conflict. Women having sex outside of marriage were, in part, protesting society's repressive restraints on their sex lives. The unbuckling of pent-up sexual drives was an integral part of the social climate. The double standard in sexual matters was under attack, and women aimed their extramarital sex at redressing sexual inequality. Emboldened by second wave feminism, women donned a defiant "If they can do it, so can we" stance. Men were no longer the only ones to enjoy self-indulgent pleasure; women dared to do the same.

The "hippie" youth counterculture proclaimed a rebellious anti-establishment cry. The social mores of free love and openness of youthful hippies filtered into the sex lives of bourgeois couples. The freewheeling social mores of the late 1960s and 1970s were reflected in the popular culture offerings.

In the 1969 hit film *Bob & Carol & Ted & Alice*, Carol (played by Natalie Wood) is married to Bob (played by Robert Culp). Alice (played by Dyan Cannon) is married to Ted (played by Elliott Gould). The foursome tries on the hippie cultural trends of permissiveness, free love, husband swapping, and sexual openness. Marriage vows are not really broken; they are revised. It is not a matter of infidelity, as no trust has been broken. Candor is the order of the day, so women feel freer to be daring and act on their sexual desires.

In the best-selling 1973 book *Fear of Flying*,[4] Erica Jong coins the phrase "the zipless fuck," a descriptor of the open abandon of her hero Isadora Wing. Even though none of her lovers satisfy her in ways other than sex, Isadora dares to defy all convention. She engages in promiscuous sexual infidelity just for sex and the fun of it. She is a woman of her times. Throngs of women readers were repulsed, yet riveted to Isadora's sexy antics and Erica Jong's explicit, no-holds-barred language.

In a popular non-fiction 1975 book, author Linda Wolfe uses the title *Playing Around*,[5] suggesting that women took a cavalier approach to extramarital sex. Oh yes, the subtitle is *Women and Extramarital Sex*, suggesting that women's affairs are more about sex than anything else. Indeed, the author tells us that this was the zeitgeist in the seventies. It seems that women of her time took lovers as freely as they changed hairdos.

The pop culture of the sixties and seventies presented quite a different picture from that of our new millennium's "moral values" message. An ethos of free love—extramarital sex as a discharge of sex drives—has been replaced by a new morality. Wives' extramarital affairs reflected in the current pop culture offerings are more about conflicts in marriage or conflicts within the individual. Such also seems to be the case in my practice with wives daring to have extramarital affairs. These wives are distressed about their marriages or themselves.

Many other cultural forces of the seventies continue to influence women's psyches today. Once women's infidelity is out of the closet, it cannot go back into the closet. Indeed, once a bell has been rung we cannot unring it. Women who stray are causing quite a stir in our more conservative culture.

Female infidelity flies in the face of the new buzzword "moral values." Perhaps the paradox of liberal sexual behavior in a climate of conservative social values is part of the mystique, and perhaps the fascination has deeper psychological meanings.

## PSYCHOLOGY OF POP CULTURE: BEHIND CLOSED PSYCHIC DOORS

Speaking of paradox and conflict, what are the psychological underpinnings of the nation's entrancement with women's infidelity? What processes in our psyches are set in motion by pop culture's deviant characters? How does pop culture reflect our innermost desires, attractions, and repulsions? Pop culture has exposed sexual matters that were once hidden behind closed doors. Nevertheless, shadowy secrets may still remain behind closed doors, locked in our minds.

Audiences love to watch others take paths they themselves secretly long for and fantasize and dream about, but would not dare to take themselves. Unaware of these desires, they may remain unrealized behind closed doors in our unconscious. We may have felt dismayed, yet drawn to deviant television and film characters living out their desires. Perhaps the paradox of disgust and fascination is part of the intrigue of The Sopranos. Indeed, these characters dare to act out our split-off parts, our sadistic, salacious sides.

We psychoanalysts have some thoughts on this paradoxical phenomenon. Here is how I see it. We usually cherish our loving, kind, sweet sides and dread our hateful, sadistic, and salacious sides.[6] We like to be thought of as "nice people"—which is in line with our sense of our ideal selves. So, at an unconscious level, we go through uncanny transformations.

We disavow our dirty, dark sides and show the world our spotless, bright sides. But our disavowed parts, hidden behind closed doors, are itching to rear their ugly heads. These disowned parts may make their appearances in disguised ways. Passive-aggressive behavior is one way of enacting split-off sides. Another way is to spot them in others, which we call projection. Still another way is to vicariously experience them through others who dare to act on their detested parts. Television and film characters are perfect vehicles for our split-off parts to find themselves. They act as a conduit for us to live out vicarious thrills with impunity.

Many of us have identified with Carmela, the female star of The Sopranos. A long-suffering mafia wife, Carmela feels stuck in her marriage. She finally throws her husband Tony out and then proceeds to take a lover. How many of us have rooted for her? I know I did. She dared to do what some of us desire, but do not do. I'll bet you were disappointed that the affair did not work out.

As for Gabrielle in *Desperate Housewives*, many of us would surely like to be in her skin when she goes for it with her sexy boy-toy. Some women dare to go for it and identify with her, whereas others do not. Still others may not be aware of their disavowed desires. Nevertheless, very few women watchers turn off the tube during Gabrielle's illicit sex scenes.

The Oedipus story that Sigmund Freud made so popular comes to mind with Gabrielle and her younger lover, John. Freud's version of the story is based on a Greek myth, where Oedipus sleeps with his mother and kills his father. Of course, his mother sleeps with him, so her behavior is equally incestuous. Is Gabrielle's attraction to a young high school lad partly due to unconscious incestuous wishes toward a symbolic son? Is John's attraction to Gabrielle partly based on his incestuous wishes for a symbolic mother? Indeed, John has won the oedipal battle with Gabrielle's husband in more than one way. A penniless high school kid claims victory over an older, successful man. Now that has got to be a mind-boggling ego trip!

What about Connie's daring behavior with a seductive sexy hunk in *Unfaithful*? Not all of us get to meet a heartthrob like Olivier Martinez or would carry on with him if we did. In some dark hidden recess of our minds, the desire for such an affair may, nevertheless, be part of why we are mesmerized by Connie's steamy affair.

Women can also play out the oedipal family drama. The gender roles are reversed. So, unconscious incestuous wishes for their fathers result in rivalry with mothers and other women. We do not get to see Connie's relationship with her mother, but we get a glimpse of her unconscious competitive fantasies toward women. She has a torrid sex escapade within eyeshot and earshot of her women friends. Connie may unconsciously wish to be exposed so that she can flaunt her winnings to her women friends.

For many women in unhappy marriages, the characters and situations played by Laura Dern and Naomi Watts sure hit home. Their dilemmas are not a far stretch for women whose marriages are failing. But not everyone in a bad marriage takes a lover. Some women may disown their desires for a lover, condemning them as morally repugnant. They may unconsciously live out their disowned desires through Dern and Watts. Other women may be more aware of their desires and openly identify with Dern and Watts.

In the film *Closer*, we get a close look at the dark sides of people. The characters in the film are not exactly "nice" people. They are nasty, noxious, conniving, cruel, sadistic; or saccharine, suffering, sardonic, masochistic, and martyring. The characters have each split off one aspect of their personalities and projected it onto another partner who enacts it. So, sadism alternates with masochism, as do power with powerlessness; niceness with nastiness; and tender, sensual sex with crude, kinky sex. This film can be a field day for our disowned and despicable traits. If we are more candid with ourselves, we can see our detested parts in these characters. There is something compelling about seeing others act out our secret, or not-so-secret, dark sides. We may harbor implicit desires, but the characters of pop culture are explicit in their daring behavior.

Pop culture, of course, is replete with sensational stories of fictional female characters. Let us see whether statistics of non-fictional, ordinary women can give us the real scoop.

## STATISTICS OF SEX ON THE SIDE

The heightened focus on female infidelity raises still other questions. Just how many women are engaged in extramarital affairs? Is there an increase in the numbers of wives having affairs? Are wives catching up with husbands? Are extramarital affairs necessarily related to marital dissatisfaction? Can statistics give us clear, consistent answers?

In researching the data, I have come across discrepant findings on the incidence of women's infidelity. At one extreme, Shere Hite (author of the groundbreaking survey *The Hite Report: A Nationwide Study of Female Sexuality*[7]), in the more recent book *Women and Love: The New Hite Report*,[8] claimed that 70 percent of women engaged in extramarital affairs, compared to 72 percent of men. Hite asserted that wives were having almost as many affairs as husbands were.

At the other extreme, the 1996 survey by the National Opinion Research Center at the University of Chicago[9] found that only 11 percent of women engaged in extramarital affairs, compared to 21 percent of men. This study revealed that male infidelity was twice that of women's infidelity, which contradicts Hite's assertion.

Somewhere in the middle, popular book authors[10, 11] estimate the prevalence of women's infidelity at 30–60 percent, with male rates of 50–70 percent, only slightly higher. Similar to Hite, these authors estimated that women were catching up with men.

In a review of the popular literature, author Carol Botwin[12] reported an increasing rate of wifely infidelity. Her evidence was based on polls taken by Alfred Kinsey in his 1953 report *Sexual Behavior in the Human Female*[13] and popular magazines including *Psychology Today* in 1970, *Redbook* in 1975, *Playboy* in 1982, *Playgirl* in 1984, *New Woman* in 1986, and *Woman* in 1989. She found that the incidence of female infidelity over a period of thirty-six years rose steadily from 26 percent in 1953 to 50 percent in 1989—almost double. The author[14] concluded that men were still having more extramarital affairs than women, but that the gap between them was closing.

The scholarly research sheds additional light. Recently, researchers[15, 16] reported that women engaged in extramarital affairs almost as much as men did. One recent study[17] showed that the incidence of female infidelity was the same as that of male infidelity. With the exception of the University of Chicago study,[18] scholarly researchers corroborate the popular literature's assertions. They also find an increasing rate of female infidelity and a narrowing of the gap between men and women.

Recently, researchers[19] looked more closely at the national random data of the University of Chicago National Opinion Research.[20] Based on the University of Chicago's data, a new study of 4,118 participants[21] found, similar to the original study, that a greater number of men compared to women reported extramarital sex. Upon examining the age factor, however, the statistics took on a different meaning. At age forty-five and younger, the incidence of lifetime extramarital sex was the same for women as for men. This finding corroborated another scholarly finding.[22] Why might this be the case?

The growing number of women in the workforce over the past twenty years[23] may be a contributing cultural factor that explains the increasing rate of women's infidelity. Indeed, women in the workforce may have more opportunities than they previously had as stay-at-home wives. Opportunity, coupled with a greater feeling of power and financial independence, may account for some of the rise in female infidelity. Men have always had opportunities in the workplace, and now women have them too; this may partly explain the narrowing of the gap.

Another age and gender factor in the above study[24] struck me as salient. Whereas younger women showed the same incidence of infidelity as men, older women did not. Women aged sixty showed a markedly lower incidence of lifetime infidelity than men showed. They reported less than one half the incidence of infidelity that men their age reported. This finding coincides with the review of the popular literature[25] cited above. The author provided evidence that women in 1970 (approximately age sixty now) reported considerably less infidelity than women in 1989 (approximately age forty-five).

The wide difference between younger women (forty-five and under) and older women (age sixty) may reflect another cultural effect. The double standard may no longer hold as much sway in today's cultural climate as it did thirty years ago. So younger women today may be less influenced by the double standard than older women were.

Women born sixty-some years ago were the first generation to experience the women's liberation movement. Many of these women born in the late 1930s were still steeped in cultural mores espousing the double standard. While many women in the late 1960s and 1970s gained a new consciousness of their sexuality, not all women did. A sweeping sea change takes time. It took much longer for the notion of sexual equality to affect many a woman's behavior. So, this may partly explain why older women reported much lower incidences of infidelity than men, and younger women reported the same incidence of infidelity as men.

The candor of people's responses to surveys may also be a confounding factor. It is unclear whether younger women really engaged in a greater incidence of extramarital affairs than older women, or whether they felt freer to disclose this information than their more conservative sisters. Indeed, the double standard may affect both disclosure and true incidence, making it hard to tease them apart.

Perhaps the strongest finding shown by a number of researchers[26, 27] is the powerful relationship between marital dissatisfaction and infidelity. Upon further examination of the relationship between marital dissatisfaction and infidelity, researchers[28] found that relationships were on a continuum. Couples who were "not too happy" with their marriages were almost four times more likely to have affairs than couples who were "very happy." Couples who were "pretty happy" in their marriages were only twice more likely to engage in affairs than those who were "very happy."

In another large survey of couples, however, researchers[29] failed to find any relationship between infidelity and marital dissatisfaction. In yet another study, the researcher[30] found that the relationship of marital dissatisfaction and infidelity was greater for women than for men.

These data suggest that marital unhappiness is a large contributing factor to infidelity. Also, the degree of unhappiness may be related to the degree of infidelity. The data also indicate that women are more likely than men to have extramarital affairs because of unhappiness in the marriage.

If your head is spinning a little by now, be assured that statistics can be mind-boggling. Taken together, in the popular and scholarly literature, there is no consistent prevalence of women's infidelity across studies. With one exception,[31] there appears to be an increase in the number of women daring to engage in extramarital affairs; and women are catching up with men. The year women were born also influences data on female infidelity. The strong relationship between marital dissatisfaction and infidelity is greater for women than men. So women, more than men, are likely to engage in extramarital affairs when they are not happy in their marriages.

Still and all, the discrepancies among studies beg a crucial question. What are some of the factors that may confound or bias statistical studies of infidelity? Indeed, unseen extraneous factors may bias even stringent research. The nature of the questions posed to participants varies from study to study. Some studies are more rigorous than others.

Another extraneous factor may contaminate all research based on surveys or polls. The attitude and feelings of people who respond to surveys about an intimate matter like infidelity may very well differ from those of people who do not respond. For example, some people who are inhibited, suspicious, or too busy to respond may have engaged in extramarital affairs and are unwilling to respond. In certain age brackets, people may be more willing to respond candidly than in others. Whereas some women may be less willing to disclose infidelity, some men may exaggerate or brag about their affairs.

A different type of person may respond to a *Playboy* magazine survey than to a conservative survey conducted by the University of Chicago. People may withhold information, minimize, unconsciously forget or exaggerate, boast, and even lie.

So, what can actually be gleaned from statistics? At best, statistics can only be a guide, but certainly not a given. Statistical data across studies are not always clear and consistent. What seems to have greater clarity is that the topic of women's infidelity is the talk of the town.

Authors are writing books and magazine stories; researchers are conducting studies; and wives on television, in films, and in my practice are having affairs. In our era of openness, teens talk freely about their sexual experiences. Open a magazine, turn on the television, and sexy symbols boldly stare out at you. Terms like *transparency* applied to political and business figures are on the horizon. In an effort to provide *in vivo*, candid coverage of wars, reporters are "embedded" with troops. No doubt, the zeitgeist facilitates frank, public discourse of hush-hush, private matters; and that shows promise. Only through open dialogue can societal change take place.

In our more open society, the influence of the double standard seems to be diminishing somewhat, and women are becoming more daring. Indeed, female infidelity is out of the closet. How did this all come about? To understand the present, it is important to understand the past. Allow me to take you on a guided tour through the pages of history. The experience is bound to provide further insight into women's desires for extramarital affairs.

# 2

# Drastic Double Standards and Daring Wives

*Those who cannot remember the past are condemned to repeat it.*
—George Santayana[1]

*For most of history, Anonymous was a woman.*
—Virginia Woolf

## ANCESTRAL ROOTS

The years leading up to the nineteenth century revealed the roots of drastic double standards and daring wives. Before we embark on a path to examine the ancestry of the double standard, let us take a slight detour. One of the factors that have profoundly influenced the double standard of infidelity is the age-old nature versus culture debate.

### Nature versus Culture

Popular wisdom tells us that men are by nature more highly sexed and promiscuous than women. According to this logic, men must be more adulterous than women. It follows then that the double standard—acceptance of male infidelity and repudiation of female infidelity—arose out of these same, unfounded leanings. A social construction simply followed genetic proclivities. Hormones came ahead of honor for men.

In our evolutionary past, polygamy was the rule of law for most apes. Yet, the male gibbon, considered to be Homo sapiens' closest relative, practiced monogamy. Indeed, the male gibbon had a "wife" to whom he was faithful. The chimpanzee, however, practiced polygamy, and the female mated with several males in swift succession. What is more, she had no ties to any of them.[2]

It is unclear whether genes or the environment led to greater promiscuity for female chimpanzees than males. What is clear is that no double standard existed in prehistoric times. Much to our surprise, female infidelity was greater than male infidelity in certain ape species.

Of course, that information relates to apes. But what about Homo sapiens? Many people have bought the notion that, even in prehistoric times, men were more promiscuous, and in turn more adulterous, than women. I thought so, too, until I researched the literature and found that early history does not really support that notion. Similar to chimpanzees, at times in early history women were more promiscuous than men.[3] Scores of women died in childbirth, leaving them in the minority and more sought after.[4] Hence, a cultural construction influenced women's sexuality.

In the medieval period, the game of courtly love became the fashion of the day for the upper classes. In this game, a high-ranking married lady took a young lover of a lower rank. Does this remind you of high-ranking Gabrielle of *Desperate Housewives* taking a lower-ranking young gardener as her lover? Courtly love was a cultural construction in the twelfth century, as it is today.

In the early era of America's settlement, women in the Chesapeake area were in the minority.[5] Knowing that they could easily remarry, they engaged in extramarital sex rather freely. The abundance of men gave Chesapeake women more opportunities for affairs with laborers, neighbors, or business partners of their husbands. Once again, a cultural construction was the contributing factor to female infidelity.

Now, let us look at another cultural factor. Throughout history, human beings clung to each other romantically in threatening times, and were more promiscuous during peaceful times.[6] This finding is supported by current research. A new study on "terror management theory" indicates that romantic commitment acts as a buffer in times of terror.[7] Another study[8] suggests that close relationships regulate fear of death.

These findings led me to muse on the effect of our current era of terrorism on monogamy. I wonder whether men and women will be more motivated to seek greater romantic and sexual fulfillment in committed marriages, rather than in extramarital affairs. After 9/11, throngs of people immediately contacted their spouses. In my practice, an estranged wife contacted her detested ex-husband, and they went home together. Some of my married women patients who were having affairs called their husbands first and then their lovers. Inevitably, they spent the traumatic evening of 9/11 at home with their spouses, not their lovers.

Overall, in early history the double standard, commonly thought to be biological, has been mainly a cultural construction. One could argue that approval of male infidelity and disapproval of female infidelity has evolutionary roots. Indeed, the female's estrus cycle limits her ability to propagate the species, so, for survival of the species, males required more females with whom to mate. But we have come a long way from that thinking; education has rendered this notion obsolete. With a population explosion placing a strain on natural resources, countries like China limit birth rates. If we are to rely on archaic genetic or evolutionary theories, we will only perpetuate gender prejudice and the double standard. We cannot change nature, but through cultural change we can modify nature—a hopeful prognosis for humankind.

## DOUBLE STANDARDS FOR STRAYING SPOUSES

The double standard goes back to biblical times. King Solomon had 700 wives and 300 concubines. In sharp contrast, if a woman strayed she was stoned to death. Tragically, we still hear of adulterous wives stoned to death in some areas of Africa and the Middle East. In the second century in Rome, Emperor Augustus instituted penalties for adultery. These penalties applied only to women, not to men. Upon discovery of his wife's infidelity, a husband was mandated to divorce her. She lost her dowry and one-third of her property and was banished. Another man wishing to marry her risked criminal offense. Consequently, she was left humiliated, penniless, and alone for the rest of her life.[9]

In ancient times, adulterous wives came to a bad end, with one exception. If infidelity with a man of a higher rank led to a rise in her station, a woman was rewarded.[10] So, a conniving woman who bettered herself through a man was held in high esteem. At that time, the only way a woman could better her station, if not by birth, was through a man. So, even though she was not punished for her infidelity, her fate was nevertheless contingent on a man.

In ancient Assyria, adulterous wives had their noses cut off or were killed at the behest of their husbands. But, this was not the case if the adultery led to a rise in her class. Semiramis, married to an officer in King Ninus's army, took up with Ninus himself. She left her marriage and married the king. When he died, Semiramis ruled though her young son. Following an affair with King David, the biblical Bathsheba left her husband and married David. Bathsheba became queen and Solomon's mother.[11] Most of the time, however, the adulteress brought misery to herself or others.

In first-century BC Greece, excising of the clitoris was practiced to prevent female promiscuity and infidelity. Much to our dismay, these ghastly practices persist among fundamentalist Muslim and African women today. A shocking statistic, reported in the *London Observer* in 1970, informs us that 90 percent of women interviewed by the Cairo Family Planning Association had had some part of the clitoris or labia removed.[12]

The Christian church from the seventh to the eleventh century had a formidable influence on people's sex lives. Sex was transformed into a sin,[13] and society plunged into the Dark Ages. The Hebraic and Greek negative view of women as sexually voracious temptresses of righteous men permeated the early Christians.[14] The Church denigrated women as primitive and as seductresses. It viewed women as the "weaker vessels," who did not have mastery over their passions.[15] The fair sex was to hide her beauty, lest she seduce men to commit lascivious sins, as Eve did to Adam. This double standard continues today in religious Hebrew and Muslim cultures and to some extent influences all Judeo-Christian religions.

The twelfth century ushered in the game of courtly love. Young men called troubadours composed love songs and wooed married women of the noble class. Class and age distinction were central features of the love songs. The romantic troubadour of a lower class was also younger than the high-ranking, older married lady. Not only was the lady of superior age and class, she was also unattainable, virtuous, and admirable.[16] Her affair with a younger man did nothing to diminish her stature; rather the affair elevated it.

In the love song, the hero struggles to become worthy of his lady. Finally, she falls in love with him. It is thought that in real life, the lady follows the song and engages in an extramarital affair. Indeed, it would be naive to think otherwise, given the love talk, illicit meetings, kisses, and ogling of each other's naked bodies.[17] If this sounds like a reversal of the double standard, it is not. Courtly love was reserved for high-ranking ladies. Of course, it was her husband who provided the lady her status.

Courtly love resurfaced in France in the eighteenth century, in which idle rich wives had affairs freely. High-ranking wives led frivolous lives, made possible by their husbands or lovers, who escorted them.[18] So, even though women seemingly enjoyed equal sexual liberties, it was because of men. Indeed, gender relations influenced the double standard.

The 1988 film *Dangerous Liaisons*, based on an eighteenth-century novel, depicts this game of love between Valmont and Madame de Tourvel. The film stars John Malkovich as Sébastien de Valmont and Michelle Pfeiffer as Madame de Tourvel. The story of passion, women's infidelity, deception, and betrayal is still fascinating in our modern sophisticated culture.

In Turkey around 1716, wives paraded openly with their lovers and their husbands. They were more respected by the rank of their lovers than their husbands.[19] In contrast, in England women's infidelity was secreted, to preserve the notion of the virtuous wife. So, different cultures had different takes on women's infidelity.

In reviewing the literature, I noticed an intriguing contradiction. The irreligious practice of female infidelity in courtly love flourished at the height of the Church's power.[20] In a similar vein, exposure of women's infidelity thrives in our current climate of conservative, traditional "moral values."

For a short time, among the noble classes the double standard took a hit. Women's sexuality was elevated, and love was ennobled. But this blow to the double standard in the noble classes did not necessarily filter down to the lower classes.

Women in the lower classes were still subjected to the double standard. Middle-class merchants called burghers in the fourteenth century locked up their money and their wives when they were away. To prevent their infidelity, wives were required to wear chastity belts for which only their husbands held the keys. Jokes about spare keys for lovers made the rounds.[21] As we well know, there is much truth said in jest. Even chastity belts did not prevent female infidelity.

Nor did the influence of puritanical ethics in colonial times prevent female infidelity. Records of adultery trials in the mid-eighteenth century reveal female infidelity in the American colonies and England.[22] In the tightly knit Puritan communities, people spied on their neighbors, and their testimony in court was enough to convict someone of adultery.[23] Titillating accounts of adultery were available for the public's entertainment, as pornography is today.

Although men could get a divorce if their wives were unfaithful, women could not get a divorce if their husbands were unfaithful. It was not until 1932 that Englishwomen could get a divorce if their husbands were unfaithful.[24] In 1631, Massachusetts enacted the death penalty for female adultery. In turn, male adultery was merely considered fornication. If that is not the double standard, I wonder what is! Nevertheless, risking severe punishment or death, some wives dared to act on their desires.

It seems that early in our history, in moralistic or puritanical cultures, the double standard reigned supreme. Yet, wifely infidelity found its way. If anything, daring women have always defied their cultures' repressive restrictions and acted on their desires. Risking so much could well provide additional thrills to the forbidden act of infidelity. Will our current culture promoting moralistic sanctions on sexuality backfire? Will history repeat itself?

Join me in a tour of the ghastly effects of the double standard on women not so long ago. You may be shocked by some of the egregious acts committed on women simply because of their gender.

## THE NINETEENTH CENTURY

*There have been women in the past far more daring than we would need to be now, who ventured all and gained a little, but survived after all.*
—Germaine Greer

### Female Fate Due to the Double Standard

The double standard of the nineteenth century had horrific repercussions on women and on society at large. Painted as a pillar of purity, middle-class wives found it flattering to be elevated. They were revered as vulnerable and virginal—as pure angels. Middle-class wives became languid, listless, and inert—wilting creatures. Their powerful, chivalrous husbands protected them from the vulgarities of the real world.[25] In turn, wives worshipped their godlike husbands, in whose good graces they were fortunate enough to bask.

A demure, delicate wife shuddered at the thought of sex. She only tolerated this "disgusting" act for her husband's gratification. She was taught—and she bought—the idea that she was undersexed, and that sex was disgusting and dirty. Sex, revolting as it was, had its place. A proper wife submitted to it solely for procreation and certainly not for pleasure. No such prohibitions on sex applied to husbands.

Making love to the gentle, pure "angel of the house" was not exactly a wonderful sexual experience for a husband.[26] Society granted license to men to engage freely in their sexual "instincts." The result was an explosion in prostitution and venereal disease in Europe and America. The dichotomous ethos of the pure woman and the fallen woman split the sex lives of women into two distinct categories. The polarities of the virginal wife and the whore had dire effects for all women.

The rampant spread of venereal disease led to a craze for virgins, adolescents, and eventually young girls.[27] At mid-century in America, some brothels offered child prostitutes. A similar social more of wives enduring sex strictly for procreation influenced southern plantations in America. To protect their wives' virtue, husbands readily took women slaves to satisfy their sexual desires.[28] How gallant!

The Mormon religion in America preached the double standard. The founder Joseph Smith introduced polygamy for husbands in 1843; Brigham Young made polygamy a central Mormon principle in 1852. Polygamy advocated that men take multiple wives, but women were not to engage in extramarital affairs. We can still find remnants of this practice here in America.

According to the influential writer Alexis de Tocqueville, the American pioneer wife was revered because of her qualities of devotion, submission, and self-denial.[29] A few writers of the time had more realistic insights into wives' desires. D. H. Lawrence described the homestead wife as a poor, haggard drudge.[30] Hamlin Garland understood that wives' repression cost them their sanity, and that they filled the insane asylums.[31] Unfortunately, these writers were in the minority, and their words were overridden by the influence of more prestigious medical physicians.

In his book *The Horrors of the Half Known Life*, G. J. Barker-Benfield[32] describes chilling accounts of the female fate due to the double standard. Prominent men like best-selling author Reverend John Todd and Augustus Kinsley Gardner, gynecologist and president of the American Medical Association, convinced the medical establishment that only men could perform gynecology. They declared that women were just too delicate to handle the horrors of medicine or to work with black women.

The result was that women were in the hands of male doctors with appalling agendas of their own. Citing Gardner's diatribe on women's "heinous sins" of masturbation, contraception, and abortion, Todd dealt a critical blow to the female fate.[33] He asserted that women's psychological disorders were the result of their sexual transgressions. All of women's problems stemmed from their physiology—their wombs. By the early 1870s, male gynecologists began to practice surgical treatment on women's genitals for all of their emotional and mental health problems.[34]

Excision of the clitoris (clitoridectomy) to cure masturbation, and female castration (removal of the ovaries) to cure insanity were only two of the atrocities committed by sadistic male gynecologists. The narcissistic J. Marion Sims, father of gynecology, by his own admission held hostile and aggressive views of women's sexual organs. In his role as the "architect of the vagina," Sims initiated cruel and inhumane surgical treatments to "help" women heal and conceive. Sims cut into these despised female organs and used them as material for his personal standing among men.[35] He believed that the uterus should be as pliant as its bearer was to the male will.[36] The gynecologist's role was to surgically shape, destroy obstacles in, and redesign the womb for optimal inward flow of sperm.[37] Never was there a thought of male infertility; the blame fell on the woman.

The Women's Hospital was founded as a demonstration ground for Sims's surgical skills.[38] His guinea pigs were poor, often Irish immigrant, women. One of his hapless victims, Mary Smith, endured thirty operations in the three years between 1856 and 1859.[39]

In his book *A Dark Science: Women, Sexuality and Psychiatry in the Nineteenth Century*, J. F. Masson draws on original French and German medical journals published between 1865 and 1900 that were written in the physicians' own words. Sadistic male doctors performed atrocious, cruel surgeries on innocent women. Masson reveals how prominent men abused their power to warp and destroy women's sexual, and sometimes emotional and physical, selves.[40]

To treat psychological problems, male physicians performed outlandish treatments and surgeries including castration (removal of the ovaries), excision of the clitoris, and surgical removal of parts of the cervix. Some of the so-called "symptoms" were vices like masturbation or an erotic smile. In one case, the patient was an innocent ten-year-old female child. The physician both punished and tried to cure her of what he called her perverse, evil ways (masturbation) by administering electric shocks to her clitoris. When that did not work, the physician cauterized her clitoris with a red-hot iron.

Another shocking true story is the amputation of the clitoris and labia minora to treat vaginismus (a constriction of the vagina, considered to be one of the causes of female frigidity). Similar horrific treatments were used to treat hysteria—convulsions, agitation, and depression—found in women. It was thought that diseased wombs caused hysteria; and so, no doubt, castration would cure the disorder. In point of fact, repressed sexual desires were the culprits of hysteria. Needless to say, these atrociously cruel and barbaric methods did not alleviate psychological symptoms, but increased and induced new and more profound psychological problems.

Part of what made this all possible was that women were convinced that education and good breeding were synonymous with delicacy and submission. The male establishment espoused that women were to regard sex as something to be endured, that they had no sexual desires, and that their sexual organs were diseased and dirty. They were shamed into accepting men's definition of them. To make certain of wives' submission to these butcheries, gynecologists got the permission of husbands, without giving full disclosure to the wife-patients.[41] After a while, the power of distorted social beliefs spread like wildfire, and women actually came to gynecologists pleading for castration to cure their ills.

Some women fared somewhat better at the hands of physicians, who were more enlightened about the cause of their hysterical symptoms. They recognized that hysteria was the result of repressed sexual desires and not diseased organs. Daring wives latched on to the idea that they needed sexual satisfaction. Because society foisted traits on them like purity and sex with husbands only for procreation, they turned to their doctors for help, and doctors helped. But whom did they help? is the question. Doctors manually massaged their female patients' genitals until the women reached orgasm. In 1880 the vibrator was invented to help doctors relieve women's hysterical symptoms.[42] I wonder who got more relief, the female patient or the male doctor!

Some even more daring wives had extramarital affairs. Mabel Loomis Todd fully enjoyed erotic experiences in her marriage; nevertheless, she had a torrid affair with her neighbor, Austin Dickinson.[43] Mabel Todd defied the double standard in the quiet college town of Amherst, Massachusetts. The cultural historian Peter Gay[44] quoted from the diaries and private correspondence where Todd recorded her plentiful orgasms with her husband and also her erotic experiences with her lover.

Mabel Todd was hardly the only instance of a woman daring to have extramarital affairs. Women had these affairs throughout the country in all classes. For the most part, women did not admit publicly to their infidelities. There were exceptions, however, even in these moralistic times. Some daring women defied cultural norms in court cases. One example is that of Susan Delashmutt who boldly told the court that she "preferred to live in adultery, than to live in lawful wedlock with her husband."[45]

Despite the artificial ideals and the double standard, wives dared to engage in extramarital affairs for love or for lust. To the naked eye it may seem like a recent trend when, in fact, wives have always engaged in affairs.

The first wave of feminists in the late nineteenth and early twentieth centuries made great strides in the evolution of women's right to vote. Between 1870 and 1910, women ran 480 campaigns in thirty-three states trying to place women's suffrage before male voters.[46] It was not until 1920 that women gained the right to vote in America, but sexual equality had a way to go.

I invite you to visit two visionary doctors of the nineteenth century who held differing views about women's sexuality. You will meet the influential father of psychoanalysis, Sigmund Freud, who both helped and hindered woman's cause. More knowledgeable but less popular, his contemporary Havelock Ellis held sway with fewer people.

### Freud Faces Off on Femininity

By treating hysteria and women's psychological problems with psychoanalysis, Sigmund Freud succeeded in taking women out of the cruel clutches of their doctors and moving them onto comfortable couches. In his therapy room, troubled women engaged in the "talking cure." Nevertheless, Freud's distorted views of women as inferior and castrated had resounding effects on the image of women. So, did Freud render women a favor or a disservice? I would weigh in on both. He advanced women's plight while maintaining nineteenth-century sexist views—a paradox indeed.

Freud brought sexuality out of the Victorian closet. His theories of infantile sexuality, sexualized family dramas, and unconscious erotic conflicts were revolutionary at the time. They are still controversial in our contemporary culture. He laid bare the centrality of sexuality in human experience. We cannot talk about sexuality without talking about Freud. His contributions to our insight into the human psyche are invaluable.

The first word on sexuality and the unconscious, Freud was not the last word. The field of psychoanalysis stands on his shoulders, with feminism using him as a springboard to launch new thought. Yet, his views on femininity left something to be desired. While he exposed the hypocrisy of the bourgeois pretensions of female purity, he did much to perpetuate the double standard.

Freud[47] described the inherent disposition of little girls as less aggressive, defiant, and self-sufficient. By nature, her greater need for affection (greater than little boys') leads her to be more dependent and pliant. He then went on to modify his sexist words by stating that individual differences outweigh these gender differences, so they are of no great consequences. But they have been of very great consequence for women.

As to psychological feminine development, Freud wrote that little girls started out as little boys until they discovered that they lacked a penis. Girls recognize this difference and "are overcome by envy for the penis." Freud goes on to explain that "women no less than men originally had a penis, but they have lost it by castration."[48] If you think this is derogatory, it is just the tip of his iceberg. Freud goes on to explain the dire consequences of penis envy and female castration. According to him, a woman's wish to hide her deformity is the cause of her shame and modesty. Penis envy leads to jealousy, passivity, masochism, narcissism, lower intellectual ability, and a deficient moral conscience.[49]

If so, what is a little girl to do? She does what any sensible little girl would do. Lacking a penis, the castrated girl turns to her father in hopes of receiving his phallus. Her father is the actor, and she is his passive receiver. She is not her own subject.[50] Femininity then means passive submission, whereas masculinity means active agency. The term *penis envy* does, however, have some validity when seen as a metaphor for women's envy of male status.[51]

To his credit, Freud qualified his lack of knowledge of female sexuality, referring to women as the "dark continent." So why expound on ignorance in the first place? He went on to show more of his ignorance when he explicated the role of the clitoris in female sexual desire. Freud asserted that the clitoris was an infantile organ, and only with the vagina could women achieve mature sexual orgasm. Of course, his theory on the clitoris has since been debunked, and the clitoris has been reclaimed as the organ of mature orgasm. Nevertheless, Freud's pronouncement did a lot to maintain women's labels of "frigid" and "undersexed."

While Freud was certainly a groundbreaker, he also brought grief to a lot of women. Despite his erudite and revolutionary thought, Freud's take on the sexes was not very far from the Victorian double standard—the inferior woman and the superior male. Visionary as he was, Freud was nevertheless a product of his sociopolitical time. Now, meet Havelock Ellis, a more enlightened doctor in the nineteenth century.

### Havelock Plays Havoc on the Double Standard

In Freud's time, Havelock Ellis, a doctor and sexologist, countered Freud and the double standard. Contrary to Victorian public opinion, Ellis held that women were not undersexed and had healthy sexual desires at any age.[52] He understood that society influenced women to repress their sexual desires. Ellis recognized that "undersexed" women were not born that way, and that they were not frigid or lacking in sexual impulses. Instead their undersexed states were cultural constructions.

To demonstrate just how natural sexual desire was for women, he observed naive young nurse-girls and adolescents whom constrictive social mores had not yet affected. These nurse-girls readily initiated sexual practices with young boys in their charge. Unlike Freud's little girls who were passive and submissive, Ellis's little girls were sexually active and agents of their own desires. Ellis also wrote about the pleasure women derived from sex, and argued that it was not merely for procreation.

If you remember, earlier in history, women were thought of as seductresses with voracious sexual desires. Like Eve, they were destructive to men. Ellis commented on just this cultural construction of women's sexual impulses. "Whereas in earlier ages there was a general tendency to credit women with an unduly large share of sexual impulse, there is now a tendency to unduly minimize the sexual impulse in women."[53]

Unfortunately, the astute and radical thinker Ellis was not well known among the powers that be. Unlike Freud, his work did not take root with wide audiences. His writing style was more stilted and formal than Freud's; that coupled with an anti-status quo message may have hindered wider influence.

Not only did the nineteenth century spawn important new thinking about women's sexuality, it also spawned a rich body of literature depicting women's infidelity. Join me to peruse some of the literature of the time.

### Ladies with Lovers in the Literature

*Art copies life, but life also copies art.*
—Angus McLaren[54]

Contrary to Ellis, whose writings did not reach the greater populace, writers of fiction did. Indeed, what better way to reach a lot of people than through stories? For many authors, storytelling was used for cultural criticism and moral improvement. Daring wives who act on their desires for extramarital affairs are the subjects of some of the great classic works of literature. There are truths in fictions.[55] Through these enduring works of the nineteenth century, we can get an idea of where the writers are coming from, historically, morally, and critically.

In *The Scarlet Letter*, Nathaniel Hawthorne[56] tells the tragic story of shame, sin, and redemption. Hester Prynne, a married woman, dared to act on her desires and to take a lover. Hester was forced to marry an older, deformed man whom she did not love, so in a sense she was a victim of her times. Her desire for passion and love were motivations for the affair. In current times, some women like Hester still marry for money and have extramarital affairs for passion and love.

The punishment for Hester's sin is to wear a scarlet letter A on the bodice of her garment. Her sentence includes standing on a scaffold for three hours to be shamed by the community. As a result, she is alienated from them and suffers in solitude. Hester's wild and rebellious illegitimate daughter Pearl is the permanent embodiment of her shame. In my practice, women still suffer guilt and shame when their husbands uncover their affairs.

*The Scarlet Letter* is set in 1642 Boston, a puritanical stronghold with strong double standards on infidelity. Hawthorne is delivering a moral message, but more importantly, his work is a cultural criticism. Yes, Hester is shamed and pained. But it could have been far worse. The sexist town fathers could have sentenced her to death. Due to her spotless background, she is spared the death gallows for her sin of adultery. Also, she finally redeems herself by devoting herself to community service with other women, suffering at the hands of sexist men.

You could say Hester was an early feminist. Indeed, Hawthorne is sympathetic to women subjected to the cultural double standard. Hester dares to go for it and loses in love, but gains in internal strength. Women in my practice also go for it, suffer, and may end up feeling empowered to make changes.

In *Madame Bovary*, Gustave Flaubert[57] writes a "realistic novel" in which he tries to depict characters who are true to life. Heroine Emma Bovary is the original material girl, who marries for money and dies for lack of it. In between she is bored with the ordinariness of her middle-class life. She indulges in inane romantic and sentimental daydreams. These fantasies provide her with an erotic and exciting existence to transcend her dull day-to-day existence. A sensual, but superficial, self-absorbed bourgeoisie woman, Emma cannot stand her marriage to a dull, plodding older man. With him, she fails to find bliss, passion, and rapture that she has read about in cheap romantic stories. She despairs and dares to look elsewhere.

Emma neglects her household duties and tries out different activities to fulfill her sensual desires. She gets bored quickly, so none satisfy her needs for erotic excitement. How is she to make her dreams come true? She could try taking on a lover or two to spice up her life. Her extramarital affairs are daring revolts at her tedious provincial life and her unsatisfactory marriage. Alas, Emma discovers that affairs are as banal as her marriage, and she fails to make her dreams come true.

Flaubert paints a portrait of a mediocre women reaching for the moon and for men outside of marriage. Both Emma and Hester have affairs; however, the likeness stops there. Unlike Hester, Emma has no redeeming qualities. She is selfish, shallow, and insensitive to others' feelings.

Flaubert delivers a scathing social commentary on the pretentious bourgeoisie, but signs of a double standard are decidedly there. Indeed, Flaubert is a man writing about a woman who dares to have extramarital affairs. His male supporting character Charles has a redeeming quality, but the heroine Emma has none. And Flaubert deals harshly with Emma by killing her off. Shamed and penniless, she takes poison and suffers a disastrous death. Flaubert makes sure Emma gets her just desserts for her adultery, materialism, and failure to live in reality.

Leo Tolstoy in *Anna Karenina*[58] gives us an up-close look at the double standard in nineteenth-century Russia. The passionate, intensely emotional Anna is unhappily married to Alexei Karenin, a rational and dehumanized man. In her quest for personal meaning she looks for true love with Count Vronsky. Anna dares to act on her desires for a lover, but her downfall is predetermined. Alas, she is still only a woman whose place is in the home caring for the household and children, not cavorting with a handsome count.

Anna is more victimized by culture than her male foil, Konstantin Levin, who finds salvation in nature and God. Whereas Tolstoy punishes Anna for her indiscretions, he elevates Levin. Anna grows cruel, vindictive, and self-destructive in her relentless pursuit of the illicit love affair with Vronsky. Tragically, Anna ends her life in a dramatic, desperate act by throwing herself in front of a train. This epic novel depicts the inner conflict of author Tolstoy between a higher moral ground for personal meaning and the desire for passion, love, and self-gratification. In this novel, Levin, a male, takes the high road and Anna, a female, takes the low road. A double standard if ever there was one!

The awe-inspiring novel *The Awakening*[59] by American Kate Chopin was published in 1899 to scandalized audiences. Libraries, including the author's hometown St. Louis library, banned the exquisitely sensitive, protofeminist book. The heroine, Edna Pontellier, is a woman way ahead of her times. Chopin draws on nature for symbolic imagery to describe Edna's strivings. "She grew daring and reckless . . . she wanted to swim far out where no woman had ever swum before." Indeed, Edna longs to have an independent life, with control over her own destiny and her erotic self. She dares to go for it, too, much like women today do.

Her infidelity is not born of dissatisfaction with her marriage; neither is it for true love, like with the other fictional heroines I have described. Her affairs are in response to her internal despair at the restricted life that culture has imposed on her. Through her extramarital affairs Edna is finally able to experience her authentic, free, passionate, and erotic self. Her lovers serve to awaken her sensual body and to empower her soul. The author describes Edna's response to her infidelity as "neither shame nor remorse."

Léonce Pontellier, Edna's husband, is the conventional nineteenth-century man who treats his wife paternalistically. Her husband's possession, Edna is required to submit to his commands. Her place is in the home. Edna, however, is not cut out for the role of mother and homemaker dictated by society.

Edna recognizes the paradox of her life, "that outward life that conforms and the inner life that questions." Edna not only questions but also defies convention, and she explores her sensual erotic desires with lovers. Her death is a triumph of will over her limited life. She drowns herself in the waters that first awakened her. So she is willing to lose all in order to find her true self.

Women in my practice also dare to take lovers and are willing to risk losing marriages, financial means, and security. Under the spell of the affair, they do not always take into account the pain suffered by their husbands and children. Rage at their circumstances or their spouses continues to motivate women's infidelity.

The portrayal of Edna is sympathetic and poignant. Chopin addresses the double standard and the plight of women, forced to conform to roles for which they are not suited. The author attacks the sexist standards of the nineteenth century in this visionary, early feminist work.

In all three novels, *The Scarlet Letter, Madame Bovary*, and *The Awakening*, the heroines' desire for extramarital affairs is about self-fulfillment and authentic erotic expression. They are all victims of society, marrying men they did not love, and desirous to survive on their own terms. The harsh judgment of women engaging in extramarital affairs is conveyed by the authors' treatment of the heroines. Indeed, death to the adulteress is meted out as punishment.

Despite the artificial ideals of the Victorian age, daring wives in history and fictional literature have defied the double standard and have engaged in extramarital affairs. Nevertheless, the double standard survived well into the twentieth century, with the help of Hollywood and television. Remnants remain today. The published researches of Kinsey and Hite, the women's liberation movement, and the counterculture's sexual revolution all helped to undermine the double standard. Join me to trace highlights of the twentieth century that will illuminate how far women have come, and how far we still have to go.

# 3

## What a Difference a Century Makes

**FEMALE INFIDELITY AND THE DOUBLE STANDARD**

*One faces the future with one's past.*
—Pearl S. Buck

### THE TWENTIETH CENTURY

The sexual mores for women in the twentieth century shifted from sexual inhibitions to free-for-alls. Cultural and political forces influenced these extremes, with women responding to changing sexual standards. Some conformed to constrictive conventions, while others dared to defy, much as they still do. Female erotic expression came out of the closet in the Roaring Twenties, only to retreat behind closed doors in the prudish fifties. The late sixties and seventies saw a backlash of seismic proportions. The second wave of feminism and the sexual revolution redefined women's erotic desires, only to be curtailed in the eighties. The AIDS crisis, aided by the morally conservative "New Right" wing of politics, contained much of the previous promiscuous sex outside of marriage.

Under the sway of social mores, women bobbed and weaved. They made strides in significant spheres, most importantly, the right to vote in 1920. Nevertheless, it took another forty years for female sexuality to enter the public eye. Yet, the double standard lingered on. While women forged ahead in the modern world, one foot stayed fixed in the repressive nineteenth century. Women's erotic desires are still seen through the lens of a male-dominated culture.

#### Roaring Twenties

Radical thinkers, bohemians, feminists, Freud, Ellis, and Margaret Sanger led the way to a new sexual era on the eve of World War I. Margaret Sanger's radical platforms for birth control, women's autonomy over their

bodies, and sexual expression helped set the stage. Freud's and Ellis's writings about the centrality of the sexual impulse sent shock waves through the
Victorian age. William J. Robinson, an avant garde editor of two medical journals, weighed in on the issue of marital infidelity. He wrote that
extramarital affairs might be imprudent, but they were not more sinful than
the gratification of other natural instincts like eating or drinking.[1]

The progressive and liberal twenties roared in and broke with the past.
In 1917, World War I sent men to war and women to work. Hence,
women's wartime labor brought greater economic autonomy to women.
Initially, most women lost their jobs to men returning from war in 1918.
Nevertheless, in a short time, the post–World War I burgeoning economy
provided sufficient work for both men and women. The war also facilitated
women's right to vote as suffragettes joined the war effort and proved
themselves equal to men in patriotic terms.[2]

Women continued to forge ahead in the sexual arena. Liberating their
bodies from tight corsets and constricted sexual ideals, women expressed
their sexual desires openly. Flappers with bobbed hair and skimpy, loose
clothes symbolized loose erotic desires. A far cry from their buttoned-
up Victorian sisters, flappers nevertheless remained unflagging wives and
mothers. Cavorting freely with men in speakeasies and jazz nightclubs,
wives smoked, drank, and danced the wild and woolly Charleston. All the
while, these wives continued to cater to husbands and children.

People flocked to see Hollywood's new moving pictures that featured
women in sensual and erotic roles. Clara Bow, the "It Girl," was sexy, hip,
and wild. Bad and baby-faced Jean Harlow, in the film *Red-Headed Woman*,
was shown in sadomasochistic scenes sleeping her way to the top. Greta
Garbo was a glamorous, elusive, mysterious sex goddess who bewitched men.
Mae West, the incomparable sex symbol, was right out there. She burles-
qued sex with her promise of sexual sin, her double entendres, and her
buxom body. "Come up and see me sometime" was just one of her quips
with which she taunted the censors.

The once shockingly explicit novel *Lady Chatterley's Lover*[3] by D. H.
Lawrence (1928) was banned from America until 1959. Female infidelity by
an unfulfilled upper-class woman and her gamekeeper is not so far-fetched
in our contemporary culture. In my practice, I hear similar torrid tales of
well-to-do wives in dull marriages having affairs with their carpenters and
painters. Then there are Gabrielle and her gardener in *Desperate Housewives*.

### Conflicts Continue

Contradictory and shifting sexual roles of female sexuality continued beyond
the twenties. The traditional wife and mother conflicted with the sensual,

erotic, and daring woman. The sexual liberalism of the twenties came to a fast halt in the thirties. The power of Hollywood, unprecedented in the thirties, helped to bring the free sexual era to a close, for a short while anyway.

In 1930, a self-regulating censorship known as the Hays Code was adopted by Hollywood to screen out movies with any type of "licentious" relationships. Banned subject matter included homosexuality, biracial male-female relationships, adultery, and even childbirth. After 1930, films were required to foster the sanctity of marriage; the double standard was back in full force. Long after women had shed the restrictive sexual mores of the past, Hollywood continued to condition women to believe that their place was in the home.[4] Women were pressured to conform to male standards of beauty and youthfulness, and obedience—the prototype for the Stepford Wives. Young men going off to war were buoyed by nude pinup calendars objectifying women's sexuality. Notably, Hollywood did a great public relations job on the psyche of women until the power of television took over in the fifties.

It did not take long before Hollywood abandoned its hegemony on female traditional roles. Perhaps the artificial morality backfired. Films soon featured tough-talking, bold, and bad girl types indulging in extramarital affairs, premarital sex, and murder. Joan Crawford in the 1931 film *Possessed* defies the double standard as she boldly states, "A woman can do anything, say anything, as long as she doesn't fall in love."[5]

Bette Davis plays yet another daring wife whose extramarital affair ends with murder. In the 1946 film *Deception*, she shoots her lover when her long-lost husband shows up.[6]

In the 1949 film *Beyond the Forest*, Davis plays the infamous unfaithful Rosa Moline. The film is an exposé of the drastic effects on women of the double standard in the twentieth century. Rosa is branded as evil simply because she refuses to accept the role society has foisted upon her. Refusing to passively accept her "natural" job of mother and wife to a boring, sexless husband, she takes action by seeking an escape. Rosa constantly bemoans her limitations as a woman; she knows that the only way out is through a man. She turns to a rich and powerful lover so that she can escape her dull traditional life. Driven to distraction by her powerful and ruthless lover, she commits murder. In the end, she dies as well.[7] So even in the late forties, the death sentence was dealt to women who dared to engage in infidelity.

Other actors portrayed passionate, empowered women. In the 1950 film *Paid in Full*, Lizabeth Scott sleeps with her sister's husband after she accidentally kills her niece. Olivia de Havilland, in the 1946 film *To Each His Own*, has a child born out of wedlock in a one-night stand with a war hero.

Barbara Stanwyck, in the 1933 film *Baby Face*, turns tricks and succeeds by sleeping her way to the top. Other films of the era that depict women exploiting men using their sexual powers include *The Strange Women* with Hedy Lamarr and *Forever Amber* with Linda Darnell. A far cry from the selfless wife and mother, these women struck out in bold, ruthless, self-serving ways.

World War II brought a different spin to female infidelity. *The End of the Affair*, Graham Greene's 1951 novel,[8] and the 1942 classic film *Casablanca* examine the pathos of relinquishing a great love affair for more noble ideals. In both cases, wives are forced to give up their adored lovers for the love of God or the love of country. In *The End of the Affair*, the heroine Sarah Miles mysteriously leaves her lover as she has a spiritual awakening and cannot live with her sin. In the classic film *Casablanca*, Ingrid Bergman tearfully gives up her lover Humphrey Bogart at his behest. She realigns with her husband Paul Heinreid for patriotic ideals. In both cases, higher ideals eclipse a woman's fulfillment in infidelity; she must give up her deeply felt desires for her obligatory pulls of morality.

The twenties roared, the thirties waxed and waned. In the next era, you will become acquainted with the prudish fifties, where the pendulum swung in the direction of conservative, prudish moral values.

### The Prudish Fifties

The Depression and the horrors of World War II left Americans yearning for economic security. The American Dream of young veterans entailed a conventional wife, children, and a home in the suburbs. Eager to get on with their lives, the rush to have children resulted in the Baby Boomers.[9]

The fifties age of general goodwill implied conformity, consumerism, and prudish sexual mores. The security of a middle-class living standard was a tradeoff for blind acceptance of the conservative status quo.[10]

America's innocence was yet to be tested. Americans trusted their government to bring them out of the war.[11] Innocent Americans got caught up in the rhetoric of the government. Paranoia about the communist specter resulted in the ruthless McCarthy era. By and large, Americans went along with the witch hunts; however, some radical thinkers tried to speak out. Arthur Miller, in his play *The Crucible*, used a disguise to expose the horrors of conformity lest he be jailed as a communist. All of this in the guise of traditional values and protecting the innocence of America!

America's innocence met with a rude awakening in the next decade. The Baby Boomers grew into the youth who led the sexual revolution. They protested the Vietnam War and rejected their parents' middle-class affluence and prudish sexual mores.

The postwar definition of femininity described a devoted wife as someone who raised her family, supported her husband, cooked, cleaned, and remained attractive and optimistic. Husbands braved the corporate world and wives maintained the homestead.[12] The false front of femininity was not too far removed from the Victorian age. Sex went underground, and conformity to artificial ideals surfaced.

Sadly, behind the closed doors of this sunny façade, a dark reality emerged. Not all men wore condoms, and women were taught to please their husbands. The result was many unwanted pregnancies. Abortions were outlawed, and pregnant women were forced to seek help to end their pregnancies in unsafe and unsavory methods. They resorted to back alley abortions or knitting needles. The 2004 movie *Vera Drake* presents a poignant depiction of this dire dilemma.

In the fifties, America became wired for television.[13] Family sitcoms promoting the bliss of traditional marriages were the rage. Television wives were not subjects of their own desires, nor did they dream of extramarital affairs. Self-sacrificing objects to their husbands and children, wives were under the dominion of their husbands.

The family sitcoms shaped and were shaped by the social and sexual conformity of the times. As mistresses of their homes, wives never worked. They were nice and neat and gratefully accepted their lives as perfect homemakers. June Cleaver in *Leave it to Beaver* wanted her son to marry a girl who cooked, cleaned, and saw to it that her hubby was happy, much the same as she did.[14] Harriet Nelson of *The Adventures of Ozzie and Harriet* shared the same noble role to make life better for her family. June Cleaver and Harriet Nelson were role models for American wives. Their purpose was to please their men. They did not question their second-class status or the double standard.

The all-American girl was pert, pretty, and not too sexy—good marriage material. Her sexual desires were not spoken about. Crinolines, circle skirts, and perfectly coifed pageboys—not a hair out of place—were the hallmarks of the sexless wife. In contrast, men's sexual desires had their day.

The vulnerable sex goddess Marilyn Monroe provided men with titillating fantasies. Although she was the antithesis of their wives, she nevertheless perpetuated the double standard. Traditional men were enthralled by this wanton/waif womanchild. They fantasized about protecting her innocence as they were bedding her. With Monroe, a virile man could instantly be transformed into a combination of Casanova and Sir Galahad. What better fantasy for a macho man of the fifties?

Hugh Hefner launched his multimillion-dollar sex empire using Monroe's nude calendar pose. The double standard allowed him to buy the rights for only $500, while Monroe got nothing.[15] A descendent of Midwest puritans, Hefner was dedicated to a more open sexuality and to exposing the hypocrisy of the period. While Hefner's slick, upscale *Playboy* nudes furthered male sexual fantasies, they also treated women as sex objects.

Then, along came a daring woman who had a different approach to female sexuality. Grace Metalious in her best-selling book *Peyton Place*[16] helped to debunk the double standard and the puritanical views of women. She exposed the sexual hypocrisy of a typical staid small American town by revealing a hotbed of sexual intrigue and female infidelity. Her women characters had sexual desires that contrasted sharply with the attitudes women were supposed to have.[17] They were not passive receptacles for men, but self-fulfilling, erotic, and independent women. Her breakthrough work helped pave the way for the second wave feminist movement.

Alfred Kinsey's landmark 1953 study *Sexual Behavior in the Human Female*[18] tore down the false façade that women hid behind. He shocked the nation by exposing what women were really doing between the sheets. Like men, women were erotic, sexual beings who engaged in extramarital affairs, masturbation, and same-sex erotic behavior. Although his previous study of male sexuality was explosive, it did not compare to the outrage that the study of female infidelity caused. Unfortunately, Kinsey was accused of deteriorating the morals of decent Americans and lost the Rockefeller grant for his new book.[19]

The double standard and artificial ideals continued to do their dirty work. The seeds of discontent and dissent were sown in the fifties. It took feminism, the Pill, and the politics of war for the inequality of women's sexuality to reach the public eye.

### Feminism and False Fronts

*A feminist is anyone who recognizes the equality and full humanity of women and men.*
—Gloria Steinem

Betty Friedan was one of the early voices to challenge the false front. In her groundbreaking 1963 book *The Feminine Mystique*,[20] Friedan revealed that thousands of women were dissatisfied with their subordinate roles of dutiful mothers and wives, propagated by women's magazines. Friedan's work began to transform women's consciousness and launched second wave feminism. She exposed the fallacy of branding women with penis envy if they showed dissatisfaction with their traditional sexual roes. Friedan went on to launch the National Organization of Women (NOW) in 1966. Women now gained a forum to lobby against the sexual discrimination of women. Gloria Steinem, editor of *Ms.* magazine, provided feminism with a voice. *Ms.* magazine was influential in reaching masses of women who resonated with the magazine's messages of sexual inequality and the erotic desires of women.

Hordes of women joined "consciousness raising" groups and discovered that the way to orgasm was not necessarily the vagina, but more likely the clitoris. Masters and Johnson's empirical research gave impetus to the second wave of feminism. Their report *Human Sexual Response*[21] showed that orgasm was achieved by stimulation of the clitoris.

Ann Koedt, in her article "The Myth of the Vaginal Orgasm," put the nails in the coffin.[22] She dealt a deathly blow to the vaginal orgasm and reclaimed the clitoral orgasm. With the discovery of the Holy Grail for women, Koedt helped to galvanize the feminist movement. Women were not really frigid; they just needed stimulation of the proper erogenous zone. Women could now satisfy their sexual desires with or without men. Or so they thought. In their zeal, some feminists failed to recognize the psychological needs of women for connections, relatedness, and intimacy with loved ones.

Radical feminists declared that sexual intercourse was simply a way that women subordinated themselves to men and that men exploited women's sexuality. Kate Millet[23] and Shulamith Firestone[24] asserted that women's sexuality served the purpose of patriarchy and that men controlled women's sexuality. The women's liberation movement, with the slogan "the personal is political," was on the march to liberate female sexuality and power from the male-dominated culture.

I will take a moment to explain just what was meant by "the personal is political." That which seems to be personal, individual experience—cleaning dirty dishes after a hard day's drudgery while your husband leisurely watches TV—does have sociopolitical resonance. These personal experiences are part of a societal pattern of male dominance and female subordination.

Second wave feminists stood on the shoulders of their earlier psychoanalytic feminist sisters. Karen Horney[25] and Clara Thompson[26, 27] criticized Freud's phallocentric views of sexuality. Freud claimed that women were deficient in lacking a phallus and thus were secondary to men. Horney contested Freud's description of women as penis envying, castrated beings. She asserted that femininity was as primary as masculinity. Simone de Beauvoir, in her celebrated book *The Second Sex*,[28] asserted that women subordinated themselves to men and were regarded as the "other" in men's consciousness. She maintained that female sexuality was a male construction. Melanie Klein[29] replaced Freud's centrality of the penis with that of the breast. She believed that early childhood experiences at the breast, and not with the penis, determined the psychology of people.

Second wave feminism paved the way for greater recognition of women's sexual desires. Soon you will see the role played by two other pivotal sociopolitical forces in women's sexuality.

### Politics and the Pill

Eager to defy their parents, the children of the staid fifties formed the counterculture of the sixties. The sex, drugs, and rock 'n' roll flower children protested the Vietnam War and prudish sexual mores. With slogans of "make love, not war," the youth counterculture rebelled against the establishment and the false fronts of sexuality. The youth of the counterculture gave free vent to open and promiscuous sex. Older Americans emulated the suggestive dress, drug use, and sexual promiscuity of their children. An era of sexual permissiveness swept across the prudish landscape of America.

The advent of the contraceptive pill fueled the women's liberation movement. The Pill helped to liberate women so that they could begin to take control of their own bodies. No longer having to rely on men to wear condoms, they gained greater autonomy and sexual independence. What is more, they could satisfy their erotic desires freely without other messy methods that required planning. But women were still not in total control of their bodies until the 1973 *Roe v. Wade* decision. The U.S. Supreme Court held that a woman's right to privacy—freedom of choice—overrode existing laws against abortion.

### Feminine Sexual Freedom

*Too much of a good thing is wonderful.*
—Mae West

Sexual promiscuity, the writings of feminists, the Vietnam War, and the birth control pill advanced the goals of the women's liberation movement to gain sexual and economic independence. In response to male domination, masses of women sought independence by going into the workforce. Married women now had more opportunities for extramarital sex. The Pill gave them the green light.

The desire to claim sexual liberation fueled some women's engagement in sex for lust, not love. Pure pleasure divorced sex from intimate relating. Women's infidelity was not in response to marital dissatisfaction, but, for the most part, was in response to the period of sexual permissiveness.

Married and single women experimented with casual sex in orgies, group sex, and sex binges. Sex became impersonal—merely for expansion of sexual pleasures. Could this polymorphous hedonism really last? Not really. Unbridled, impersonal sex was not an enduring phenomenon. Women, then and now, desire love along with erotic expression. Most desire the commitment of marriage and motherhood. When they stray, their desires are psychological and relational, and not strictly for sexual expression. With the exception of seriously disturbed women, few wives today desire impersonal sex; they desire sex with a specific person.

### Pullback to More Prudent Sexuality

Reacting to the galloping sexuality of the sixties and seventies, forces in the eighties pulled in the reins. Alarmed by the corrupting power of sex and the gains of feminism, sexual conservatives fought for the return of traditional moral values. Political and sexual conservatives joined religious fundamentalists to form the New Right. They went on a crusade to purify the nation's erotic lives. Ronald Reagan ran for re-election and adopted a platform accusing liberals of promoting casual and cheap sex. He described the sex act as "the means by which husband and wife participate with God in the creation of a new human life."[30] Does that sound familiar? Indeed, old habits die hard, and the repressive sexual restraints of the nineteenth century lay waiting just beneath the surface.

The National Right to Life Committee voraciously attacked women's right to choose abortion and control of their own bodies. Female sexual gains of the twentieth century were in peril in the eighties, much as they are currently in our political climate of conservative "moral values."

To clinch the sexual panic, AIDS made its lethal appearance in the eighties. AIDS—originally thought to be sexually transmitted by gay men—did not bypass women. Thousands of women were infected. Needless to say, female prostitutes were accused of transmitting the disease to men. In fact, men transmitted the disease to them.[31]

Monogamy was one form of protection against the virulent AIDS epidemic. One is less prone to be infected if in a longstanding sexual partnership. Before having sex with new partners, people were cautioned to practice prudence and to disclose tests to their partners stating that they were not infected with the AIDS virus.

The scourge of AIDS put a damper on casual and carefree sex. Women were at risk just as well as men, so women's infidelity became more prudent. Conservative sexual mores also appealed to some of the female population, including religious wives and wives who wished to stay home and devote themselves to their families. Overall, the sexual revolution of the sixties met with a sexual counterrevolution in the eighties.

Women began to rethink the sixties notion of sex without intimacy. They found that sex lost its allure without the substance of love, romance, and commitment. Hence, the desire for women to engage in extramarital affairs has become a more serious matter. The lure of free sexual expression out of marriage has undergone a transformation.

The desire of women for extramarital affairs in our current climate is mainly in response to unresolved childhood issues, marital problems, and fear of intimacy, or as a catalyst for change. I say *mainly* because some women still desire extramarital affairs as an escape from internal demons, or to experience novelty in sexual expression. Indeed, there does not appear to be one single portrait of women who dare to engage in extramarital affairs.

What does seem clearer is that the double standard persists, and female infidelity is judged more harshly than male infidelity. Not so long ago, in 1990, a woman in Wisconsin escaped a criminal trial for infidelity by agreeing to perform community services and attend parenting classes.[32] Can you imagine this sentence for an unfaithful husband in 1990?

It does not take much imagination to shudder at the travesty of the Anita Hill case of 1991 when she accused Clarence Thomas of sexual harassment. By discrediting Hill, male supremacy and male power won, and Hill lost. Thomas was successfully appointed to the Supreme Court.

Despite second wave feminism's identification of gendered power relations as key to the subordination of women, male power continues to dominate in the twenty-first century. What did traditional "moral values" do for the nineteenth and twentieth centuries? I would say not much, other than harm.

We are now in the twenty-first century, and "moral values" threaten to undermine gains made by second wave feminism. In response, a third wave of feminism is peeking through to assert female sexual power. A daring, frank, in-your-face sexuality is brewing. Let us take a glimpse at these young women, moral values, the threat of terrorism, and women's infidelity.

## THE TWENTY-FIRST CENTURY

### Third Wave Feminism

*After thirty years of feminism, the world we inhabit barely resembles the world we were born into. And there's still a lot left to do.*
—Jennifer Baumgardner and Amy Richards[33]

Loose collections of young women born around 1970 have emerged with a goal of furthering women's equality. They call themselves "third wave feminists." These young feminists of the new millennium stand on the shoulders of second wave feminists of the sixties and seventies. Like their second wave feminist mothers, they have adopted a platform of gender equality and women's rights, and abhor male domination of women. In some ways, however, they are rebelling against their feminist mothers. In yet other ways they are pushing the envelope of female sexual power.

Second wave radical feminist slogans resonated loudly with statements from some little known feminist rebels like Irina Dunn. She wrote, "A woman needs a man like a fish needs a bicycle." In contrast, third wave feminists believe women do need men. They hold that women desire romance, commitment, and marriage. The difference is that their desires are based on choice and not need. They do not need to rely on a man to be valued or to survive economically.[34] They desire love, family, intimacy, and erotic sex with men. This all sounds great to me, but it does not always work out this way. In my practice, many women intellectually know all of this, but emotionally, a part of them still defers to and depends on a man.

The new feminist in the postmodern world describes herself in multiple terms, including *feminine sexual power, girlie, pro-sex, Prada, working class, Marxist, lesbian, married, transsexual, young, old*, and *feminist*. She wants to be described broadly rather than constricted by the narrow term *women's rights*.[35] In a similar vein, the women in my practice who have extramarital affairs are much more than straying wives. They also want to be understood, described, and recognized in multiple terms.

The new feminist takes a surprising stand on the objectification of women's sexual bodies. Rather than feeling like sex objects, they feel empowered by showing their bodies and rendering men powerless. So men become women's objects; and women, by virtue of their sexuality, are subjects. Madonna, a powerful sex symbol, exploited men by packaging her sexual power. She was assertive, self-reliant, and ruthless. Sound like a man? You bet. Attacking the double standard, Naomi Wolf wrote about how *slut* should be recast as *rebel*.[36] My young women patients are in accord with these sentiments and complain that promiscuous males are described as "players" and females as "sluts."

The new feminist contention is that when women show themselves in seductive ways, it makes them feel powerful. Sexuality is not aimed at getting a man to desire them; rather it is because the new feminist desires a man. What a fantastic about-face! In my experience, however, it is still hard to get this reversal of sexual power across to women. So many of us revert to experiencing ourselves as objects and not subjects, as you will see shortly.

Now let me try to explain the term *girlie*, to which Arnold Schwarzenegger erroneously referred. A girlie is not a silly, childish, giggly girl. "Girlie" power is a rebellion against the false idea that if a woman does not want to be exploited, she does not want to be sexual.[37] Indeed, new feminist women desire to be sexy, tough, and to speak their minds; they can show cleavage, skin, piercings, and tattoos. "Putting out makes you smart, in control of your sexual power, rather than a victim of it," wrote Elizabeth Wurtzel.[38]

The new girlie culture is also stereotypically feminine, with manicures, hairdos, cooking, and domestic duties. Girlies want to reclaim the feminine trappings that their mothers discarded during second wave feminism.[39] So, the new feminist movement is both a rebellion against their mothers and a tribute to them.

As an aside, some second wave feminists struggling against a sexist society in the seventies hung on to their feminine, sexy styles. Sexuality was a stamp of power and not submission for some women back then. We all differ from each other with multiple expressions for power, conformity, and sexuality. Indeed, not all wives in the twenty-first century subscribed to feminism. Some wives were swayed by the current culture of "moral values."

### Moral Values and the New Millennium

Although not a part of the platform, third wave feminism may be partly a rebellion against the ominous artificial ideals of traditional "moral values" propagated by right wing factions in the twenty-first century. The right wing conservative branch of the Republican Party aligned with religious fundamentalists to elect and re-elect George W. Bush president. The specter of repression hovers overhead.

A woman's right to control her body by choosing abortion is currently in peril. A billion-dollar federal program, paid by taxpayers, discredits condoms and advocates "abstinence only." How unrealistic and dangerous! Instead of less government, there is more; not for social, welfare, or environmental programs, but for intrusion into our private sexual lives. Yet, some wives adhere to the rigid, unrealistic, conservative "moral values"; and they follow the traditional gender split of homemaker wife and breadwinner husband.

In our era of greater openness, we run the risk of turning back the pages of history to dark and dire periods. Should female infidelity go back behind closed doors, punitive and pernicious measures threaten. As I have recounted, throughout history some women refused to conform to unrealistic traditional sexuality advocated by the status quo. There has never been a match between women's true sexual desires and the artificial ideals of "moral values." To shed light on women's desires for extramarital affairs, it cannot be shrouded in secrecy and shame. We have been there, done that; it did not work then, nor will it now.

Engaging in extramarital affairs may not be a prudent choice, but it is not a moral flaw, nor is it a sin. It is a human reaction to multiple factors. In our postmodern world, women's desires for extramarital affairs are related to various factors. Partly a cultural construction that shifts with the social and political climate, partly a desire for personal fulfillment and sexual expression, and partly in response to marital problems, women's infidelity has always been on the American scene.

Join me in my therapy room as I work with wives who dare to act on their desires, throw caution to the wind, and chance hurting husbands and children to pursue fulfillment with extramarital affairs. I have found that extramarital affairs rarely last after they have been exposed. The affairs that seem so romantic, exciting, and fulfilling lose their allure once reality hits home. Yet, daring wives over the centuries risk so very much for so very little.

In our post-9/11 age of terrorism, the security of attachment is comforting, so women's infidelity is, for the most part, not just for fun. Marriages missing attunement, mutuality, or reciprocity seem to be central factors in wives' decisions to have affairs. Internal conflicts, fear of loss of identity, existential angst, unresolved early faulty relationships, escape from boring lives, depression, anxiety, and fear of intimacy are other problems you will encounter. You may find aspects of yourself in these case studies, and hopefully be inspired by the solutions that we attempt.

# 4

# Not So Sweet Home

## STAY-IN-THE-ABODE WIVES

*Love thy neighbor—and if he happens to be tall, debonair, and devastating, it will be that much easier.*
—Mae West

*The weak can never forgive. Forgiveness is the attribute of the strong.*
—Mahatma Gandhi

## DOMESTIC DISCONTENTS

While many wives today have children and go back to work, many wives make other choices. Some prefer part-time work, and others choose to stay home. Stay-at-home wives may fantasize about idyllic lives—the joys of motherhood and marital bliss, along with the high art of homemaking a la Martha Stewart. Then reality sets in, and home sweet home may not be so sweet.

Twenty-first-century housewives, influenced by feminism, want more out of marriage than their grandmothers did. For starters, they want understanding, romance, and sex. Stay-at-home wives may have left fun social lives and jobs where they felt valued, recognized, and empowered by earning their own money. Giving all of that up is giving up a lot. Indeed, housewives often feel theirs is a thankless job, with no power, no pay, and not much pleasure.

Stuck at home, they exist in tedium with one day not too different than the one before. The same drudgery—food shopping, cooking, cleaning, chauffeuring—stretches on ad infinitum. Many housewives feel trapped, powerless, bored, lonely, depressed, or anxious. They fear losing their identities in children and husbands.

When husbands come home from work, they feel tired, stressed, and just want to crash. They regard home as a safe haven from the busy, competitive world. They look to their wives to provide this type of solace. Wives look to their husbands for excitement, fun, and games. After dinner, wives may find their hubbies glued to the TV instead of them, or worse still, asleep on the sofa. At the end of a dull day of diapers and dishes, housewives are itching to go; they want attention and validation. Instead they feel neglected and emotionally empty. Mutual recognition of needs and desires has gone out the window. Instead of attunement and intimacy, there is separateness and distance. The magic of marriage has worn off.

To top it off, their husbands are out in the exciting world, where they experience autonomy, independence, and power. Not so for housewives. They feel dependent on their husbands and tethered to the needs of their families. Feeling powerless, stay-at-home wives could easily grow envious of their husbands.

Misunderstanding his wife's frustration, a husband may grow critical of her. He is under the illusion that she has it easy. He just does not get it. The wife's resentment and envy of her husband turns to rage. She may withdraw or strike out. Communication has broken down, and alienation has taken its place. Trapped wild animals have been known to chew off their own limbs in a desperate attempt to release themselves from their traps to gain their freedom. Now modern desperate housewives would certainly not consider losing a limb for freedom's sake. So to what could a desperate housewife resort?

Along comes an attentive, sexy admirer, and bingo! A passport to freedom; he is the answer to her despair. An exciting adventure into the forbidden and dangerous promises, a spicy distraction from a humdrum, frustrating life. Imagine being transformed overnight from a drab housefrau to an exciting, colorful woman!

An act of passive aggression never felt so good. Indeed, the best revenge is a good life, and she seemingly has it all. Not only that, her affair is a hot power play where she is in charge, leaving her husband out in the cold. Can this fantasy really work? The following case study of a daring wife will tell us more.

### Daring Debra

Long, streaked blonde hair cascaded over a blue-gray sweatsuit that matched her eyes. With little to no makeup, Debra looked unpretentious and natural—like many a young housewife in the suburbs. She could be your next-door neighbor. Nothing about her appearance stood out, until you looked further. Her left hand sported a sparkling diamond ring (at least five carats) and a designer watch. Well, come to think of it, she still looked like the girl next door—in an affluent suburb, that is.

Married for eight years, Debra was the proud mother of two young children. She described her husband Don as a good guy who worked long hours to provide his family with a comfortable life. Debra decided to be a stay-at-home mom, which met with Don's approval. They had purchased a beautiful home, with two acres of grassy land, a swimming pool, and lots of playground space.

"My life's perfect. I don't have to work and I've got time for my adorable children. My kids are great. I can't understand why I have these panic attacks," Debra told me. She looked perplexed.

"Can you describe your panic attacks?" I asked.

"My heart pounds very fast, I can't catch my breath, and I'm sure I'm dying. I've tried everything and nothing works." Her clear eyes clouded over.

"What have you tried?" I inquired further.

Her rapid-fire explanation quickly switched to a helpless cry. "I breathe into a paper bag, and tell myself it's just anxiety, and that I won't die. I went to a cardiologist; he said my heart was in excellent shape, and that it was due to stress. So I went to yoga, tried meditation—not for me. I'm just too anxious. So I'm here. Can you help me?"

"Maybe we've got to dig deeper to see what's going on," I suggested.

She whispered like a little lost girl. "Is it going to hurt? Actually, it doesn't matter. I'll do anything you suggest. I'm desperate."

"The process of getting to understand yourself can be painful at times," I explained in candor, hopefully setting the tone of the relationship.

"I'll take it. Bring it on," she said without flinching.

*She'll do anything that's painless. But she's daring. In desperation, Debra is willing to submit to my power and probable pain in the therapeutic process for possible gain. Does this dynamic play out in her marital relationship? Does she submit to her husband's power for gains, like material ones? A twenty-first century Madame Bovary?*

I inquired about her relationship with her parents. As a child, Debra's mother and father worked hard. She remembered crying bitterly when her mother went off to work. Although she had fun in daycare, she was nevertheless traumatized every morning when she separated from her mother. She pleaded with her mother to stay with her, but her childish efforts were spent in vain. Her mother prevailed; Debra conformed. In tears, Debra revealed that she wet her bed well into her preteen years. Other than her mother, I was the first person to whom she disclosed her humiliating experience.

*A shameful, painful revelation that she hid all these years! And she's en-trusting me with her secret! I'm encouraged with the budding trust, candor, and her bravery. Looks promising.*

"I wonder if this has something to do with the choice you made to stay home and not work?" I ventured.

"You're right; it fits. I want to give my kids everything I didn't have. I want to be a full-time mom who's with them when they go to school and when they come home. I want to give them a home where each kid has her own room, the schools are good, and it's safe. Don wants the same things I want. We're in agreement on this. So why do I have these panic attacks?" she implored me.

Slowly, Debra revealed her inner feelings of boredom and feeling trapped by the sameness of her existence. Every day was similar to the one before.

"I miss the exciting life I led before moving to the suburbs. I held a powerful position on Wall Street, where the market went up and down, and every day was different from the one before. You never knew what to expect. That's where I met Don—he's still working there with all the adventure. I got stuck here in suburbia, shopping, cooking, cleaning, and carting my kids around. I'm at everyone's beck and call. I feel like I'm los-ing my identity. Is that all there is?" Her anxiety mounted as she began to articulate her dilemma. At thirty-eight, Debra sounded like a disenchanted older woman facing an existential crisis. She also feared losing herself as a separate person.

"How would you identify yourself?" I continued to probe.

"I'm Charlie and Allison's mother and Don's wife." She looked dismayed as she began to gain insight into her problem.

"Not a very powerful place for you," I interpreted.

"Don gets a lot of power in his job, people value him, he gets good feedback, and it makes him feel good about himself. I remember how it felt. My kids don't exactly give me thanks; it is a thankless job." Long strands of hair covered her face as she lowered her head.

"It sounds like you resent your husband's power that he derives from his achievements," I interpreted.

"I don't resent him—you're wrong." Brushing her hair away from her face, she bolted upright. Her face turned red with rage.

*So she's resisting, maybe afraid of losing her identity here? She's clearly angry with her husband. Is she angry with me, too? Does she envy my power, my life as a married woman with her own identity and career?*

Before exploring her feelings about her husband further, I went for her feelings about me. We found that she did indeed envy what she considered my "having it all." Part of her wanted to write me off as a tough career woman, but the other part felt warm feelings toward me. The latter seemed to win out, for now at least. Debra told me I was a good role model that she could aspire toward eventually.

*Debra's alternating feelings of envy and admiration seem to be a common-enough conflict with which other women patients struggle. Often I hear their projections—that I am envious of them and hate them. Tolerating the ambiguity of hating and loving is part of the therapeutic process for both of us. I too must tolerate their shifting feelings and projections toward me.*

"Now that we've begun to talk about our feelings toward each other, maybe it's time to talk about your real feelings toward Don," I suggested.

"Don works real hard for us, but I feel like it's not all just for us. A lot of it's for him." She was getting warm.

"How's that?" I wanted more.

"Don gets off on his success. His achievements make him feel important; like a somebody." Debra brushed her hair back defiantly and took a deep breath.

"And you?" I turned the dialogue to her.

"I feel like a nobody." Her defiance was dashed. "Making a lot of money and providing a good life for his family's a power trip for him." Eyes sparkling, Debra smiled as she glanced at her dazzling diamond.

"You have good insight into your husband's feelings. What about your feelings?" I asked.

"I have it good, and I should appreciate it all, and I do. But, I feel lonely and undesirable," she whispered shyly.

"So you have mixed feelings," I suggested.

"They're not so mixed." She resisted my interpretation.

"Hmmm," I uttered.

"Don's too tired and involved with his career to pay much attention to me. He comes home late, eats, and watches TV. Most of the time, he falls asleep on the sofa. Not too romantic. Don used to be fun, and I felt sexy with him. Now I feel dead. I miss feeling alive." A tear trickled down her cheek.

"So, you don't like his neglect of you." I tried to give her greater agency.

"No, I don't like it at all. He has all the fun. It's not fair." Debra pouted like a petulant child. Suddenly she broke out into a nervous giggle.

"I see tears and rage behind the laughter," I commented.

"I'm sad and annoyed with him." Clenching her fists, she tried desperately to control herself. Her shaking torso gave her away. Silence filled the room.

"Annoyed? How about enraged?" I chose to break the silence and confront her authentic feelings. Finally, Debra responded.

"I don't know what else to say," she uttered quietly.

"Are you afraid to disclose more of your angry feelings?" I suggested.

"It may be too much," she replied.

"Too much? For you or for me?" I asked.

"Maybe both of us." Debra's authentic response was refreshing.

"How was anger handled by your parents when you were little?" I wondered.

"When I lost my temper, my mother burst out in tears, and enlisted my father. He hit the roof, screaming at the top of his lungs, and threatening me with his belt. Sometimes he hit me." Debra's sobs were, undoubtedly, a replay of early childhood feelings of helplessness.

"Where was your mother in this scene?" I asked.

"She fell apart. Mom wasn't strong enough to stand up to him," she replied sadly.

"We can see from where fear of aggression stems. Your father abused his power, and your mother collapsed. He was too much for you and for her. It seems that you believe your aggression is destructive, like your father's," I interpreted.

"I'm not comfortable with aggression. I can't even assert myself," she explained meekly. The good little girl showed her face.

"So you've learned the hard way that girls ought to be good little girls, or else. But boys can be bad as bad can be. They sure have the better deal." I interpreted her internalizations.

"I like to think I'm a good woman. Aggression doesn't fit the picture of a good woman," she concurred.

"How's Don with assertion?" I queried.

"Great," she quipped.

"How is that?" I inquired.

"Well, he's ambitious, powerful, a little macho, but I kind of like that. He's used to calling the shots at work, and he does that with me." She showed her displeasure.

"How do you feel about that?" I asked.

"I don't like it." She seemed clear about that. "I've tried standing up for myself, but he always wins. He reminds me of everything that he gives me— the jewelry, a BMW, a gorgeous home, and private schools for the kids. He yells and threatens to leave me penniless if we split. I'm scared and I end up apologizing. So, he wins all the time. He's so controlling." She was clearly perturbed.

"A little like your mom and dad." I made the connection.

"Yeah, I married my dad. They both have explosive tempers. I guess I'm a little like my mother." She confirmed my thoughts.

"How do you mean?" I inquired.

She shuddered. "She didn't know how to assert herself and neither do I. I never thought I'd turn into my helpless mother."

"How are you feeling right now?" I wanted her to articulate her feelings.

"I feel very, very sad," Debra reflected.

"It sounds like you're enraged with him and yourself." I wanted to ferret out more of her rage.

"I don't know; all I know is I'm not happy. I'm afraid my marriage isn't going to make it." Debra's worries took center stage, leaving her angry feelings in the wings. She was not ready to address angry feelings just yet.

"Would you consider some marital therapy for both of you?" I suggested.

"I don't want him in therapy with me. I've got to be honest with a therapist, and if he comes in I can't do that. I haven't told you everything," she blurted out.

"Honest?" I asked.

"I'm having an affair. If Don ever found out, he'd divorce me. I'm terrified about what could happen. Will I lose my kids? Will I really be penniless?" Her anxiety mounted and she began to gasp for breath.

"I see we've hit a sore spot that's bringing you a lot of anxiety," I remarked.

"Well, the affair's not making me anxious. The affair's my salvation. Without Rob I'd go crazy. I'm just scared the affair will get out," she continued.

"Tell me more about how the affair's your salvation," I inquired.

"I couldn't stay in this marriage without Rob—he's my lover. He's saving my marriage. Don gives me all the material things, but I feel empty, dead, and insignificant with him. Rob makes me feel important, like a somebody. Rob listens to me; we communicate and he's so romantic. He's into me, and he lets me know it. I get so excited with butterflies in my stomach when I'm going to see him. He takes me away from my boring life, and I feel desirable and sexy." Debra's bluish-gray sweatsuit seemed to take on a clear blue-sky hue.

"Wow, this affair's heady!" I joined her enthusiasm.

"Yeah, like I said, Rob's great. But, I'm scared Don will find out. My friend had an affair, and her husband found out. He wants a divorce, and she stands to lose a lot," Debra explained, looking down at her bejeweled left hand once again.

"Any misgivings about the affair?" I wondered.

"No, I wouldn't say that. I don't feel guilty, if that's what you mean. Don is just not there for me the way Rob is. I'm in seventh heaven with Rob." She waxed rapture.

"How often do you see him?" I asked.

"I only get to see him once a week, but we talk every day. He calls and listens to me. He can tell what mood I'm in as soon as I say hello. Sex is over the top, everything goes, and I lead. Can you believe that?" she asked.

"Why not? I'll bet there are many ways you can lead," I ventured.

"I don't know. I feel on top of the world with him, and then I feel down in the dumps. I'm scared." Debra was gaining insight into her dilemma.

"So, there's no free lunch," I remarked.

"No," she agreed.

"Rob's like a vacation, an exciting adventure, a fantasy. Unfortunately, you have to come back to reality. And you go up and down like the stock market when you worked on Wall Street," I interpreted.

"Lately, I'm more down than up. I'm so scared that Don will find out. And I can't give Rob up either. I tried and I was miserable. I'm stuck." Debra was torn between the devil and the deep blue sea.

"What a dilemma," I commented.

*Amazing! Where are her guilty feelings? Diane Lane in the film* Un-faithful *was rent with guilt. Debra's only concern is fear of her fate. What about Don? What about hurting him? What about hurting her children? Is her anger toward Don split off, so she enacts it in this passive-aggressive way? Is her concern for others obliterated by her rage?*

As we continued on our journey together, Debra began to see that her anxiety was related to her inner conflicts. She got in touch with her rage and envy of Don's exciting life. Direct expression of her aggression was not her strong suit; it was Don's. In childhood, she failed to get the message that love could be greater than aggression. When her parents fought, her mother caved in, her father was the winner, and the marriage was the loser. Her parents knew no mutuality or understanding of each other's feelings. So, aggression was dangerous for Debra.

As Debra began to articulate her mixed feelings, magically her anxiety and panic attacks subsided. She remembered her volatile father throwing furniture and punching holes in walls while yelling invectives at her mother. Her mother did not respond outwardly, but she did inwardly. Turning her aggression inward, she suffered from depression.

As a little girl, Debra cringed and tried in vain to tune them out. At times, she tried to intervene by pleading with them to stop fighting. They simply ignored her; she was a mere child. Debra felt powerless in her efforts to help her parents. Her feelings of insignificance in early childhood were replicated in her marriage with Don.

She had always thought she would not become her helpless mom, and that her children would not suffer like she did. But, unwittingly, Debra did repeat the pattern from her childhood. She internalized a self that was helpless. Reenacting the past, Debra felt powerless in her attempts to reach her husband, so she gave up. But internally, she remained enraged with him. Disavowing her feelings of rage, Debra enacted them by engaging in infidelity.

Rob, her personal trainer, came to the house when her husband Don was not home. One day, Don came home unexpectedly for lunch and almost caught Debra and Rob in the act. Debra had managed to get her shorts on, but her top was unbuttoned. She explained that she was sweaty and had to change her top. Rob was not quite dressed either. Don did not really buy the story; he was suspicious, constantly checking on her. It was just a matter of time before Don would discover the affair.

In therapy, Debra began to explore what could happen to her children. She feared the consequences of exposure of the affair on her children. Debra worried that her children would hate her, that they would lose respect for her, and that they would stop trusting others. Her worries were not exactly warranted. I have found that children react in the moment, but with good-enough parenting, they can soon see the bigger picture. Indeed, in the long run, a child will love and trust her mom more for standing up for herself than if her mom continues to live in quiet desperation. Instead of relating to a weak, ineffective, helpless mom, when her mom takes a stand—even if it is with an extramarital affair—her mom is doing something to end the marital strife. So, a child has a more powerful, effective mom with whom to identify.

Daring Debra did do something drastic to end the marital strife. While her solution for saving her marriage with an extramarital affair was not working, it empowered her to make changes. She became aware that she had to save herself. Then she would tackle her marriage. We worked on articulating her desires as a separate, active subject, and not merely as a self-sacrificing object serving the needs of her family. That was her mother's self-definition, but it need not have been hers. This approach helped her allay her fears of getting swallowed up by her powerful husband and the needs of her children. Together, we found avenues of expression where Debra would begin to feel autonomous and independent and still devoted to her family.

Aggression was still a stumbling block. Debra kept protecting us from her rage. We worked on channeling her aggression into assertion of her passions and accomplishments. It proved to be an arduous journey.

One of Debra's buried treasures turned out to be her passion for the arts. Upon the discovery that her heart and soul soared at the prospect of sculpting,

she decided to give it a try. A beginner's sculpting course offered in the local museum was just the right thing. The joys of molding something out of
nothing provided her hope of molding her own self. She wanted to be a
somebody, not a nobody. By sculpting massive women with powerful limbs,
she began to recreate herself symbolically. The process and the product of
Debra's art were active expressions of her inner strivings that helped to
contain and transform her anger.

In time, Debra dared to express her anger directly, which freed her to
express her sexual desires. She began to tell Don what she desired in sex,
what turned her on, and what he could do so that she would orgasm. Don
did not know what had hit him, and he resisted at first. While he was
suspicious of Debra, Don was also intrigued by the change.

Slowly, Debra began to feel more independent, empowered, and responsible for her actions. Her guilty feelings emerged, and she began to hate what
she was doing with Rob. After all, Don was trying to be a better lover, and
she was enjoying sex with him. That was a plus for the marriage. Their
relationship, however, still had a long way to go.

Debra realized that the affair was a passive-aggressive power play. She
desired more intimacy, but the affair was no way to arrive at it. Her affair
was not about intimacy; it was an escape from reality, her boring life, and
her domineering and neglectful husband. Alas, her affair was not realistic.
Debra and her lover did not share the same toothbrush, nor did they wipe
snotty noses, or throw out the garbage.

A real intimate relationship may not be as glamorous as a forbidden
affair, but there are comforts and joys—even romance and sex—couples
can share. Debra had built a life with Don that needed repair. She and
Don had created history together, with good times and, lately, not such
good times. They had never really tried to work out their differences. She
held on to her frustrations, let them simmer, and acted out secretly. Don
maintained his power by ignoring her and demeaning her, much as her
father had done.

She realized that before she could embark on marital therapy, it was
crucial that she end the affair first. After numerous stops and starts, Debra
finally ended the affair with Rob. Debra and Don have entered marital
therapy where they are learning how to understand each other, and how to
meet each other's needs.

Intimacy means openness and honesty. A secret act, infidelity is a betrayal
of trust. Infidelity is also a power play for the betrayer, as it leaves the
betrayed spouse disoriented.[1] Debra's greatest fear was exposure of the affair,
so honesty as the road to intimacy was exceedingly dangerous. She showed
her daring side and disclosed the truth in marital therapy.

Not so surprisingly, Don's fury and humiliation knew no bounds. He vowed revenge. Debra was soon able to recognize that rage was Don's antidote for the terrible pain she had inflicted upon him. In tears she begged forgiveness, but Don was not ready to forgive her. He needed time to process his anger, and Debra understood she would have to bear up and withstand his assaults. The affair was devastating for both, but it also provided a platform from which a more meaningful relationship could spring.

As hurtful as the affair was to Don, it was also a wakeup call. He loved his wife, but he was not aware of the emotional impact of his neglect and his controlling ways. In marital therapy, Don is learning how to listen, and Debra is learning how to communicate in direct and assertive ways. Mostly, they are beginning to gain mutual understanding and empathy. They are still in marital therapy, and Debra sees me individually. She is calmer these days, more assertive, and more hopeful.

Like Debra, many wives find that they are not satisfied with domestic life, and they miss the excitement of their careers in the outside world. Debra partly used the affair as an exciting escape from her boring existence. She also envied her husband's powerful position as the provider. Debra submitted reluctantly to her husband's power as she had done in her childhood with her father. Fearing her aggression, she disavowed it and then enacted it with an extramarital affair. The affair was a daring attempt to empower herself.

Debra desired—but did not enjoy—a romantic, exciting, sexually satisfying marriage. So another motivation in reaching outside of the marriage was satisfaction of her desires. She believed the extramarital affair made it possible for her to tolerate the marriage and used the affair to save her marriage. Ironically, she was almost right—the affair brought everything to a head. Once the affair was relinquished, Debra was able to work on herself and her marriage. She came into therapy looking for painless fixes, only to find that pain and suffering were an integral part of living life fully. In marital therapy, Debra and Don are working on transforming the pain into a more pleasurable life together.

## SUBJECT OR OBJECT?

Wives today are grappling with feminist thought advocating that they be subjects of their own desires, sexual and otherwise. We are not merely objects to children, or sex objects to men, but desiring sexual subjects in our own right.[2] I use the word *grappling* because so many of us wives are in conflict about our desires and our needs. We got a glimpse of this conflict in the above case study, where Debra desired an equal relationship, but was caught up submitting to her husband and serving as an object to her family.

Indeed, wives need nurturance and devotion to loved ones—this is central to femininity—but, they also need power and achievement—traditionally the domain of men. The desire for power and achievement, however, is not a gendered one, but a human trait of both men and women.[3]

For some wives, the desire for power, independence, and separateness—to be a desiring subject—conflicts with the wish for the protection, comfort, and security provided by powerful husbands. In an abortive attempt to have both, a wife may forgo her desires, submit to an idealized powerful man, and derive her power vicariously through him. This is a setup for male domination and abuse of power.[4]

The more he dominates, the less she has of her own self, her own subjectivity, her own autonomy, and her own power. He becomes the master and she becomes his slave. Disappearing in him, she ceases to exist, and he remains alone. Merged without separateness, there are no longer two people in the relationship, but one. Erotic relating, however, requires two equal subjects who are separate and interrelated.

Erotic union is achieved in the tension of separateness and fusion—where two subjects lose themselves in each other, without loss of self. The experience of erotic merging achieves its intensity precisely because self and other are not merged.[5]

Wives today desire to be recognized and acknowledged, not only to recognize and acknowledge their husbands as they did in the nineteenth century. Nevertheless, history has left some indelible marks, and continues to color intentions of wives. So wives may still desire to be protected, but not want to be dominated. How does one manage this sweet deal?

In the following case study, you will meet a housewife who marries a submissive man, dominates him, and pushes him to achieve, so that he can provide her with comfort and security. Then she lives vicariously through her achieving, powerful husband. His dependability and reliability provide the safety and protection for which she longs. But human nature is complex and fine-grained, with nuance. Alas, she finds that she is not so thrilled with her construction. So, what does a girl do for thrills? She looks elsewhere.

### The Power behind the Throne

A downpour threatened floods in the neighboring oceanfront town where Tara lived. Drenched and shivering, Tara bolted into my office. She refused my offer for a dry towel. I had been seeing Tara for the last four months, trying to help her cope with alternating states of despair and hope. Her feelings about her housewifely role went from fulfillment to frustration. She either experienced admiration for, or fierce envy of, her husband Roland.

Tara either loved or she hated. She had not developed the capacity to hold onto ambiguity, the tension between contradictory feelings of love/hate, good/bad, separateness/difference, self/other, and subject/object. So she veered from one pole to the other. Tara's world was black and white, with no grays, no nuance, only binaries.

"So you want to suffer today. You refused to dry yourself," I commented.

Short, cropped dark hair, now soaked, framed the contours of her sculpted face. A wet lace-trimmed prim frock clung to her body, revealing ample curves. Her olive skin was flushed, and her dark eyes sunk like black coals in a red-hot fire. Something was smoldering.

"No, I hate suffering. It's against my religion," Tara quipped sardonically.

"I see you brought your sense of humor along with the rain," I commented.

"Yeah, I'm gonna need it." She burst into uncontrollable sobs. "I'm miserable," she moaned.

"Miserable?" I asked.

"I've always loved the rain; it matches my sad feelings, but today I can't stand it; I can't stand anything." She continued to shiver as the water dripped down from her head.

"Like what?" I inquired.

"Like myself. I can't stand myself," she responded.

"Hmmm," I said.

"I hate myself. You see, I'm cheating on my husband, and I hate myself for it." Anguished cries swept over her. Salt and rainwater mingled.

"Let's talk about it further," I suggested.

"My father warned me that pretty girls had to be very careful, to look ladylike, not trampy or sexy, because boys would take advantage of us. I dress down, if you notice," she explained.

"I notice. So your Dad didn't validate your sexuality; instead he encouraged you to hide behind a demure woman's skirts. Maybe your mother's skirts?" I interpreted and queried further.

"I don't know much about my mother, but she was anything but demure. Mother was a wild, wanton, evil woman. And I'm following in her footsteps. When I was two, my mother left my father for another man. Dad never got over it. I later found out Mother was a junkie, and she ran off with her drug-pusher boyfriend. Dad was strict, and raised me to be a good girl: no drugs, no sex before marriage, and no bad boys. He loved Roland." Tara's pensive mood placed her need for self-blame on hold.

"I think you told me Roland's like your father—responsible, dependable, and sober," I offered in an attempt to soften her punitive superego.

"Yeah, they're alike, so what I'm doing is even more despicable." She was determined to punish herself.

"Why do you think you're like your mother?" I asked.

"My mother, my horrid mother. We're both cheats." She blushed in shame.

"She abandoned you for another man. Do you think you're abandoning your family by having an affair with another man?" I inquired.

"No way. I'd never leave my kids, but what I'm doing's still a sin." She continued on her path of self-destructive punishment.

"A sin?" I asked.

"Yeah, I'm Catholic and adultery's a sin," she explained.

"Uh, huh," I uttered.

*So today she's all bad and Roland's all good. She's punishing herself and sparing me. I guess I'm all good today. Just three days ago, she was yelling at me for not understanding her. Maybe I wasn't. Maybe we co-constructed an impasse. I darted and she dodged. I didn't stay with her; instead I proclaimed my separateness by pointing out her resistance. It led to an argument, maybe a power struggle. Today she's letting me into her world, and we're in a more mutual power place. She's piqued my curiosity. Can I pique hers? Can we go for some nuance?*

"Roland's such a good guy?" I tried to engage her curiosity.

"Well, yeah, he is, sort of," Tara said thoughtfully.

"Sort of?" I asked.

"Actually, Roland is boring. And I don't respect him," she revealed.

"Why not?" I asked.

"Roland's a wimp," she responded.

"A wimp? I don't get it. You've told me he's a successful businessman." I was baffled.

"Well, he didn't want to go to business school, so I pushed him. Then he went to business school and got his MBA. When he graduated he took the first job offered to him, even though it was a lousy job. I insisted that he leave and take this other job. If not for me, he'd still be there, pushing papers around and making $40,000 a year. He listened to me. And see what happened? He's doing great, making five times that much now." She beamed.

"So you're in charge, and he abides by your dictates. And you derive material benefits from his power. How does that make you feel?" I inquired.

"Good. I like being in control. I feel powerful. But he doesn't always listen to me. Like now, he's afraid to go the next step, to move up to upper management. He doesn't like to make waves, except with me." Tara spewed out her angry words.

"How is that?" I inquired.

"He controls me when it comes to spending money. He wants me to give him a written account of every penny I spend—even for groceries. He calls me a spendthrift. Sure I like nice things. So what? What else can I do for fun? Roland's not fun; he's boring. And he's so stingy." She bemoaned her fate.

"How do you address your discontents with him?" I was curious to see how she asserted herself.

"I try to hash it out with him, but he ignores me. I can't get him to listen to me. He controls the relationship," she complained bitterly.

"So you're the power behind the throne. Only, the king has a mind of his own. And he defeats you. He takes center stage. How's it to be backstage, directing a defiant actor?" I interpreted and inquired further.

"I see where you're going. He's really got the power, not me." Tara sighed wistfully.

"He's the powerful actor after all, and you're the powerless reactor. He dominates you and you're forced into submitting. And you don't like it. Living vicariously through his power's not working." My interpretation was a reach. But then again, why skirt the issue?

"He's abusive verbally. He calls me lazy, frivolous, that I spend his hard-earned money recklessly. Maybe he's right," she chimed in, while rearranging the folds in her dress. Ignoring my interpretation, she continued her lament.

"I feel worthless. Maybe I'm really lazy. After all, he's competing in a tough, rough world, and I get to stay home, safe and sound." She was entertaining a new thought. "But why don't I like it?" she inquired in bewilderment.

"Perhaps his world out there's giving him more satisfaction than yours," I suggested.

"Roland's life is exciting. I'm left at home, bored and unappreciated. He comes home after a satisfying day where he's appreciated, so I resent him." She certainly was not skirting any issues.

"You look angry and miserable," I noted.

"Why shouldn't I be? He comes home late, tired from work, and doesn't talk to me. I have his dinner ready and waiting for him, the house is spic-and-span, and the kids are bathed and ready for bed. I feel like a servant. I wait on him hand and foot. He plays with the kids if they're still awake, and after dinner, he's ready to conk out. He's so boring," she complained.

"Sounds frustrating, to say the least," I said.

"I also work hard, but he doesn't recognize me. I'm alone with the kids all day, and I'm bored. I want adult company, some excitement, and some romance. And I'm going for it." Her dark eyes danced as she smiled mischievously.

"Anyone I know?" I wondered about her reverie.

"No, but I know." She was teasing me.

"Want to let me in on the secret?" I went along with it.

"I'm not fooling you. You get me, Carl gets me, but Roland doesn't. Oh yes, Carl's my lover," she explained.

*She's getting it, and letting me in, so we're both in on it. It's nice to be on equal footing with her. It doesn't sound like she feels equality in power with Roland. Is her affair a means of gaining power?*

"Tell me more about your affair," I suggested.

"Carl's so different from Roland. Carl's cool. He's a lead guitarist in his own rock band. He's exciting and fun. I always loved to sing, but Dad wouldn't give me lessons. He was afraid I'd land up singing in a nightclub like a floozy. Carl lets me sing with his band once in a while. That's the greatest!" Tara sighed dreamily. She waxed exhilaration.

"Sounds like you two make beautiful music together. I notice that you said, 'He lets me sing.' So he's in charge. Sound familiar?" I asked.

"No, Carl's not anything like Roland. Carl's tattooed with pierced eyebrows and nipples. He fascinates me. Carl does coke. I tried it, and I like it. With coke, I feel confident and alive." Tara was telling all, or was she?

"So, he's showing you another side of life," I interpreted.

"Carl is sexy and a risk taker. He's been arrested a few times. Tells me jail's not so bad, that the drug highs are worth it. I don't know about that. The idea of jail freaks me out." Fascination, then disgust, filtered through as she cringed. The jail she constructed in her marriage was enough. She did not need another one.

"So, you've split your men into good boys and bad boys. Roland's the good boy and Carl's the bad one. It sounds like you love Roland, but you desire Carl," I interpreted.

"Yeah, I do love Roland, even though I don't respect him. I desire Carl, and I respect that he takes risks." Tara confirmed my thoughts.

*She reminds me of the madonna/whore complex that was so powerful a force in Freud's nineteenth-century world—the split between the angel of the house and the prostitute. Only now, the genders have been reversed. So many women today struggle with a similar split between love for men they see as good, dependable, and reliable, and desire for men they see as exciting, reckless, and dangerous.*[6] *It's amazing how countless good women want bad boys!*

"You've split love and desire," I interpreted.

"I really want both, bur I can't get it from Roland, so . . ." She stopped to consider my interpretation and continued. "If my father ever knew about Carl, he'd turn over in his grave." She squirmed, scrunching her eyes into tiny dark dots.

"What about Roland? What would he do if he knew?" I asked.

"I think he knows, or at least suspects it. He's asking me a lot of questions lately," she explained.

"So you've got him off guard. Now, that's got to be a powerful place for you. You've got a secret, you know about it, and he's left guessing," I said.

"It's not right, not fair to Roland. I do love him, and I wish I desired him. I feel like telling him the truth." She was on the right track.

"For whose sake would that be? Yours or his?" I asked.

"For mine, I guess. It'd help ease my guilty conscience." She was candid, all right.

"Maybe your confession would help Roland to feel relieved that he's not crazy, that something's really going on. It could also help the marriage to become more honest, more open, and more intimate. You might get to really understand Roland and he'd get to understand you. Who knows? You might find Roland to be stronger and sexier," I suggested.

As we continued to work, Tara began to gain more insight into her desires for an extramarital affair. We mined multiple layers of meaning for her decision. There was no one answer or one solution. Clarity came at a price, a path on which she dared to embark. Alas, Tara was about to discover that clarity was muddled with murky waters of ambiguity and uncertainty— a central goal in our work.

Tara decided that she would weather the storm with Roland for the possibility of peace of mind. After ending the affair with Carl, Tara confessed to Roland about her infidelity. Roland was not really shocked, as he'd suspected it all along. He felt vindicated, and determined to punish Tara for her infidelity. In his mind, he was upright and moral; she was decadent and immoral. Roland called Tara every name in the book, cursing and comparing her to her "adulterous, dirty, junky, whorish mother." Nothing could be more painful. By meting out the ultimate punishment, he felt somewhat vindicated.

Valiantly, Tara suffered his vitriolic onslaughts and begged to be redeemed. She did not counterattack or construct excuses for her behavior. Finally, Roland found forgiveness in his heart and he joined Tara in marital therapy.

Tara remained in individual therapy as well, whereas Roland refused to do any individual work. He was not ready yet.

In therapy, Tara recognized the affair for what it was—mainly a vehicle for her to embrace her raw sexuality, her daring, dangerous, and dark side. She had split off her vivacious, desiring subjectivity and enacted it with exciting and dangerous Carl. Her marriage became lifeless and dull. Excitement was split off from security, and love from sexual desire. Indeed, people in our time, like in Freud's time, may find it hard to see that two opposing emotional states can coexist. So they split love from sexual excitement, and commitment from passion.[7]

As the power behind the throne, Tara was left holding the crown for Roland. He wore the crown and she resented his power. Roland was the subject of his own desires, and Tara was his handmaiden. Despite efforts at dominating Roland in order to live vicariously through him, she remained at his mercy. He was not such a benevolent dictator. He held onto his sovereign power by criticizing her and treating her like a servant.

Another one of Tara's conflicts revolved around her dependent housewifely role and her desires for independence. She struggled with seeing herself as an active subject of her own desires, and not a passive object to her husband. Wishing to flee from the clutches of her constricted childhood and controlling husband, she escaped with an extramarital affair. Her defiant act did not really do the trick.

She decided to pursue an old interest of hers where she would derive separateness and fulfillment. Singing lessons, forbidden by her father, were now a godsend. Tara is beginning to feel more comfortable about exercising her own autonomy.

The affair brought Tara and Roland closer and they worked at hearing each other's perspective. Nevertheless, trust had eroded. Roland was insanely jealous of Tara's voice teacher and the prospects of her performing to admiring men. A little like her father? Indeed, with the extramarital affair, Tara unwittingly recreated the possessive, jealous relationship with her father. Only this time, she saw her role in the construction and felt remorse.

We worked on tolerating the ambiguity and uncertainty of two opposing feeling states that existed simultaneously. In childhood, Tara experienced her mother as the irresponsible, decadent, self-indulgent one and her father as the responsible, innocent, moral one. On the surface, she identified with her proper father and married a proper husband. Deep down, Tara disavowed her exciting, self-indulgent parts and enacted them by having an affair with a risky, dangerous man.

A goal of marital therapy was to arrive at a relationship where Tara and Roland could endure the tensions of commitment and passion, comfort and erotica, security and excitement, love and desire. Another goal was to learn mutual recognition and empathy for one another's desires. In communications work, Tara and Roland took turns listening to each other, paraphrasing what the other said and responding. This exercise helped them to place themselves in each other's shoes—the basis of empathy.

The communications exercise also highlighted how the couple wanted sameness by obliterating differences. In the marriage they had taken turns in the dance of power, domination, and submission. In marital therapy, Tara and Roland are working on articulating differences and bridging them without assigning a right or wrong to either one. And that is pretty much where they are now.

The struggle for power—who is to blame, who is taking advantage of whom, who is exploiting or exploited—is exceedingly difficult. Fighting for who is in the right places the marriage in the wrong. Who is right or wrong does not matter in marriage; what matters is getting along.

Tara resisted the reinstatement of romance that they had enjoyed early in the marriage. She felt tied to her children and reluctant to leave them overnight with a baby sitter. They decided to go slowly and start with romantic dinners and dancing. One evening, Tara got up and sang with the band. Guess what? Roland applauded proudly. Sure, he watched the men watching his wife and felt insanely jealous. But he contained himself and they talked about it afterward. The marriage survived this act of separateness. Though tempted, Tara did not run off with the winsome piano player. She returned to her husband's embrace.

## BOTH SIDES OF A COIN

*When I'm good I'm very, very good, but when I'm bad, I'm better.*
—Mae West

Do you see any of yourself in the above cases? How about fears of losing your identity in your housewifely role? What about power, domination, and submission? Or frustration in not getting your emotional or sexual needs met in the marriage?

Feeling unfulfilled in marriage was a prime motive for infidelity in the above cases, which is consistent with recent research.[8, 9] Neither affair was intended to augment the marital relationship, but rather to supplement it. The affairs were mainly attempts to get the missing elements in the marital relationship. Nor were the affairs merely for expulsion of sexual desires as in the 1960s. Sex was a part of it, but not the prime motivator.

The housewifely role in which women stand to lose their autonomy, separateness, and identity may be a source of fear, anxiety, malaise, and existential angst. Like other wives in past history, many housewives today devote themselves to nurturing their families while their husbands make their marks in the business world. Rather than being subjects of their own desires, they become objects to others.

In our current culture, however, housewives hold other expectations from marriage. They desire mutual understanding and power. They also desire sexual and emotional engagement with husbands. They want romance and intimacy, yet it seems to evade them in the marriage. So they may turn to an affair. Alas, securing romance and intimacy in an affair is a myth. Why then are romance and intimacy so hard to sustain?

A chief factor in maintaining romance and intimacy is the ability to be comfortable with ambiguity. The arena for romantic, erotic excitement lies in the tension between separateness and merger, sexual passion and commitment, excitement and security, love and hate. Unfortunately, difference may signify separateness, and separateness signifies loss of the other and the relationship.[10] To avoid abandonment, one partner dominates and the other submits.

In both the past and the present, housewives are most often the partners to sacrifice themselves. Indeed, male domination with female submission has been coiled into women's experience over the years.[11] A dynamic of power and submission, however, is not where we find the other and the relationship. Rather, it is how we lose the other, and how both partners are left lonely and isolated.

Unconscious templates of early patterns of relating interfere with our ability to sustain intimacy and romance. Women continue to disavow their aggression, as seen in Debra's story. Not so for men. Women tend to split off their detested traits like hate, envy, and bad-girl aspects. For many of us, bad girl parts are discordant with our culture, our internalized childhood templates, and how we wish to be seen by others. Negative qualities, however, do not disappear; they are biodegradable. They go underground, only to resurface in other forms. Bad-girl parts stay behind closed doors, only to come out to play with bad-boy lovers, as seen in Tara's case.

Muriel Dimen,[12] the brilliant relational psychoanalyst and feminist, writes about the importance of multiplicity to replace dualisms in sexuality and women's development. She tells us that aggression, hatred, envy, competition—bad-girl parts—must come forward lest we remain locked in a false good girl model of femininity.

How can you resolve some of these dynamics? There are multiple constructions and equally multiple solutions. I have found that many housewives need a "room of their own"—a separate place where they can experience their authentic, creative, and powerful selves. They need a sphere where they can be subjects of their own desires and passions without resorting to extra-marital affairs.

Infidelity may threaten the marriage and needs to be examined carefully. The affair, however, may be a catalyst for marital repair, as in the above stories. Marital therapy is essential for healing from hurts, and to restore romance and passion. Most often, couples have not learned to articulate their feelings and work them through without help. Their parents did not leave them with a working model for resolving differences and for intimacy.

Can you fall in love with your husband again, and can he reciprocate? For the most part, I believe it is possible. To increase the probability of success, you and your spouse must commit to some hard work; and hard work never hurt anyone. Working through adversity can strengthen the marriage and result in mutual understanding, openness, love, and desire—real intimacy. Not every marriage, however, can be repaired. Nevertheless, hard work will strengthen the partners to go on with their lives separately. They will acquire the tools for love and fulfillment in or out of the marriage.

Speaking of hard work, how about wives in the workplace? Are they feeling more autonomous, independent, and powerful? Do working wives have it all, achievement and families? Not necessarily, as you will see in the following chapter. Indeed, working wives may have their own issues, feel desperate, and also dare to engage in extramarital affairs.

# 5

# Wanderlust While They Work

## WORKING WIVES AND OUTSIDE ROMANCE

*I generally avoid temptation unless I can't resist it.*
—Mae West

## DUELING ROLES

*Too many women still martyr themselves rather than risk upsetting the marital apple cart.*
—Karen J. Maroda[1]

Scores of wives have assumed working roles in and out of the home. Notwithstanding the stress, strain, and drain of the workplace, wives derive certain benefits. In the workplace, they get satisfaction by recognition and validation of their work and their personalities. Earning one's own money can also be empowering. Unlike their stay-at-home sisters, at the workplace, wives fulfill desires for autonomy, independence, and separateness. At work, they feel freer to compete and assert themselves.

At a deeper level, however, wives may still be ill at ease with these culturally defined masculine traits. For eons, women have been more comfortable with cooperation than competition.[2] Across the generations, wives have opted for gentleness over toughness, nurturance over aggression, and devotion to loved ones over achievement in the world. It is easy to see how some modern-day working wives may feel conflicted about their dual roles of power and devotion.

Historically, husbands have been threatened by wives' separateness, power, and independence. By assuming powerful roles, working wives may fear rejection by their husbands. Husbands may wish to assume power over their domestic diva wives. By tending to husbands' needs before their own, wives may unwittingly collude with their hubbies' needs.

In order to preserve the marital status quo, wives may feel compelled to conceal their desires for power and success.[3] Working wives often feel guilty about deserting children and household duties. So, after a hectic day at work, they go overboard at home, frenetically cooking, picking up messes, chauffeuring children, checking on homework, and comforting bruised knees and feelings. While they are knee deep in drudgery, their hubbies are free to watch the network news. Essentially, husbands are off the hook, and wives are left sinking. In silence, working wives struggle to be heard.

In the sixties, when wives went back to work en masse, husbands promised to help with parenting and household chores. They did not help then, nor do they help now.[4] Indeed, even among young couples today, in 70 percent of cases, wives do 70 percent of the work whether they are working or not.[5] So, the burden falls on working wives, with untold pressures.

With wives feeling overwhelmed, exhausted, and fed up with husbands, romance and sex are degraded. Collapsing in the arms of a willing, comforting, and convenient co-worker promises a romantic respite; and romance in the workplace is not hard to find. The workplace offers tempting opportunities for racy romances. Suddenly, lagging spirits are revived. The following case study depicts a working wife's stresses, the fading of romance in her marriage, and the temptations in the workplace for a convenient and romantic extramarital affair.

### Sarah's Stresses

"How soon can you see me?" a soft voice beseeched me.

"What seems to be the problem?" I asked.

"Everything. I'm stressed out and ready to explode. It's my job, my husband, my . . . I just can't cope." The words tumbled out frantically over the telephone wire. I gave her an appointment for the next day, and she sighed in relief.

Sarah arrived a half hour early, and patiently stayed in the waiting room. Strawberry blond hair tied back, in a cream-colored, tailored suit with contrasting accessories, she was outfitted for business. Her smudged mascara and wringing hands suggested otherwise. Her shiny freckled face was yet another tip-off. Our urbane, sophisticated lady may not have been so sophisticated after all.

"I'm sorry I'm early, but I was afraid I couldn't find your office, so I left lots of time," Sarah explained apologetically.

"How can I help you?" I asked.

"I don't know." Her slim, petite body caved in.

"On the phone you spoke about your job and your husband. Why don't you begin by telling me more about your job? Then we can talk about your husband." Work for women seems to be less emotionally charged than intimate relationships. So I inquired about her job before her marriage.

"I work for an advertising agency. Actually, I'm a vice president. I'm under constant pressure to make tight deadlines to please my accounts and to keep expenses down. It's a stressful job, but I love it." She sat up straight, filling every inch of her five-foot, hundred-pound frame.

"What do you love about it?" I inquired.

"I like making my own money. My husband Charles makes good money, and he doesn't want me to work, but I need it for my sanity. I'd go crazy in the house all day long. I tried it and we almost got divorced. So I went to work where, yeah, it's hectic, but I like the challenge. I like the idea of my high-power job. Am I selfish?" She equivocated.

"Why are power and achievement selfish?" I inquired.

"Well, I should be home for my kids after school; instead they go home to a baby sitter. I feel guilty about leaving them. I try to be a good mom and wife, so I do what I can for my family—the grocery shopping, cooking, cleaning up afterwards, helping my boys with the homework, and getting them ready for bed. Then I'm pooped." She delineated her burdensome role at home.

"I can see why. Does Charles help you with any of this?" I wondered.

"No, he doesn't do a thing around the house. He plays with the kids and leaves the discipline to me. He's a big spoiled kid himself. His excuse for not helping is that I chose to work. It's my problem, not his. So why should he help? If I stayed home, I'd have plenty of time, and not be so stressed," Sarah blurted out.

"You seem angry with Charles," I noted.

"I shouldn't be angry. I chose to work; he's right," she replied tartly.

"How's he right not to support your desire to achieve satisfaction as a separate person?" I showed my anger, which she had disavowed.

"I think he's threatened by my work, where I have a separate, independent life. He'd like me under his thumb, where he can treat me like a dependent child, dole out money to me, and keep me tied to him." Her neat suit began to show wrinkles.

"Now we're getting somewhere." I validated her candor.

"Not really. I feel like I'm stuck, going nowhere," Sarah spoke tearfully.

"It sounds like, at home and at work, you're Superwoman. Only you're not flying; instead, you're faltering. But, Superwoman had an assistant. Do you ask Charles for help?" I tried to get her more in touch with her dilemma.

"I've tried, but he doesn't listen. It's funny. At work, I'm in charge of fifty employees, and at home I can't get my husband off the sofa to help me." She was right on.

"So, you're a lion at work and a mouse at home," I suggested.

"You could say that," Sarah laughed.

"It seems you're more comfortable with devotion to your family and nurturance of their needs than your desires for autonomy, power, and achievement at work," I interpreted.

"I need to think about that." Sarah pondered my interpretation. "Speaking of desires, I have a lover." Briefly emboldened, Sarah soon retreated into a timid schoolgirl. She meekly asked me to excuse her while she used the bathroom.

*Are my daring, frank words encouraging her to be more daring and outspoken? Is she dismayed about her daring revelation? She's been timid about her desires with me. At home, she probably denies her desires for power, separateness, and independence by plunging headlong into housewifely duties. I wonder if she sacrifices her desires for fulfillment to preserve the marriage. How about her desire for a lover? No wonder she's stressed. She's a complex woman—a challenge.*

"How does your lover fit into all of this?" I was curious.

"He doesn't. Larry, my lover, works at the same agency, only he does PR." She wasn't making any connections.

"So the affair has nothing to do with any problems in your marriage?" I kept at it.

"I didn't look for an affair; it just happened," she replied innocently.

*It just happened? Often wives feel that way. With deeper insight, however, they uncover multiple problems that led to the affair. Then they can see that the affair wasn't merely a happening—a passive response—but an active act of will and desire. That's more hopeful. Once we acknowledge agency, we're in control, and we can make changes. A happening places us in the back seat, whereas desire puts us in the driver's seat. How empowering desire can be!*

*I'll try to see why she keeps herself in this powerless position. Has it got to do with a penchant for denial of her desires? What about self-blame? Her unnecessary apology to me for coming early may be a clue to a propensity for self-blame. Perhaps she goes on automatic pilot to blame herself unduly, like so many of us women. Years of society placing blame on women for either too much or too little sexuality have their impact.*

*Her double load of home and work stresses may well be a part of her desire for an affair. Her anger with Charles for not lending support to her desires must figure into it. We have just begun, and already so many directions to pursue. My head's spinning. I guess hers is too. No wonder she's stressed.*

Upon returning from the bathroom, Sarah explained she had to leave early and asked for another appointment soon. We made one for two days later.

In the following sessions, Sarah let her hair down literally and figuratively. She wanted to talk about the affair.

"I want to tell you more about my relationship with Larry. I think it'll be good to get it off my chest," she explained.

"Is the affair adding to your stresses?" I wondered.

"No, not at all; it's just weighing on me. I don't know why. Oh, yes, I found out that Charles is having an affair. He denies it, but I know." She changed the subject.

"How do you feel about Charles having an affair?" I was curious.

"How can I feel? It's not like I'm not doing the same thing," she explained rationally.

"I see." I did.

"Like I said, I wasn't looking for the affair; it just happened. It was all just so tempting." Sarah was determined to keep it there.

"How'd it happen?" There was no reason to fight her, so I joined her.

"We work together on certain accounts; it's been a great working relationship. We each have a say, and respect one another's point of view. One day, Larry invited me to lunch to talk about a big, important, and difficult account. We both opened up about our frustrations and how we had a hard time dealing with stresses. One lunch led to another, when we began confiding in each other about problems in our marriages. We had a real good, close friendship before any sex happened. We met for six months before we went to bed." She explained the evolution of the affair, not the underlying meaning as yet.

"So you both have problems in your marriages," I clarified.

"I guess so. Maybe we'd just be good friends if I had a better love life with Charles." She thought about it.

"How would you describe your love life with Charles?" I asked.

"We don't have one. For Charles a love life is just sex. He wants sex all the time, only I don't. When I'm done for the evening, I'm too tired for sex. Anyhow, Charles doesn't turn me on. He's not understanding or romantic. He doesn't want to talk, or listen to me, to hug, or be close to me. He just wants to do it," she complained.

"Hmmm," I murmured.

"Charles calls me frigid, that I don't like sex, that I'm cold. Little does he know," Sarah smiled wryly.

"You don't seem cold to me," I noted. Indeed she sat on the couch close to me and made good eye contact.

"Well, I'm not. For a long while, I believed Charles, but I found out differently. It took Larry to open my eyes. Making love with Larry is super. We spend time talking, laughing, and delighting in each other before any sex. I love his sense of humor, and we have fun together. We have pet names for each other. I'm his little cabbage, and he's my bunny wabbit. Larry and I kiss a lot, he caresses my body all over, goes down on me till I orgasm, and then he enters me. I can't even have one orgasm with Charles, but I have multiple orgasms with Larry." She stretched out in a catlike pose of pure, unadulterated pleasure.

"So you feel like a desiring woman with Larry. Do you love him?" I asked.

"Yup, I love Larry. Like I said, it's not really about sex; it's about our friendship. He's my best friend." She was intent on denying her sexual desires.

"You seem intent on denying your desires for power at work and for an erotic relationship. I wonder how your mother handled her desires," I interpreted. Then I asked for greater clarification.

"I don't think she had any desires of her own. Dad ordered her around, and she didn't fight him. It was his way or the highway, so she didn't have much of a say. Mom was a dutiful housewife and catered to her family. Sacrificing herself for her family, she grew dependent on my Dad. That's partly why I work—not to be dependent on Charles." Sarah was making connections.

In the following sessions, Sarah and I explored more of her family history. Her mother had suffered from debilitating depression, with several hospitalizations. Her dad had been a powerful trial lawyer, winning large sums for his clients. It was well known that he carried on with his secretaries and sometimes with his clients. Sarah harbored conflicted loyalties about his adultery. While she admired her father's strength, success, and achievements, she also blamed him for her mother's illness. She abhorred her father's voracious desires for power and sex. Sarah also felt protective of her weak mother. Her father was a powerful, autonomous, achieving man, and Sarah identified with him in some ways. Nevertheless, his power and success were dangerous and hurtful, so Sarah denied the powerful, autonomous parts of her own self. Hence, some of the genesis of her inner conflict about her power and success.

Sarah's father came home late and had little time for her. His domineering ways were not confined to his wife, but they also affected Sarah. An authoritarian parent, he shouted out his commands to little Sarah. In grand lawyerly eloquence, her father won all disputes with Sarah. Rather than gaining recognition of her own opinions, Sarah's separateness and power were met with punishment. She felt compelled to apologize to her father and beg his forgiveness. Therein lay the origins of part of her self-negating and self-blaming behavior.

Standing by her man, Sarah's mother agreed with her father. In doing so, Sarah's mother failed to validate Sarah's strengths, too. Her mother encouraged her to be demure, sweet, and innocent, and said that the right man would take care of her. Sarah did find a man to take care of her, but dared to differ from her mother. She was determined to take care of herself with independence at work and at home. Part of her failure in securing Charles's help at home was her fear of dependence.

Whereas Sarah's mother was nurturing and gentle, her punitive and powerful father was not. Unable to identify with her passive, submissive mother for a sense of agency, Sarah identified with her father for subjectivity and power. Like her father, Sarah became successful in a high-powered job, and engaged in an extramarital affair. In her marriage, Sarah identified more with her mother, overdid her caring, denied her power, and was helpless in getting her needs met with Charles.

As to Sarah's marriage, for every jar there is a lid. Charles sealed the jar. A domineering man much like Sarah's father, Charles did not recognize his wife's strengths. Instead he undermined her. His masculinity was tied into being in charge, so that Sarah's marriage resembled her parents' marriage. Fortunately, Sarah was determined not to meet the same fate as her mother.

Armed with greater insight, Sarah tried to work on the marriage. But, one person alone does not make or break a marriage. Charles persisted in defending himself and blaming Sarah for their problems. He was unwilling to look at his role in the problems. He blamed Sarah for rejecting him sexually and "making him" have affairs. Of course, no one makes anyone do anything. Well, that was the last straw. While Sarah had an affair, she took responsibility for it. But Charles's arrogance was too much for her. Sarah filed for divorce, and they are now battling it out. Seeing as the marriage showed no promise, Sarah never told Charles about her affair.

What happened to Larry, her great love? Sadly enough, when she filed for divorce, Larry got cold feet. He said his wife was too fragile to handle a divorce, and that she wanted too much money. Larry promised to keep trying and pleaded with Sarah to continue the relationship with him. Sarah declined. She began to see that Larry was not the man she thought he was; he simply wanted an affair, not a real relationship.

Sarah dared to take her life into her hands and make changes, but Larry did not. She dared to let go of both men, and to go on with her life. She is more confident and comfortable with her power, independence, and separateness, as well as her nurturance, gentleness, and caring. Also, Sarah is hopeful about finding satisfaction of her desires for a mutually reciprocal relationship with another man. She feels she is able to make better choices and to assert herself in an intimate relationship.

In this case study, the extramarital affair served as an illusory love to bolster a dead marriage. An affair with a co-worker was also convenient. Indeed, the workplace is a tempting ground for infidelity. With enough problems in the marriage, temptation is hard to resist. Sarah's stresses at work and home brought her into therapy, but it was far more than that. Childhood history had hard-wired Sarah for denial of power and success at home. Cultural history of denial of women's power and sexuality had its impact as well. Her history also primed her for an intransigent, domineering man.

The above story illuminated multiple layers of meaning—cultural history, childhood history, temptations in the workplace, problems in the marriage, and each partner's role in wrecking the marriage. Sarah's daring side fueled her desire for an extramarital affair. It also empowered her to leave both the affair and the marriage in order to seek a more meaningful and fulfilling relationship. Are there stresses ahead? I hope so; without stress we cannot have success.

## WHAT WORKING WIVES WANT

*But why is it that some of our stars ignite and burn themselves out, falling to earth as little more than ashen rock, while others, muted over time, continue to float gracefully through space.*
—Jody Messler Davies[6]

Although wives go off to the workplace to fulfill various inner desires, they may also need the money to make ends meet. Two-income families are not uncommon in our current economy. Desires for financial independence, emotional independence, autonomy, separateness, and appreciation may be still other motivators for wives working. Or, a wife may simply work to get away from the home and her drab, dull housewife life. She and her husband have worked on the marriage, so that there is interplay between romance and commitment, erotic desire and love.

Then there are those wives who feel that romance in the marriage has faded, that their lives are limited and narrow. That is not to say they do not love their husbands. They do, but they want more, much more. Safety, security, comfort, caring, and commitment are not enough. Many a wife yearns for adventure, excitement, novelty, passion, and sexual and personal growth.

Frustrated in not fulfilling these desires in the marriage, the workplace beckons seductively. Imagination, the handmaiden of desire, has no bounds.

A wife may fulfill herself and expand herself at work. She may also explore new creative areas for a capacious self. By the same token, she may find limitless romance and passionate desire in the workplace. The innocent, young trainee may be smitten with her. Or she may attract a distinguished, dashing older associate. The stunning sexy superior may even go for her. So many tempting possibilities! Do you remember the movie *Thelma and Louise*, which featured two daring women on the road to sexual and personal freedom and self-expansion? Much like Thelma and Louise, wives today leave home to explore their selves. But, unlike the two movie heroes with wanderlust on the highway, wives may remain in the marriage with wanderlust in the workplace.

It is these wives whom I want to examine—the wives who believe that romance in marriage does not last, that it is normal for steamy sex to cool down and for marriage to become merely familiar and comfortable. They believe that intense, passionate desire in the early phase of marriage diminishes as deep affectionate love and security take over.

The sexy voice of desire and the steady rhythm of love simply cannot coexist in one relationship. Does this discordant note sound familiar?

In his last book prior to his untimely death, Stephen Mitchell,[7] a leading figure in relational psychoanalysis, left us with some brilliant and fresh insights on the topic of lasting romance. He opined that romance and erotic relating did not diminish in marriage; they became increasingly dangerous. So we go into a risk-management mode and degrade passion and romance in the marriage. It is not that romance fades; it is that we, unwittingly, destroy it. But why is romantic, sexual desire so dangerous?

A partner who can satisfy our desires over time is risky. We begin to need them for fulfillment of our desires. Placing ourselves in the perilous position of depending on our partners raises all kinds of fears. Mitchell goes on to say that in a monogamous marital relationship you select only one partner, which dramatically increases your dependency on your partner.

Dependency on only one person leaves you feeling vulnerable. You are now hostage to your partner's feelings and actions. Human nature is constantly in flux, and people change. Knowing you well, your partner may lose interest in you, detest your fallibilities, betray you, or leave you. There are risks, but there are no real risk-free meaningful relationships. Yet, we try to escape hurtful risks.

Mitchell[8] argues that we struggle to curtail dependency by constructing limited marriages. One way of achieving this is to bring mundane reality to the foreground and push excitement and romance to the background.

Together with our partners, we collude to keep devotional love alive and let sexual desire die. By focusing on commitment, safety, and stability—components of love—we lose sight of adventure, excitement, and spontaneity—components of desire. But real love does not lie in either love or desire; it is in both. Real love lies in the tension between love and desire. The inability to sustain adventure and safety, sex and security, excitement and commitment degrades romance. By collapsing one pole into the other, we squeeze the life out of marriage and real love.

If romance in marriage is dangerous because we become dependent on our one and only partner, is not a second or third partner safer? As the age-old adage goes, "It's not safe to put all your eggs in one basket." Which begs the question, If monogamous marriage cannot maintain sexual desire, novelty, and adventure, why not look elsewhere? What more enticing place for prospects is there than the workplace?

Daring to act on desires for an extramarital affair is one way to go, but there are others. The hopeful aspect of Mitchell's theorizing is that once we understand how we construct and destruct relationships, we can assume responsibility and change our self-defeating patterns. He believes that love and romance can endure. It is up to us.

In the next case study, meet a working wife who wanted more out of her dead marriage and dull life. Unaware of her self-destructive efforts to protect herself from the risks of real love in marriage, she did what many of us do. She looked for love outside of the marriage. But if you've opted for margarine over butter, we have new findings. It turns out that soft margarine is a far greater health hazard than sweet, creamy butter. There is something about the real thing that no substitute can replace.

### Alicia in Wanderland

One of those long, twelve-hour days at the office was finally coming to a close. Not that it was a bad day; it was simply draining. Emergencies, trauma, and pain marked the hours, with little respite. A hot bath and soft bed promised sweet surrender to slumber. The repeated knocks on my door suggested otherwise. In stumbled Alicia. Wild red hair disheveled, scarlet lipstick smeared, short wrap skirt askew, she looked like she had been shot out of a cannon.

"I thought I should see you." Nonchalantly, Alicia meandered over to the couch.

*No apology, no appointment, no warning, no recognition of me. As usual, it's all about her. Where's she been, looking like that? Her attire's unusual, even for her—a hemline and cleavage that almost meet! What am I thinking? I feel like her protective father, or worse still, her chastising, envious mother.*

"Why now?" I asked.

"You seem angry with me." She pouted tearfully. I thought I smelled liquor.

"Yup, I'm angry with you, Alicia. I also have a life, it's late, and we had no appointment." I tried to explain that we were engaged in a relationship, which entailed both of us, not just her.

"I know you have a life, but I don't." Groggily she tried to get up, only to fall flat on her face. On her descent, she threw up on my new rose-colored carpet. Then she passed out.

*So, I'm not only her parents, I'm her maid! I knew she downed some shots here and there, but I never saw her dead drunk. I wonder what's up. She sure knows how to get to me.*

*Alicia wanders in and out of marriages, moods, and men. Last week it was casual chic—skin-tight designer jeans, midriff-cropped tops, and dangling jeweled earrings to go with her belly button jewel. She giggled, cooed, and moaned about her lover, Tony. The week before, she was the epitome of sophistication—sort of. Her long, black, slinky dress was one thing, but her rose tattoos encircling her ankles were another. Somber and dramatic, her sonorous tone denounced Tony. He was new on the scene; others had come and gone.*

*You'd think Alicia was a fickle adolescent. Hardly. She's pushing sixty-five! Unpredictable, wild, and wanton, she's oblivious to others' needs. Alicia sure is a challenge. But why am I even contemplating seeing her at this time of night? Is she that entertaining, that colorful, and captivating? She reminds me of my younger days. I must keep in mind the analytic frame, and refrain from breaking the boundaries.*

I managed to move her and clean up her mess, when she woke up.

"I'm so ashamed of myself. I need to talk to you," she wailed.

"Alicia, I think you're in no condition for us to talk. I'll call a cab and see you tomorrow at our scheduled appointment." After Alicia left, I went upstairs to my home to the familiar comfort of my hubby and my two kitties. A cup of chamomile tea helped.

The following day brought a refreshed Alicia, looking surprisingly alert and ready to work.

"You're looking chipper," I remarked.

"I called in sick and slept all day. I couldn't believe what I looked like last night when I got home," she explained.

"What happened?" I inquired.

"So much happened. I don't know where to begin." She was quizzical.

"Wherever is just fine," I suggested, giving her agency to make the choice.

"I got drunk last night, it was a bad night all around. Tony warned he'd leave unless I got a divorce from Ernesto. I told Tony that Ernesto would never give me a divorce, so he threatened to take care of Ernesto." Oddly, Alicia looked calm.

"Is Ernesto in danger?" I asked.

"I don't think so. Tony's passionate and cavemanlike. He wants what he wants when he wants it. But he's all talk." She seemed certain about that.

"So, he's bluffing. You said Ernesto wouldn't give you a divorce. Do you want one?" I was calling her bluff.

"No, I don't want a divorce. I've made so many mistakes. This is my fifth marriage and I'm determined to make it stick. Like I told you, I had affairs in each marriage. Not a good record; I'm ashamed of it. I didn't want to cheat in this marriage, so I went back to work." Alicia's pensive mood surprised me—pleasantly, that is. Indeed, for people like Alicia, thinking before acting shows progress.

"Why'd you think working would prevent an affair?" I was puzzled.

"I don't know. All I know is, I didn't want to get into trouble again." She spoke earnestly.

"From the looks of it, I'd say you did." I was candid.

"Yeah, I keep getting into hot water over and over." Alicia began to tell one of her failed-marriage stories. "In my first marriage, my husband Tom was devoted and caring, but dull. He was an accountant, and real good with figures, except for mine. We rarely had sex, and when we did, it was the same monotonous routine. I withdrew, got depressed, and landed in the hospital. Tom's a bore, but he's a born caretaker. He nursed me back to health."

"How'd you feel about Tom then?" I wondered if she would give him an inch.

"I'm indebted to Tom, but I didn't feel any passion, excitement, or erotic desire. He was more like a father than a lover." She was not giving him a centimeter, let alone an inch.

"Uh huh," I joined her.

Her saga continued. "So, I went after my passion for design. I got a job as a graphics designer and threw myself into my work. I ended up having an affair with my art director, Alex. He encouraged my work, inspired me, and taught me a lot. He was so sensuous and tactile. Our working relationship evolved into a wild romance. We smoked pot together and made mad, passionate love. Sex with Alex was erotic, spontaneous, and exciting; every fiber of mine was alive. I wasn't depressed anymore, but I became a pothead. Slowly I deteriorated, and couldn't think straight."

"Are you still doing pot?" I asked.

"No." She did not offer any more.

"How'd you stop?" I was curious.

"My husband Tom came to my rescue and got me into a fancy rehab. I was cured, but Tom found out about the affair. He was understanding and forgave me. I still wasn't happy, so I divorced Tom to find a more exciting life with romance." She looked sad.

"And Alex?" I wondered what had happened to her heartthrob.

"I wasn't smoking pot anymore and he was still smoking. Who needs a pothead? He was really a loser." She condemned her playmate.

*So, Tom cleaned up her messes like I did when she threw up; and she bifurcated her desires. Alicia imbued her lover with sexual desire, excitement, and novelty, and her husband with anti-erotic, dull familiarity. She doesn't see that by breaking down into depression or drugs, she had constructed her marriage as a recovery center. Her extramarital affair became her risky caper.*

"In your marriage you enlisted a devoted, sober caretaker cleaning up your messes, and in your affair you enlisted a sexy, stoned lover. Comfort and safety were reserved for the marriage, and risky adventure for your affair. Do you think you may have unwittingly set it up that way?" I tried to direct the dialogue to her inner motivations.

"No, that's not it. It's just that they're both opposite. Tom's boring and banal, whereas Alex is exciting and off-beat." She was not having any of my interpretations yet.

"I'm sure there's something to that, but we often orchestrate a marriage where we degrade romance and passion. Perhaps your breakdowns had something to do with Tom's role as a devoted caregiver. I guess his caregiver role wasn't sexy or fun for you." I stayed with it, trying to show her that it was not really the men who were different, but the situations that she created.

"A devoted old fogy accountant sure isn't sexy. Anyhow, I was too sick for sex." She stuck to her guns.

*Was she afraid to give credence to me, lest she depend on me? Will she dampen me down, so I become her dull caretaker, cleaning up her messes? She pretty well did that tonight, and I colluded.*

"I notice that like Tom, I too clean up your mess. Will I become a dull, old fogy?" I threw out the bait.

"You're nothing like Tom." She wasn't taking the bait. Did she fear I'd reel her in?

"Are there any similarities with the other husbands?" I was curious to see whether my hypothesis of a pattern would be supported.

She spoke quietly. "They're all different. In my second marriage, my husband Raphael was a professional gambler. Unlike Tom the dull accountant, Raphael was exciting and risky. I loved his sense of adventure. He made me laugh, and we had fun till the kids were born. After birthing, I sunk into a heavy postpartum depression. I couldn't care for the kids, so Raphael had to, but he called me lazy and kept insulting me. So he changed. Instead of the carefree boyish charm, I saw a critical, controlling man, just like my father. Raphael no longer turned me on. The anti-depressant meds didn't help my sexual libido either. I wasn't feeling sexy any more. Romance had faded."

"That's sad," I empathized.

"Yeah, but I didn't give up. I live for romance, for passion. So if I couldn't get it at home, I figured I'd go back to work. Then I met a sexy illustrator, and I cheated again. I'm not proud of it, but I did. Only this time my husband didn't forgive me. Raphael was humiliated, enraged, and pleaded poverty. His gambling winnings didn't show up on tax returns, so I had no way of proving his ability to support us. He fled to South America, and I got a divorce." Tears rolled down her cheeks, streaking her makeup.

"That must've been tough," I commiserated.

"It sure was. I couldn't cope; I broke down and was hospitalized again. That's where I met my third husband, Patrick. He was visiting his ailing mother, and I could see how steady and good he was to her. A social worker, Patrick knew how to empathize with me. He came to visit me daily. When I was discharged, Patrick professed his love and promised to take care of my kids and me. I needed him; he was so responsible, not like Raphael. I knew him for two months before we got married." She wiped her tears only to begin crying again.

"I guess that didn't end well either," I suggested.

"No, I got better, but I felt trapped and lonely in my marriage. Patrick worked late hours and I felt neglected. He came home tired and fell asleep on the sofa. He was definitely not sexy or fun. I also worked but I was raring to go." She waxed ecstatic. "At work there was this young trainee. He was my boy-toy. Wow, what sex! This loveless marriage only lasted six months, more like a long date. But my boy-toy—what passion, what sex!"

"So the pattern's the same. You have security and devotion at home, and adventure and sex at work," I interpreted.

"But, I want it all—comfort and caring and excitement and fun, but I don't think you can have it all in marriage," she responded regretfully.

"Why not want it all?" I asked.

"I don't know, only I've never had it all. Actually, with my fourth husband, I almost had it all, but that didn't work out either. I'm on my fifth husband, and things don't change." She despaired as she took stock of her dismal failures.

"So you keep changing men, but things stay the same. We can't change things by changing situations; we only carry over our old selves from place to place. It's not the situation that has to be changed, it's you." I was brutally frank.

"Yah, it's me all right. I don't know who I am anymore," Alicia wailed. I dared to be candid, and she dared to take responsibility. Alicia was on her way to greater definition and meaning.

Alicia wandered in and out of marriages like women wander in and out of stores window-shopping. She did not really try the marriages on for size; she never gave them a chance. In her serial marriages, Alicia followed suit— same cloth, new color. Her enigmatic charm and wild side attracted stable, dependable men. If they were not so steady and reliable, she coerced them into these dull caretaker roles. By falling apart, Alicia elicited their reliable, caretaker sides, or their controlling, critical sides. Neither scenario was sexy. Degrading passionate and erotic romance in the marriage, she felt compelled to fulfill her desires elsewhere.

Did she fear intimacy? Indeed, she did—big time. Alicia became dependent on her husbands for sustenance during her illnesses. What she failed to see was her fear of dependency on only one man for real love and romance. The poles of sexual desire and devotional love in one rod spelled danger for Alicia. The rod may be fragile; it could break and she would lose everything. She broke instead. Alicia constructed devotional love while diminishing romantic passion in marriage. Like many healthy all-American women, she did not want to settle, and so she sought outside help in the workplace. Like many all-American men, her coworkers were available for fun and games.

In examining Alicia's family background, we saw how her parents constructed a marriage without romance and passion. Early in the marriage, her mother, a glamorous runway model, was the darling of her father's desires. Alicia recalled her young mother as playful, quick-witted, stylish, and unpredictable. She remembered her engineer father as an earnest, reliable, serious, but old-fashioned man. Theirs was a storybook marriage—at first, anyhow. Over time, Alicia overheard their virulent fights. Her laconic father, in terse and certain terms, always won, leaving her mother weeping and apologetic.

One day, when Alicia was ten years old, she overheard her mother's hushed and seductive voice on the phone to a man. A precocious child, Alicia guessed her mother was having an affair. Her mother swore Alicia to secrecy about the clandestine relationship. Alicia's mother went on to complain about her rigid, dull husband, and how he could not satisfy her sexually or emotionally. Honored by this grown-up intimacy, Alicia felt closely bonded to her mother. She dreamed of them together, in high heels and sophisticated clothes, listening to jazz in swank nightclubs.

By her mother's inappropriate confidentiality with her young daughter, she reversed the roles. At an early age, Alicia took the maternal role and advised her mother, whereas her mother became the child. Her mother cried on young Alicia's shoulders, looking to her for support and comfort. Aging runway models were not in vogue, and her mother's career was truncated. Her suave looks lost their luster and she lost her verve.

Developing diabetes, Alicia's mother deteriorated and became dependent on her father. They now slept in separate rooms, and Alicia no longer saw signs of desire or romance. Instead she heard her father boss her mother around, and her weak dispirited mother submit to his demands.

Alicia's adolescence was fraught with turmoil and trouble. Her passion for sex, drugs, and rock 'n' roll in her turbulent teens was, partly, a reflection of the sexual revolution of the sixties and seventies. Another factor that fueled her wild and willful teen years was an unconscious wish to keep her parents together. She created a lot of messes for her parents to clean up. Her misbehavior gave them a common goal—to straighten Alicia out.

Alicia tested her father's moral values. Her father condemned her display of sexuality, and her mother chimed in, scolding Alicia with, "You're asking for it. You're a tramp." It seems her father could not handle his erotic feelings toward his daughter, so he disparaged her emerging sexuality. Alicia's mother envied her youth and sexuality, and so she demeaned her daughter.

With her extramarital affairs, Alicia maintained her close childhood bond to her charismatic mother. She also identified with her mother's sense of adventure; her risky behavior; and her choice of safe, reliable husbands. Disdaining her father's stodgy, controlling ways, she rejected all of him, including his steady, reliable parts. She threw out the baby with the bathwater. Without internalizing the tools for maturity from a secure, consistent parent, Alicia was catapulted into pseudo-maturity. She fantasized a wonderland where wishes came true—a strong stable prince who was also romantic and passionate.

Alicia's desires for extramarital affairs had multiple meanings. She identified with her mother in her height of intense passion and in her decline of abject dependency. But she wanted more than her mother had gotten. Without a parental model of real love, Alicia did not have faith in marriage. Why then did she keep remarrying? Alicia would say she liked being married, as she identified with her father's strict moral values. She did not believe in living with a guy. Would you believe that? Well, she believed it. I believe she was trying to get it right, was more daring than most, and in her way, was more persistent and hopeful.

Once we understood the connections to her family, Alicia began to see her true self better, her influences, and her choices. At sixty-five, she still had a lot of growing up to do. One of her goals was to find security, stability, and dependability within herself, so she would not be so dependent on a man for sustenance.

In time, her moods began to stabilize; her depression became less severe and manageable. Alicia also learned to think before she acted and to react in a less-impulsive manner. She dyed her hair back to its natural dark blonde, but her wardrobe remained funky. No retiring shy flower, Alicia held on to her alluring, elusive side; only now, she reached for a steady anchor within herself. Alicia was on her way to command of her inner self—the key to relating in a deep, meaningful way.

Feeling on more solid ground, she found that wandering was now a waste. Her bright, colorful desires, now more variegated, revealed undertones of gray. A consistent, committed marriage with spontaneity and sex presented a challenge. With greater insight into her desires for extramarital affairs, Alicia dared to face the challenge of her failing marriage. She relinquished her lover Tony and entered marital therapy with Ernesto.

Her fear of dependency on a man stemmed from her mother's abject dependency on her father. Clarification of how she degraded romance in marriages helped her to take responsibility. When Alicia assumed greater sober, mature responsibility, Ernesto's colorful, sensuous qualities began to play out in the relationship. Marital therapy helped the couple realign their patterns of behavior so differences and similarities could cohabit. Ernesto learned about how he colluded in this dead dance of degraded romance. Together they are working on constructing a marriage where romance and love can coexist and endure.

You may be thinking that Alicia is an anomaly, that she had serious problems that precluded intimacy. You may not ricochet like Alicia; instead you may be bound by commitment to a long-term dead marriage. Nevertheless, we all have our ghosts that come out to haunt us in marriage.

Marriage is not a miracle; it takes insight, work, and more work. Transforming these ghosts to ancestors with whom we can live is one goal of healthy relationships. Another goal is close scrutiny of self-defeating patterns in which you and your partner participate. You may well find that you can reconstruct a marriage in which romance lasts.

Whereas Alicia was influenced by a culture of sexual permissiveness in her youth, young wives today have other cultural influences. Inspired by second wave feminists, a new brand of bold young feminist wives has stepped onto the scene. In contrast, some young wives today continue to hold onto traditional marital roles. But their idea of marriage is updated. Notwithstanding cultural influences, ancestral ghosts also haunt many young wives today. Their mothers, grandmothers, and great grandmothers have left legacies, some of which they love and some of which they hate. In the following chapter I will examine the dilemmas of young daring wives and their desires for extramarital affairs.

# 6

# Young and Restless

## THE WORLD'S THEIR OYSTER

*Love is or it ain't. Thin love is no love at all.*
—Toni Morrison[1]

*Toughness doesn't have to come in a pinstripe suit.*
—Senator Dianne Feinstein, D–Ca

## NOT FOLLOWING IN MOTHER'S FOOTSTEPS

Earlier in the book, I discussed the phenomenon of third wave feminism[2]—young women proud to be called ballbusters or barracudas. Historically, powerful and competitive women have threatened men. So women have curbed these traits.[3] Third wave feminists, however, compete openly with each other, their mothers, and men. Yet, many want the feminine trappings that second wave feminists dismantled. Unlike their mothers who rebelled against objectification of their sexuality, third wave feminists embrace their sexuality as symbols of power. They flaunt their sexuality as a powerful expression of their desires. As such, they construct their selves as active subjects of their own desires, and not passive subjects desired by someone else. They may even compete with each other for a man.

These young, third wave feminist wives wear makeup; polished long nails; skinny, sexy clothes; and a chip on their shoulders. They complain that their parents shortchanged them. They feel their working moms deprived them of a nurturing maternal figure. Often fathers were absent also. Hence, both parents valued work ahead of them—or so they believe.

In the sixties and seventies, their parents' marriages may have suffered from newly defined roles. Historically, the breadwinner role concomitant with power and autonomy has been assumed by husbands. In turn, wives' roles as angels of the home[4] rendered them passive and dependent. Not so for many wives in the sixties. Their desires for equality and mutuality disoriented many a husband. Indeed, negotiating changing roles takes several generations. Marriages in the sixties were new at this shift in power, so that discord and friction may have ripped some families apart. Romance and passion may have diminished. Losing their luster, many marriages limped along for "the sake of the children" or died in divorce courts. Such was the legacy of second wave feminism for some children.

On the other hand, if their mothers were traditional housewives and deferred to their husbands, young third wave feminist wives feel they were deprived of strong female role models. They perceived their mothers as sexless, powerless, and pathetically dependent on powerful fathers. No matter the love, attention, and encouragement from mothers, daughters are up in arms about their mothers' shortcomings. Third wave feminist wives complain that their mothers are too intrusive or too distant, too home-oriented or too career-oriented, too present or too absent. Mothers cannot win. Young third wave feminists are determined not to become their mothers.[5]

Young wives desire commitment in marriage, children, and security along with romance, passion, and sex. Separateness, autonomy, and power should not preclude merger and sexual surrender. They desire reciprocity and equality in marriage. They want to sink their teeth into steamy, succulent, exotic fare and still have their meat and potatoes. They want it all, and they go for it. The world is their oyster.

It seems times are changing. But are they really? Have women changed that much? Despite wishes not to follow in mother's footsteps, are young wives forging new paths? Not entirely. Wishing does not make it so. Cultural and personal histories influence expression of desires. As nurturers and caretakers, wives over the centuries have taken a backseat to men.

A look at one of the major forces in second wave feminism sheds light on a remarkable woman who maintained her traditional role as caregiver. The feminist Gloria Steinem was a caregiver to her infirm mother and to her progressive movement.[6] This strong, optimistic woman who influenced the world refrained from following in her mother's frail, non-functioning footsteps. In part, Steinem's poignant personal history provided her with the impetus to help change the consciousness of a world.

Despite the force of feminism, twenty-first-century young wives are only one generation away from skewed gender power relations. One rosebud does not make a rosebush. Growth may be strangled by unruly weeds or starved by deficient sunshine, water, or rocky soil. Prickly thorns may make pruning difficult. Indeed, family histories may not have provided a fertile ground or solid gardening tools.

If not firmly rooted, when romance fades a young wife may grow restless and reckless. In the next case study, meet a young wife—like many of us—who found that her marriage bed was not made of roses. Like many of us, she searched for a bed of roses in another man's bed.

### Mary, Mary, Quite Contrary

"I must talk to you. You come highly recommended, and I need expert help. I saw you at the library. I'm the one who lost her library card; you were standing behind me. We smiled and I felt a connection right away. Do you remember me?" A familiar, soft voice was reaching out to me.

*Do I remember her? How could anyone not remember her? Skin-tight jeans, glitzy belt, and spike heels—racy and raring to go—in our conservative, laid-back library! It seems Mary desperately wants to connect with me. She was flustered then, and it sounds like she's flustered now; and she's flattering me. I wonder what this says about her relationship with women, with her mother.*

"Yes, I remember you. How can I help?" I asked.

"I'm strong, so this is not like me. I don't know what to do. I'm desperate." Her quiet voice took on intensity—the dark intensity of despair.

I gave her the first open appointment available. She arrived fifteen minutes late. Annoying, yes, but she also gave me time to drink in the fragrance of lilacs wafting through the window. Spring was here! When I was a child, Canadian spring promised carefree, lazy summer days in the Laurentian Mountains, where my parents rented a cottage. Her arrival brought my reverie to a halt.

"You're late," I noted.

"I almost canceled. I don't think I can do this; there's so much. It'll take a lifetime." Mary looked hurriedly around the room.

"I see you scanning the room. Are you looking for a fire exit? Do you expect things to heat up?" I joked in earnest.

"I'm told I'm too hot to handle." She played along.

"Maybe we could explore that side of you. It could be exciting, even a daring adventure," I suggested in eager anticipation of a real relationship.

"Yeah, I'm daring and adventuresome, all right. I'm so daring, I'm having an affair with Brett—the librarian. I hate myself for it. It's a sin." Tears welled up in Mary's hazel eyes as she condemned herself.

"Why's it a sin?" I asked.

"It's not the only sin. I had an abortion last week, and that's a sin. And it's not the first one I had. This is my third abortion. Each time, I beat myself up." Her tears rolled down her smooth cheeks. Bejeweled, slim, long fingers intertwined as she wrung her hands.

*She's revealing so much so soon. Unusual—what's next? Is this a case of loose boundaries, or desperation? Perhaps her despair's about her "sin." This could turn out to be springtime of redemption and renewal.*

"As human beings we aren't perfect, and we make mistakes." I tried to comfort her.

"Well, I keep making mistakes. That's the story of my life. Deep down, I know Brett's not for me, but I can't give him up. He's the reference librarian, and he's been helping me with my book. I heard you're also writing a book." She made yet another connection to me.

*I know Brett. He's a pale, lanky, studious, tweedy fellow. He reminds me of a Sunday school preacher. She wasn't exactly decked out in her Sunday best—more like her sexy best. Is she the teacher's pet?*

"What's your book about?" I inquired.

"It's about a Nigerian woman who leaves home and immigrates to this country. It's loosely based on my mother's and my experiences. But lately, I can't focus on it. It's impossible." She brushed her curly dark hair off her face. Her café au lait skin glistened in the sunshine streaming in through the window.

*So she's writing about her mother, and I'm feeling a warm glow. She may be searching for a transformative mother figure. That may well be the connection I'm feeling.*

"So, you're writing about your mother and you. It sounds like a worthwhile topic. When you're feeling better, perhaps you can resume the writing." In an attempt to offer hope, I suggested that she had something to look forward to.

"I can't imagine ever being able to focus or write again. This is disastrous. My husband found out, and he's leaving me. I don't blame him, Brett keeps calling the house, and when he doesn't, I call him. We can't stay away from each other." Mary leaned over to get a Kleenex, and her skin-tight top and jeans separated. She tried to yank her top down to meet her jeans, but it continued to ride up.

"It sounds like you've got a dilemma," I commented.

She went on with her story. "It's a dilemma all around. Brett's married too, and he promises to leave his wife, but doesn't. He keeps breaking his promises, and I'm losing respect for him. He's a wimp. I should give him up, but I can't. I love him."

"Aside from breaking up two families, why else should you give him up?" I inquired.

Her face contorted in anger. "Like I said, he's not for me. He thinks I'd get bored with him; maybe he's right. But I want him to leave his wife. I've got to win."

I tried to clarify her actions. "So you're competing with his wife."

"I can't believe he'd choose her over me. She's old and dowdy." Mary ignored my interpretation and attacked her adversary.

I tried to add some reason and nuance. "Maybe it's not about choosing you, but choosing his marriage over an affair. He could also be considering other issues."

"That's what he says. He says he couldn't afford me, and that I'd never be happy with him in a two-room apartment." She agreed and continued. "I still want him to leave her. I have to win." She pounded her fist in the air.

*She's not opening her mind to any other possibilities. Reasoning with her isn't working. What has reason got to do with emotion anyhow?*

Rather than reasoning with her, I tried to flesh out her feelings. "If you won, how would you feel?"

She shook her head defiantly. "I'd feel good. I love him and I'd get what I want."

"So winning's a powerful feeling for you," I interpreted.

"Of course, winning's powerful." She shot me a what-else? look.

"What about your two families? How do you feel about them?" I asked.

"I feel bad, guilty, terrible about my husband. Henry's a good man, and I care about him. I love him, but I'm not in love with him. I hate hurting him. Brett's wife's another story. I hate her and I don't care about her." Tenderness gave way to toughness as she spoke about the spouses.

"I understand winning is a powerful place, but this win comes with a lot of losses. Perhaps we can find other ways for you to feel like a powerful winner," I suggested.

"Like how?" she asked.

"Like from within yourself rather than from outside of you. We would explore your authentic self with your inner strivings. Before we go there, tell me more about your personal history. Perhaps we can get some understanding of your compelling need to win," I proposed.

Over the next few months, Mary and I explored her childhood experiences and made connections to her current dilemma. That took some effort. Mary digressed from our exploration by obsessing about Brett. On a mission for him to leave his wife, Mary, the fierce fighter tried everything. Obsessed with calling Brett's wife and threatening to tell his children, she stopped short of pulling the plug on his job at the library. The quiet, quaint library would never tolerate a screaming scandal; it would be instant dismissal for Brett. Interspersed with her current dilemma, Mary talked a lot about her mother.

When Mary was two years old, her mother emigrated from Nigeria to America. She left little Mary with her grandmother in Nigeria until she could secure a job, a husband, and a home. Three years later, when Mary was five, she rejoined her mother and her stepfather in America. Mary's fond memories of a warm, loving, kind grandmother flooded her. Separation from her beloved grandmother proved to be a grievous loss. By age five, Mary had endured two central losses.

Her grandmother told Mary that her biological father had died. But Mary later found out that her parents had never been married, and her father abandoned her pregnant mother before Mary was born. Her mother assured Mary that she was a child born of a great love. Lamenting her lost love, her mother described her father as sexy, smart, and exciting.

Mary suspected that her mother married her stepfather for security and not for love. She saw no passion, desire, or outward expressions of romance in their marriage. Mary's stepfather was hardworking, earnest, and steady—the exact opposite of her biological father.

A force to reckon with, Mary's stalwart mother dominated her meek husband. She badgered and intimidated him into doing her bid. One day, Mary's mother discovered that her husband was leaving them for another woman. So he was not so meek after all. Mary loved her mild-mannered stepfather, with whom she had established a warm, loving attachment. He was the only father she knew.

At age ten, Mary suffered her third central loss. She held her mother responsible for her stepfather's abandonment of them. Mary believed her mother was too aloof and controlling for any man. Rather than holding her father responsible for his actions, she blamed her mother. Because mothers become salient when fathers disappear, they often get dumped on by children.

Mary's mother, a tall, handsome, robust woman, was endowed with numerous attributes, including a hair-trigger temper. While working days, she attended night school and got her doctorate in sociology. Not able to give Mary the attention she needed, she sent her to a private boarding school for girls. Mary felt lonely and unwanted. She pleaded with her mother to come home, but her staunch mother remained firm. Mary would get a good education and go on to have a good life.

A second wave feminist, Mary's mother joined the women's liberation movement and taught her daughter about feminism and racism. While Mary admired her mother's accomplishments, she felt deprived of a nurturing, warm, and affectionate mother. Mary longed for a close, cozy mother-daughter relationship.

At an unconscious level, Mary transferred her wishes onto me, so that I represented the mother she felt she missed. Our good working relationship greatly facilitated the work.

*Is her idealization feeding my narcissistic needs? I wonder what will happen when her idealization of me comes to a halt. I may be toppled. Well, that would be more grist for the mill.*

But Mary surprised me—she stayed firm. She was intent on seeing me in a reassuring, bright light, and her mother in a menacing, dark shadow. So she split her mother figures into the all-good mother and the all-bad mother. Much of her grumbles centered on her wish for a strong and present father figure.

As to a strong father figure, Mary's father figures were elusive—the vanished biological father, the divorced stepfather disappearing from her life, and phantom would-be fathers whom mother dated. Mary blamed her mother for these losses that deprived her of a permanent father—one of her grievances. Another grievance was her mother's accomplishments.

Mary placed the blame for her mother's absence on her quest for achievement and power. By the same token, she respected her mother's accomplishments in the academic and literary worlds. No matter Mary's intelligence and sensitivity, she feared she could not compete with her awesome mother. So, Mary—silently and not so silently—rebelled against her mother.

In childhood, Mary conformed to her powerful mother with stellar academic achievements in grammar school and then in high school. But college was another story. Influenced by her mother's feminist teachings, she pursued third wave feminist thought. There she explored her sexuality with men and with other women. She knew she preferred men, but she also desired women. She wanted it all. Her hunger for love fueled her sexual desires. She found men and women who were only too happy to indulge her desire for a threesome. What better way to satisfy her needs for a symbolic mother and father?

Mary began to cut classes and frequent bars, picking up willing sex partners. Whereas her mother was intent on success, Mary was hellbent on failure. Despite her intelligence, her truancy did her in. By dropping out of college and going off to work as a bartender, Mary enraged her mother. Things got so heated that her mother threatened to disown her. By the time Mary was twenty-two years old, her rebellion was in full flower.

In her bartending job, Mary met various and sundry men and women. One of the men whom Mary took up with was an ex-convict. When he was arrested once again for dealing drugs, Mary dropped him. Pregnant with his child, she decided on an abortion. Remorse and guilt about the abortion overwhelmed her. Estranged from her mother, she felt alone, and sunk into a deep depression.

Topless dancing gave Mary a high. On top of the bar, with men clamoring for her body and filling her G-string with dollars, she was Queen of the May. She described the feelings of power she felt as she rendered these men powerless. In her quest to hold men captive by her sexy display, Mary unconsciously competed with her mother, who could not hold onto a man. She would outdo her mother in this arena and entice a lot of symbolic fathers. She also competed with other women, as the men lusting for her were often married. At an unconscious level, by ensnaring the forbidden father, Mary competed with her mother.

She developed a cocaine habit and fell in love with her pusher Sam. He was the owner of the bar, but not of his self. Another woman owned him. Alas, Sam was married. What a challenge for Mary! Sam fell for Mary, and together they made mad, passionate love.

In response to Mary's repeated pleadings and threats to leave him, Sam finally left his wife to live with Mary. She felt powerful in winning Sam from his wife. But, as it turned out, her gain was merely a pyrrhic victory. After a tumultuous year together, Sam announced that he was going back to his wife and children. The affair ended with Mary once again pregnant. She feared her cocaine abuse had harmed the fetus and so she aborted it.

From the depths of despair, Mary found the courage to grow. Indeed, sorrow is inevitable, but we need not drown in it. Mary's guilt and disappointment were excruciatingly painful. She tortured herself with self-blame. Finally, she decided to turn a new page in her young history and to realign with her mother.

Resuming a relationship with her prickly mother was stormy, but they forgave each other and tried to move forward. Feeling overshadowed by her mother, Mary struggled to find her own voice. She resumed her education and earned a master's degree in literature. Her burning desire to write fiction was supported by her day job as a journalist. So she created a balance between her idealistic desires and pragmatic considerations. Her mother heartily approved of Mary's goals, and finally Mary felt warm and fuzzy feelings with her.

Mary married a sweet, reliable, financially secure man with his own plumbing business. She described him as warm, generous, and handsome, but a simple, black-and-white thinker. He did not understand her needs, nor did he recognize her as an intellectual, emotionally complex woman.

He viewed Mary as a good wife and mother—nothing more. Mary complied by leaving her job to be a stay-at-home mother and lavishing her love and caring on her two children. Distancing herself from her ambitious mother, Mary put her family's needs ahead of hers.

She almost had it all—a secure marriage, a dependable husband, and a promising career that was on hold. Yet she missed the excitement of her former life, her adventures into the unknown, her risky behavior, and her sexual prowess. At the ripe age of thirty-four, Mary wanted more. Wishing to expand herself in a multitude of ways, she grew restless and reckless. Throwing caution to the wind, she pursued Brett, the librarian, relentlessly. She was ready to hurt her cherished children, the husband who adored her, and Brett's family, not to mention her mother.

With Brett, Mary was certain she could have it all. He was intellectual, emotionally sensitive, savored nuance, and surprisingly sexy. While his attachment to his wife enraged Mary, it was also a vehicle to compete with another woman—her symbolic mother.

Once Mary gained greater clarity about herself, her hunger for love, and her competition with and defiance of her mother, a cloud began to lift. She tried to stay away from Brett in order to see whether he would volitionally leave his wife. Unable to maintain her resolve, she continued to give him ultimatums. Under the pressure, Brett broke and was hospitalized for mental exhaustion. Under doctor's orders, Brett refused to see Mary.

The last Mary heard was that Brett had reunited with his loyal wife, who nurtured him back to health. Mary realized that Brett was not the strong man that she envisioned. With increased self and other awareness, Mary was able to mourn this loss with greater equanimity than the prior losses. Forgiving herself for the pain she caused others was a long, anguishing journey. Out of this morass of agonizing feelings, Mary forged herself a stronger and more centered woman. She was on a path of renewal.

Mary did not reunite with her husband Henry. She wanted a fresh start with a more suitable man, but she was not desperate. She felt a burning desire for fulfillment professionally, and so she resumed her writing. Her characters had greater dimension, with a strong underlying feminist voice. Her relationship with her mother took a more cooperative and less competitive turn. Instead of rejecting her mother's help as she had in the past, Mary accepted her offer for an introduction to a publisher. Her proposal for a semi-biographical novel was under consideration.

To her surprise, Mary's mother doted on her grandchildren. Mary wondered if her mother had really changed. Her mother might have been feeling guilty about her less-than-optimal parenting with Mary. She might have been trying to repair herself through her grandchildren. Whatever her mother's motivations, Mary could finally provide her with a second chance for both of them. Her mother would not live forever, so time was of the essence. A more loving relationship was in the offing, perhaps the penultimate chapter in her book.

In the above story, we met a young and restless wife who wanted it all. Determined not to follow in her mother's footsteps, she faltered and fell flat on her face. In her desperate attempt to defy her mother, she remained inextricably bound to her. Indeed, we are just as attached in hate as we are in love, in defiance as in compliance, and in envy as in gratitude.

Mary split her world into binaries of good and bad mothers, good and bad men, and good and bad self-states. Unable to tolerate the ambiguity of two coexisting feelings, she failed to experience nuance and complexity in her interpersonal relationships. Not only were nuance and complexity essential for her personal life, they were essential for her work as a fiction writer. Our work together focused on her fears of uncertainty and ambiguity that facilitated the quest for her true self. Not until we find our inner selves—our autonomous and independent selves—can we find fulfillment and meaning in love and work.

It takes an enlightened path to arrive at real love, with emotional, intellectual, and sexual reciprocity. The path, however, may be overgrown with wild weeds and fallen branches. The way must first be cleared of old hurts, mistakes, regrets, despair, and excruciating guilt. While it is necessary to visit the road traveled, we cannot stay there. Coming to terms with the past is essential for us to move ahead and pave new paths. Moving ahead also entails compassion and repair for those you hurt and for yourself. Spring is then not far off.

## MORAL VALUES A LA MODE

Second wave feminism was certainly a force to reckon with; however, some wives in the sixties and seventies rejected feminism's tenets and held tight to traditional values. While their husbands gained power and success as breadwinners in the outside world, housewives gained their pinnacle of success at home, nurturing the next generation for success. The women's liberation movement that inspired masses of women to gain independence threatened traditional housewives' cozy, comfortable lives. Whereas many wives of the sixties embraced the sexual revolution, the freedom, and the self-exploration, other conventional wives declined these liberal values. They chose to follow in their grandmothers' shoes and raise their children with conservative, moral values.

Traditional family values offered certainty in uncertain times, and safety in the wake of the Cold War of the fifties and the Vietnam War of the sixties, and now the ever-menacing terrorist threat of the twenty-first century. Raised with the steady assurance of continuity with the past and wisdom of the ages, children of the sixties felt a sense of security. Conformity to the status quo promised greater equanimity than the chaos of free choice. The wish for protection by a powerful husband, however, reduced traditional wives to dependent, submissive, self-sacrificing conformists. Housewives may have lived vicariously through their husbands' and children's achievements. Such was the legacy of the nineteenth century that persisted well into the twentieth and twenty-first centuries.

Raised by traditional mothers, not all young wives today accept the precepts of third wave feminism. Young wives caught up in the "moral values," consumer-driven culture often adhere to traditional, materialistic lifestyles. But their interpretations and their mothers' interpretations of "moral values" differ somewhat.

Their mothers may have shrugged off their husbands' dalliances with a "boys will be boys" attitude. They may even have convinced themselves that sex was more important to men than women. In effect, the sexual desires of their conservative mothers were often restrained, while husbands' sexual desires were indulged—the double standard. But as we know, wives throughout the ages, even in prudish, traditional eras, dared to have extra-marital affairs. Historically, society condemned wives' extramarital affairs. Not so for husbands; their affairs were condoned.

The influence of feminism has managed to filter into the consciousness of even young, traditional wives of the twenty-first century. But they are not all that comfortable with the double standard. Whereas they adhere to the traditional splits in roles—provider husbands and stay-at-home wives—they, nevertheless, want updated relationships. Unwilling to throw the baby out with the bathwater, daughters admire their moms' devotion; however, they also impugn their martyr roles.

Young, traditional wives may hold conservative "moral values" close to their hearts and still maintain liberal souls. Unlike their martyr mothers, they want to be recognized, appreciated, and understood by their families. Instead of a relationship of male domination and female submission, they may struggle to construct a more equal power relationship.

Now, a modern traditional wife, no matter how she was raised, has feelings like any other wife. Missing mutuality, equal power, and autonomy in the marriage, she is torn between her upbringing and her desires. The conflict clouds her feelings, and she may be tempted to step over the line and fish in clearer waters. In the following story, meet just such a traditional young wife.

### Morally Modern Millie

I had been seeing Millie to help her with feelings of depression and anxiety that began during her last pregnancy two years ago. Postpartum depression is common, but depression during pregnancy is rare. Sudden hormonal changes after birthing are partly responsible for postpartum depression. During pregnancy, however, hormones favor good moods. Millie's ongoing depression stemmed mainly from psychological factors.

Millie met Moshe in medical school, fell in love, and married. She dropped out of school to go to work and pay for Moshe's education. Millie sacrificed her career for Moshe and opted to have babies. She achieved the feminine status of motherhood, and he achieved the masculine status of a successful gynecologist. At the time, however, Millie did not believe her decision was a sacrifice. She told herself that motherhood was the highest achievement of womanhood, and that she did not need to be a doctor. Moshe was better suited for it. Over time, she began to regret her decision and to resent Moshe.

Moshe had changed; initially they were both observant modern Orthodox Jews, but Moshe had grown more religious, rigid, and closed-minded. On the other hand, Millie had grown more liberal and open-minded. Their changing core belief systems placed distance between them. Moshe's personality had also changed. Mary described him as full of himself, arrogant, and controlling.

Their sex life suffered due to Moshe's ultra-religious views of marital sex. He believed that sex was only for procreation, not for pleasure. With the exception of Millie's fertile period, he expected them to practice abstinence. Sex was stilted and desire suppressed. When they had sex, Moshe refused to look at his wife's naked body, and so the act was done in the dark. During her infertile period of two weeks, Moshe barricaded himself from Millie with a board so they would not be tempted to have sex for pleasure. Millie missed the spontaneity, the excitement, and romance in the marriage. She hated how Moshe used her as a vessel to bear him children.

Inwardly, Millie seethed with fury, but she did not fight back. By turning her rage inward, she complied with her Orthodox mother's teachings and kept the peace in the marriage. Enduring her ordeal in silent desperation, Millie compromised her peace of mind. Like her religious mother, grandmother, and great-grandmother, Millie assumed the role of the all-suffering, subservient, pious wife—to a point.

Millie refused to wear a wig, and unbeknownst to Moshe, went on birth control pills after the birth of her last baby. She had two little children and felt a third was too much. In a passive-aggressive way, she defied God's will and her godlike husband. That was only for starters. There was much more to her story of woe.

"I feel so terrible today. Moshe wants a divorce from me because he thinks I'm not fertile enough. He has no idea that I'm on the Pill. That's funny, because he's a gynecologist and thinks he knows everything." Millie seemed less despondent.

"So, you're outsmarting him at his game," I suggested.

She sobbed. "It's not working. I don't want a divorce. My kids would be left with the scars from a broken home. I can't do this to them, but I don't want more children."

"Any other reasons you don't want the divorce?" I tried to bring some more light to her darkness.

"My babies are young, and I'd have to go back to work and leave them. I love being a mother. I guess I'm like my mother that way. Her life was her kids. I can't hurt them." The pain in her eyes showed as she slouched forward.

*I remember all too well the pain I felt after my divorce. Seeing my little boy cry as I left him with a nanny to go to work is as heartrending today as it was some twenty-five years ago. Unlike religious Millie, I'm a secular woman. Indeed motherhood—a mark of femininity—crosses religious, ethnic, and racial lines.*

"So a great part of your identity centers on motherhood, as it does for many women." I empathized with her pain.

"I think it's harder for me because of the example my mother set for me. She was a Supermom, religious, and some balabusta (mistress of the home *par excellence*). My mom has eight children and twenty-three grandchildren. And she caters to each and every one of them. When they come over she prepares each one their favorite dish. Can you believe that?" Her freckled fair skin turned a light shade of pink.

"Did she have help?" I was curious. Her mother brought back memories of my martyr mother.

"No way. Mom does everything herself. She refuses help, gets exhausted, and lands up in bed for the rest of the week crying about how hard her life is. My mom's a martyr." Sitting up straight, Millie tossed her reddish-brown hair back and straightened her long, flowing dress. The sheer printed frock subtly revealed the curves in her voluptuous body. Full-breasted and broad-hipped, there was no way she could hide her sexuality. Maybe at some level Millie did not want to.

I smiled. "Something tells me you don't want to be a martyr."

"I want to be like Mom in some ways, but I'm tired of being a martyr and letting Moshe push me around. He thinks he's God, and that I should worship him. I won't do that anymore." Her face flushed a bright shade of red. Her anger suited her; she looked vibrant.

I interpreted her conflict. "I see good energy. I think you desire to reclaim your authentic self and gain Moshe's recognition of you as a separate person from him. Given your background, you are conflicted between your traditional values and your emerging desires for autonomy."

"I'm a modern wife and I want an equal power relationship. At the university, I met people from all over the world, with diverse belief systems. I read about feminism and opened my mind to liberal ideas. What an enlightening time for me!" Sheer delight emanated as Millie drew a deep breath and exhaled. I wondered if this pleasure was just too much for her.

"I notice you delighted in expanding yourself," I commented.

"I sure loved that life, and I miss it. But then, there are my kids. It's confusing, because I was raised with conservative values, and I'm drawn to liberal ideas." Her conflict quickly dampened her delight.

I clarified her discordant feelings. "So you're stuck. You feel trapped in this unsatisfactory marriage, yet you resist getting out. You feel you'll hurt your kids if you get out, and if you stay you're killing yourself."

"I'm not exactly dying in this marriage," she responded coyly.

I punched home my points. "You're not? It sounds like Moshe squeezed the life out of the marriage: no romance, no mutuality, no recognition of you as a separate person."

"Yeah, all of that's true, but there's someone else who does give me all those things, and more." No blushing this time, as Millie's daring side was showing.

"Uh huh," I uttered.

"I'm having an affair. Would you believe it, a modern Orthodox Jewish wife having an extramarital affair? In my religion, only men do that sort of thing. I'd be stoned to death if Moshe's religious High Hat friends heard of this." Pretty Millie was never prettier. She shone glorious in the sparkle of her devilish, dangerous behavior.

"You look radiant. You're defying the double standard that's central to ultra-Orthodox circles," I commented on my observation.

"That's only part of it. I'm in love with Aaron. We were high school sweethearts, but my parents wouldn't let me marry him. Aaron was a secular Jew, and he wanted to go to film school. My parents disapproved as he was not religious, nor did they think he'd make a good living for me. They wanted me to marry a rich doctor, so of course, Moshe was a good catch," she explained.

"Do they know about your marital problems?" I asked.

"No, I don't want to disturb them. They're not kids anymore."

*Her consideration and devotion to them was considerable, but once again she was losing sight of her needs. She's not so different from many of us.*

"You said they weren't kids anymore. You've got a point there. They're older and maybe wiser, so they may surprise you and empathize with your plight. Who knows? Maybe they would support your needs," I suggested.

In my experience, when their children have marital problems, loving parents side with their children and not their spouses. Of course, that presupposes loving parents. Millie's recollection of warm, loving, and devoted parents bolstered my confidence in making this suggestion.

Millie responded calmly. "I guess no one else knows about my affair. It's not something you discuss with friends or family. But I'll think about disclosing it to my family."

The aim of some of the following sessions was to mobilize Millie's inner strength so that she could break the impasse she had constructed. As Millie's and Moshe's differences were irreconcilable, work on the marriage was not an option for her. Not only would she be cheating herself out of a rich life with romance, love, and free expression of sexual desire, she would be cheating Moshe out of a marriage with a more suitable partner.

In time, she could recognize that in her despair she could not fulfill her maternal role. No matter what she did for her children, her tumultuous state of mind intruded on their development. Indeed, it is not what you do for your children, it is who you are that counts. Aaron wanted some answers also, and she felt she was not fair to him either. Stuck in an unsatisfactory marriage, Aaron wanted to divorce his wife and marry Millie.

Pressure mounted, and she felt hard-pressed to make some decisions. A dream brought some clarity to her. Millie dreamed of an angel in dark clothes sitting on her right shoulder. On her left shoulder a light green leaf held a tiny baby. She romped through a thriving field of clover, and bent down to pick a wild flower. In the background a high mountain rose. She tried to climb over the mountain, but could not. The baby was now a grown woman, and she teamed up with the angel, now golden, to help Millie over the mountain.

Millie sorted out some of the symbolism, and together we mined some meaning. The dark angel was her guilty conscious that she transformed to a golden angel who helped her to surmount the obstacles. Millie understood that she was the creator of her dream, and so the mountain was her creation. If she constructed obstacles to her progress, she could also demolish them.

The tiny baby symbolized her infantile state, from which she grew to become a powerful woman. We thought I was the field of clover, the fertile ground that she used to nourish herself. As to the wild flower, I will let you guess who that could symbolize. It might be a facet of Millie, someone else, some other wild card, or all of the above.

After much continued deliberation, Millie decided to tell her parents. To her surprise they supported her beyond her wildest dreams. They insisted she move in with them, return to medical school, and obtain her degree. Millie's mother volunteered to babysit with her two children while she went to school. Her father contacted his brother, a marital divorce lawyer, who took on Millie's divorce case pro bono. Millie promised to repay him when she became a doctor. As to Aaron, she decided that breaking up one family was all she could handle.

In the above story we saw how religious and cultural belief systems conflicted with the inner desires of a young, modern, traditional wife. Family tradition handed down over the centuries is a formidable force, but so are stirrings of the heart, body, and soul.

As to the concept of "moral values," who is to judge what morality is really about? It is decidedly not a pious, ultra-religious, domineering man who dismisses his wife's needs and desires in the name of God. This is merely a distortion of God's will. Moral values may reach out to understand the plight of a frustrated wife who dares to fulfill her desires with an extramarital affair. She is not immoral, but simply human. Such rigid, artificial values have not satisfied sexual desire. In Millie's case, we saw that her traditional parents, who also believed in moral values, were filled to the brim with love and tolerance. So, open-minded and unprejudiced moral values embody a multitude of meanings.

In the above chapter, you met two types of young wives from opposite lifestyles who made different choices. Numerous other young wives with differing lifestyles make still other choices. Not only do young wives make daring choices, but older wives do so also. Numerous older wives with sacred, profane, and secret lives also make daring choices. One of these choices for older wives may be an affair with a younger lover. Older wives who choose younger lovers will adorn the pages of the following chapter.

# 7

# Older and Bolder

## UNDERCOVER WITH A YOUNGER LOVER

*You're never too old to become younger.*
—Mae West

*Sex is more fun than cars, but cars refuel quicker than men.*
—Germaine Greer

## WHAT'S AGE GOT TO DO WITH IT, ANYHOW?

A groundswell of Baby Boomers has come of age—middle age. In the next two decades, 40 million women will experience menopause.[1] Stereotypes of midlife and sexually neutral older women with sensible shoes, short gray hair, and shapeless bodies are a thing of the past.[2] Baby Boomers, influenced by second wave feminism, see aging in a different light. Older women today glow with youthful, sexy, and vibrant hues. Sixty-eight-year-young ageless beauty Jane Fonda, and sixty-something, sexy-legged, energetic Tina Turner shine brilliantly.

Yet, the double standard persists. Older men loving younger women are a given. Not so for older women. Older women loving younger men are seen as robbing the cradle or harboring incestuous oedipal wishes. Needless to say, older men are not denigrated with these unseemly labels.

Over the centuries women have strived for sexual equality. Popular writers claim that relationships between older women and younger men are increasing rapidly. Perhaps older women are challenging the privilege of aging men to love younger women. Older women may want to have the same privilege as older men by challenging the patriarchal inequality between the sexes.[3]

There are many other motivations for older women to love younger men. Fantasies of a last chance for desires to be met go with the territory. With greater experience and less time left, older wives may think, "What have I got to lose?" Exploring their sexuality with a younger man, older women may fulfill their fantasies before it is too late.

Older women and younger men are more sexually compatible. As women get older, they get better. Sexual dysfunction affects aging men more than aging women.[4] Whereas men peak sexually in their teens and early twenties, women's sexual peak is the late thirties.[5]

Older wives may continue to have sexual desire, but in long-term marriages, sexual desire could easily fizzle. Fading romance, diminished excitement, and novelty dampen sexual desire for wives. Security, comfort, and commitment without romance are the steak without the sizzle. To feel sexy, wives need the sizzle.

Other age-related psychological issues interfere with sexual desire in marriage. A woman who perceives herself as over the hill is not apt to feel sexy. Our youth-oriented culture with superficial values impacts older women. The media bombards us with youthful sexual images, from belly-button-baring singers to Botox.[6] So, how sexy can an older woman feel?

At midlife and older, we face a crucial crossroads, with fear of growing old and dying—existential angst.[7] Fading youth raises a fearsome red flag that signals aging and mortality. Fear negates sexual desire, so a wife in the throes of an existential crisis may well think her sexual desires are a thing of the past. She may believe that her flame has died. She may desperately want her hubby to shore up her faltering sense of sexuality. He may not, however, rise to the challenge. So what is an aging wife to do? Among many choices, she could choose a young flame to light her fire.

Aging parents heighten our anxieties, which affect marriage. Wives need supportive, romantic, attentive husbands more than ever. Husbands are not always receptive. They may be preoccupied with their own fears of aging, financial worries, or health issues. Along comes a carefree, smitten, robust young Romeo. Now, how can an aging Juliet resist him?

Older wives and younger lovers are not exactly an invention of the twenty-first century. Earlier in the book I wrote about the practice of courtly love way back in the fourteenth century. At that time older noble wives had extramarital affairs with young troubadour lovers. Elizabeth I of England and Catherine the Great of Russia had young companions and lovers as they aged.[8] So did Gabrielle in the TV series *Desperate Housewives* and Diane Lane in the movie *Unfaithful*.

By engaging in extramarital affairs, aging wives over the millennia have defied the double discrimination of ageism and sexism. When faltering marriages or frightening existential issues encroach, older wives today may also find solace with younger lovers. Unwittingly, they are also defying the double discrimination of ageism and sexism. In the following story, meet just such a daring older wife.

### Lighting Farrah's Fire

Farrah was married to Liam for thirty-eight years. They enjoyed a solid marriage with three lovely children, the comforts of a sprawling suburban home, and a pied-à-terre in the city. Nevertheless, passion had faded. Farrah had reached the ripe age of sixty-four, but felt something vital to her had died. In therapy, she was trying to figure out whether the flame inside of her had died, or whether the flame inside the marriage had died.

Farrah and Liam had met in the sixties at the height of second wave feminism. Farrah was active in the women's liberation movement, and Liam was a sympathizer. Early in the marriage they experimented with an open marriage—other sexual partners—but found it did not work. Rather than bringing them closer, jealousy and fierce fights only served to create distance. The experience, however, did awaken the desire to keep excitement, romance, novelty, and spice alive in the marriage. They worked on keeping the flame alive within and between them.

Their lives were filled with the joy of children and satisfaction in their careers. They also managed to find time to play and make love with each other. Resolving differences was still troublesome, but they were working on it. Their personality styles were at opposite ends of the pole. Farrah was loose as a goose, and Liam was tight as a drum. They were working on respecting each other's needs and desires and recognizing each other as separate but intertwined. Their goal was to enjoy a mature, intimate union with love and desire. Farrah recalled thinking she was the luckiest girl alive and that her marriage had been made in heaven. Alas, even heavenly marriages meet with earthly obstacles.

As Farrah aged, unwanted and unexpected changes occurred. Sure, her skin sagged, her back ached, and her memory missed a beat here and there, but there was much more than that. Farrah's elderly mother suffered a stroke and was now living with Liam and her. While the lifelong bond between Farrah and her mother was a loving, close one, now it was being tested. Her infirm mother had grown cranky, clinging, and demanding. Farrah's siblings lived at considerable distances, and so she became the appointed caretaker.

While Farrah assumed the responsibility of caring for her mother—and she did so out of love and gratitude—she was buckling under the stress and strain. Farrah stopped going to the gym and neglected her nutrition and her grooming. Sex was the last thing on her mind. Her flame had died.

Turning to Liam for much-needed support and understanding met with cold, unfeeling, pedantic lectures and criticism. Flexibility was never Liam's strong point, and now as he aged, he was more rigid and stubborn than ever. He resented the intrusion of her ill mother into their marriage and the burden it placed on his wife. His solution was a nursing home, but Farrah just could not do that. Her mother had done so much for her, so this was her time to give back. Her mother would have no part of anyone other than Farrah.

Farrah longed for warmth and intimacy with Liam, but he was too furious to make love to her. Liam's excuses included the lack of privacy, his diminishing sexual drive, and her unreasonable demands on him. His rejection and criticism sent her faltering sense of sexuality and adequacy plummeting to a new low. Tense and despairing, she cried at the drop of a hat.

I suggested marital therapy, but Farrah chose to work on herself instead. She did not know whether she wanted the marriage. We both agreed she was in no shape to make that decision now. The work was plodding, as Farrah's feeling of hopelessness blocked anything positive. My interventions met with disdain, and we were clearly at an impasse. She felt inadequate, like a failure, and so did I.

Suddenly, the dark cloud that hovered overhead for months gave way to a ray of sunshine. In a canary-yellow sweatsuit, Farrah sauntered into the room. The tall, stocky, matronly looking Farrah I thought I knew was replaced by a willowy, curvaceous, and youthful one. The smile on her face was outlined with a bright shade of lipstick. Her gray, stringy hair was dyed a warm shade of auburn, with soft waves that framed her face. The familiar slouched body was now on proud display. The transformation was stunning!

*I like to think I'm a keen observer. How has her weight loss escaped me? I knew she hid her corpulent self from the world with a loose, sexless wardrobe. Did she hide her diet plans from me? Is that why I didn't notice it? What else did she hide?*

"You look great!" I exclaimed.

"I feel great. All the work we've been doing's paying off. I want to thank you for your patience. You've helped me so much," Farrah complimented me.

*From a help-rejecting complainer, she's become gracious overnight! It's not making any sense. Something's up. I like to think I'm good at what I do, but not this good.*

"How have I helped you?" I asked.

"I know I've been a pain in the you-know-what. Then I thought to myself, if you could stand me, maybe someone else could. After all, Liam couldn't even tolerate my voice," she explained.

"And, who's this someone else?" I was curious.

"Josh, my mother's speech therapist, has come into my life." She beamed. Her dark eyes shone as she disclosed her daring secret.

"How's he come into your life?" It was like pulling teeth. She wasn't giving me the scoop so easily.

"I'm having an affair with him," she declared and leaned forward eagerly.

"So, what's that like?" I could see she was itching to tell me.

"It's wonderful. Josh is wonderful, and I feel wonderful." She swooned, like the bobbysoxers of our youth.

*She's hitting all the bases with three wonderfuls in a row. Where's she heading? To home base, or is this only a first base soon to be struck out?*

"Tell me about Mr. Wonderful," I suggested.

"I thought you'd never ask. Josh is nineteen years younger than me, but who's counting? He's smart, sensitive, romantic, and so attentive. He hangs on every word that I utter, and we really communicate. He's warm and understanding; not like Liam, who's cold and critical. He loves my sophistication and wisdom. He's no fool either, so a compliment from him is really great. And is he a lover!" The sun shone in through the window, bathing the room with a warm glow.

"So, he turns you on in a lot of ways. I see you're not feeling low anymore," I commented.

"No, but I still have my moments. I love Liam and we've built a life together. So, I sometimes have a hard time reconciling what I'm doing." A fleeting shadow swept over her countenance.

"I can understand that." I empathized with her. When in a long-term marriage, an extramarital affair is bound to bring excitement, but also distressful, conflicted feelings.

"I don't really understand it. I feel so alive, young, and vibrant with Josh. I thought my sexual desire was kaput, but not so. Josh lights my fire, whereas Liam snuffs it out. I desire Josh, and he desires me," she explained, trying to make sense of things, to gain clarity of her muddle.

"So now you know the fire inside of you is burning brightly, but the fire in the marriage is dying." I reiterated her thoughts.

"I feel so sad when you say that. I don't want to end the marriage. Liam and I have a lifetime of memories, children, and two homes. I'm not ready to give up on Liam, but I'm not ready to let go of Josh. I need Josh now. He helps me to cope with Mom, and I feel he really cares about us. Liam only cares about himself." She kept trying to find answers to her conflict.

*I guess she wants both worlds: the best of the marriage and the best of the extramarital affair. Who doesn't fantasize about this delightful infantile duo? Infantile wishes are the foundation of creativity, but when enacted in marriage, they shake the foundation of the relationship.*

"Ah, wouldn't it be divine to engage in the two worlds of an extramarital affair and a marriage unfettered by doubt or guilt?" I shared my musings.

Farrah turned the discussion back to Liam-bashing. "I guess I'm not one of these people. I can't have an affair and a marriage without doubt or guilt. I feel like a heel. But there are so many things about Liam I can't stand. Like I said, he's so self-centered."

"Has Liam always been self-centered?" I asked.

"Ever since he retired, he's gotten old and self-centered. He's a hypochondriac, always complaining about himself." She looked perturbed.

"How do you feel about getting older?" I asked.

"I hate it." She was clear on that.

"It sounds like you and Liam are both plagued with existential issues, fears of getting older, and your mortality. Rather than getting closer as you age, you're pushing each other farther away. His self-involvement and lack of empathy are how he deals with it. Your affair with a younger man is how you deal with it. Both of you are placing wedges between you, eroding romance, desire, and passion," I interpreted.

"I guess I got my answer. The flame in the marriage died, and all that's left is ashes." Tears flooded her eyes.

"Perhaps you can construct something meaningful from the ashes," I suggested.

"That's a lot to consider. I'm so attracted to Josh." She was receptive, but tentative.

"And this did not happen overnight, so it won't be resolved overnight," I explained.

In the subsequent sessions we worked on Farrah's feelings of inadequacy and her fears of her fading youth. Her mother's aging and illness were stark reminders of her mortality. Farrah began to see that escape with a younger man was a tempting option, but not a prudent solution. While it was heady, her affair also disoriented her. Coming to terms with her aging and focusing on her gains rather than her losses helped her to regain her equilibrium.

Facing her mortality could have undone her, but Farrah was determined to find a way out of her quagmire. I emphasized that coming face to face with our mortality presents us with an urgent cry to live fully, with meaning and love.[9] With less time to live, every moment was precious, so she would have to go for it. She dared to do just that.

Ending the affair with Josh took a lot of willpower. Bolstered by her burgeoning sense of self, she summoned up her courage and told Josh it was over. As usual, Josh understood her feelings, and wished her well. They decided a new speech therapist for her mother was in order, and this time, Farrah found a mature woman. She was not taking chances. Then Farrah decided she wanted to work on the marriage.

Farrah and Liam are in marital therapy, where we are dealing with their existential issues. Liam's feelings of inadequacy after retirement are not uncommon for men. He is looking at how his feelings of worthlessness were projected onto Farrah. Farrah is also looking at how she placed her mother's welfare ahead of the marriage. Rather than dumping on Farrah, Liam is looking for new ways to build his self-esteem, and Farrah is, too.

Not so long ago, they enjoyed a lively romantic and erotic sex life together. Seeing as they had a really full love before, their past good experience provided a platform for future good experience. Reclaiming the old passion is on the horizon. They are researching and practicing ways to relight their fire. It may take longer to get it going, but slow-burning embers maintain heat longer. The warm glow between them is promising.

In the above story you met an older and bolder wife with a set of existential and marital issues. Farrah's fear of aging was exacerbated by her aging, infirm mother. Caring for an aging parent elicits strong feelings about our own mortality.[10] She reeled and reached out to Liam; however, he was plagued with his own existential angst. His self-involvement, rigidity, and fear of aging were issues that prompted his rejection of Farrah's request for empathy.

Although the marital system was in dire need of realignment, Farrah chose to ignore the situation and do what many other older wives do in the face of marital discord. She found a young, flexible, empathic lover—her mother's speech therapist. Not only was Josh good to talk to, but he embodied other virtues. Miraculously, her flagging spirits and dying flame were rekindled.

Alas, miracles are not everlasting, and her actions brought her back to reality. Farrah was not able to carry on with both a lover and a husband. So, she made a choice to work on the troubles in the marriage. Her extramarital affair served a lot of masters, including her need to feel young, alive, and sexy again. It also acted as a signal of trouble in the marriage.

In the next story, you will meet another older and bolder wife. At midlife, she was struggling with an empty nest syndrome. Like Farrah, her husband was part of the problem. Like Farrah, she found a younger man to fill her in.

### A Feather in Her Nest

A distraught male voice beseeched me. "Doc, you've got to see my wife. I don't know what's come over her. She's never been like this."

"What's 'like this'?" I asked.

"She's always been a homebody, and now she's never home. She rolls in at all hours of the night, reeking of cigarette smoke and liquor." Enrique's voice trembled.

"Would you ask her to call me?" I suggested.

"I already did, and she said she didn't need a shrink. What should I do?" Panic resounded over the wires.

I responded to his anxiety. "You sound terribly anxious. Perhaps you should come in."

"Who wouldn't be anxious? I don't need help." He was emphatic about not needing any help.

"So we're at an impasse," I said. What else could I say?

"Okay, doc, I'll see if I can talk some sense into her." He seemed resolute to keep the attention on her.

*Sounds more like his child than his wife. I wonder if this is a macho man or an overwrought husband. He's going to talk sense into her! Whose sense are we talking about—hers, his, or mine?*

Two days later Enrique called back even more agitated.

"Doc, I found out she's having an affair. I lost it and I hit her. It was nothing, but she called the cops. They said it was a domestic problem, and that we should go to counseling. So, she's going to call you." He sounded strangely calm.

*His story doesn't seem to faze him at all. I guess he won his point. He got her to come in to see me. Not hard to guess who's got the power in this marriage!*

His wife Rosita did call and made an appointment to see me. She then called back to change the date. It seemed she was hesitant to see me, which is often the case when a child comes to therapy at the behest of a parent.

"My husband wanted me to come in, so here I am," Rosita announced. Finely lined porcelain skin with delicate features stood out in sharp relief against gray-streaked, dark, shoulder-length curls. Designer jeans, a jeweled belt, and a pink skin-tight top adorned her petite frame.

"How do you feel about coming in?" I turned the dialogue to her.

"I was scared. But you seem warm, and I love your office. Mauve pink's my favorite color." Her warm brown eyes met mine.

"What were you scared of?" I asked.

"That you'd think I was disgusting." She averted her gaze.

"Do you think you're disgusting?" I asked.

"No, but my husband does. He called me every name in the book. Then he threw me up against the wall. I hit my head on the bookshelf, and had to go to the doctor the next day. The doctor said it was a concussion. It hurt a lot, but I'm better now." Tears welled up, but she valiantly held on.

Concern turned to alarm. "How awful! Have you had these types of fights before where he strikes you?"

"He broke my nose once, but that was my fault. I saw him throwing the chair. I should've ducked." She was losing ground on her attempts to stay composed.

I spoke frankly. "It sounds like domestic violence and that your husband's the perpetrator. Yet, you're blaming yourself."

*I'm appalled at this tale of woeful misplacement of blame. This aging, diminutive, waif-like wife reminds me of a delicate damsel in distress. Will my rescue fantasies obscure my judgment? I'll have to watch for it.*

"I provoke him. I'm lonely lately. I'm always begging him to be with me. He calls me a nag and uses the C word. I hate that word. When I try to stand up for myself he shoots me down, and we get into a rip-roaring fight." Her eyes deepened and shone brightly.

*There's more spirit here than meets the eye. I'll try to help her harness her strength, so that she's a survivor and not a victim of domestic violence.*

I began to interpret. "I'm glad you fight back, even if you back down. You have inner strength that you're not aware of. So, you submit and he dominates you."

Her soft voice neared a whisper. "He sure does. Enrique thinks he's the king and I'm his servant. He says I should kiss his feet for what he does for me. He pays the bills, and when I ask, he gives me money to spend."

"He gives you money when you ask?" I emphasized the inequity.

"He treats me like a child." Rosita got it.

"How do you feel about that?" I wanted to hear her feelings about the power differential in the marriage.

"I feel like a child. Maybe I am a child. I can't stand being alone. Enrique travels a lot, and I can't stay in the empty house. So, I go out to the local bar. He's furious and says a decent wife shouldn't be at bars. I don't get it. He's always going to business trips, and who know what he does." Her voice was now more forceful.

"What do you think he does?" I asked.

"He probably cheats. He keeps accusing me of cheating, but I wasn't—until recently. I didn't mean to. It's not like I was looking. It just happened. Enrique found out, and he's threatening to divorce me. He doesn't understand that I'm lonely and that I need him. But he's not there. I've been so depressed. Then I met Claude." She looked away dreamily.

"So, Claude's helping your loneliness and depression. Aside from Enrique's travels, are there any other reasons for your recent loneliness?" I was curious about whether any other midlife issues might have been at play.

"Overnight the kids grew up, and they're all out of the house. The house is empty and I feel empty inside. When they left, I thought, it's just Enrique and me, which could be a good thing. I thought it was our time now. But, he's got other ideas. He's still busy building empires, so he can retire rich." She was more than disappointed.

"You're disappointed," I suggested.

"It's not like we're hurting financially, but money's his god. Not mine; love's my god. Enrique says he loves me, but I don't believe him. His words are empty." She looked sad and defeated.

"So, your nest is empty, and Enrique's not helping you fill it in. He's abusive. His response to your needs is frightening." I was clear about my position.

"I'm frightened, all right. Not so much about his physical attacks, but I'm scared of being alone. If he leaves me, I'd be lost," she whimpered in a little-girl voice. The thought of abandonment filled her with terror.

*Her pale skin and dark hair add to her Snow White appearance. Is Claude her Prince Charming to the rescue? Does he fulfill her fantasies? That's one thing, but there are more pressing problems that require attention— powerlessness, surviving domestic violence, fears of abandonment.*

"Why would you be lost without an abusive man?" I inquired.

"Enrique always controlled me, but he wasn't abusive till the kids left home. I miss them so much," she explained tearfully.

"So, things weren't so bad until the nest was empty. How much of you was invested in the children?" I wanted more.

"All of me. Enrique's a good dad, so we were both involved with the kids. When the kids left, I told him 'the best is yet to come.' But, the worst came. I began to cling to Enrique, and he became abusive to me." Rosita explained how the contract in the marriage had changed.

"It sounds like the focus of the marriage was the children, but not just the two of you. And maybe you had other things you placed between you two to keep a safe distance. Now that the children are gone, and it's just you two, the contract has been broken. You want more closeness, and Enrique is rejecting you," I interpreted.

"Enrique was never really emotionally or sexually attuned to me, but I had my children, their activities, their school work, their hurts and joys, so I was fulfilled. I knew I was missing something with Enrique, but I stayed for the children." She articulated her feelings.

"Are there any other reasons that you stayed?" I wanted more.

She looked down. "I'm financially dependent on Enrique."

"I can understand that. If you could support yourself, would you still stay with him?" I inquired.

"I don't know. Claude is much younger than Enrique—actually, he's fourteen years young than me—but he's a very successful architect. He's helping me to rebuild my confidence as an older woman. Claude's so loving, romantic, and sexy. He's always telling me how beautiful I am, and he thinks I'm smart. He really appreciates me, not like Enrique. Claude wants me to leave Enrique and live with him. Claude's the answer to my prayers." Her face radiated warmth and comfort.

"So with Claude you can fulfill your fantasy of a Prince Charming coming to your rescue." I did not know how this interpretation would go over.

"You're being sarcastic, like Enrique." She glared at me.

"I see you can stand up to me. Maybe you're stronger than you think. You feel dependent on Enrique, but unless we work on your independence, you'll repeat the same pattern with Claude. After all, we can change our circumstances, but we bring our old selves along." I gave her something to think about.

She smiled. "I'd like to work on being more independent. I really want to give this a try with Claude."

"How do you think Claude would respond to your greater independence and autonomy?" I was curious to hear how she regarded equality in gender roles.

"He's already encouraging me to go back to school. I've always wanted to be an interior decorator, and he said he'd pay for my education," she explained calmly.

*So, she's not so powerless; she's plucky. It augurs well. Our Snow White has some dark spots. She's scrappier than I thought. She's got her ducks lined up. Our waif wife sure is wily! Now we can roll. I feel hopeful she can transform her aggression to assertion and work toward autonomy, agency, and strength.*

"So, Claude's supportive about your developing independence. What do you think Enrique would say about you going back to school?" I asked her.

She explained his narrowness. "Enrique doesn't understand me. He tells me I have everything, so I should be happy."

In our following work, exploration of her past revealed how Rosita was repeating old patterns of relating that she learned in her family. Her mother had come from a long line of dependent housewives who were subservient to their husbands.

Rosita's mother's life was her children, her home, and her husband. She derived her power vicariously through him and by serving others. Rosita's father was a hardworking construction worker who took orders from his boss. At home he assumed the boss role, with Rosita's mother as his employee. Beer-drinking, demanding, and criticizing his wife, he usurped the role of the dominant player in the relationship.

Her mother danced around her father, trying to please him, her children, and others. Often, little Rosita comforted her despondent, subservient mother. When Rosita showed her contempt for her father, her mother silenced her. She warned her that forceful behavior was unfeminine, and that no man would love her.

Rosita identified with her mother's concept of femininity and repeated the old dynamic. Femininity precluded any male traits—independence, autonomy, active agency, aggression, and separateness. Rosita split off these male parts and lived vicariously through Enrique, a domineering macho man like her father. She hated her father, so she could not identify with his maleness. Her mother was not in touch with her male parts, and Rosita was not either. Alas, Rosita had neither an autonomous, independent mother who accepted her own masculine traits, nor a strong, kind father with whom she could identify.

Accessing Rosita's aggression, her spunky, steely side that was disavowed, became a central part of the work. As long as she was dependent on others, she was an emotional hostage to them, a passive victim without agency or will of her own. Fortunately, Rosita desired her freedom. As her sense of independence grew she gained more confidence in becoming the actor, rather than remaining the reactor. Her split-off aggression was slowly coming into awareness and transforming to assertion.

One day Rosita informed me that she had filed for divorce and was moving in with Claude. She knew the move was premature, as she had a lot of growing to do. Rosita also wanted a break from therapy to test her newfound autonomous self.

*She's made strides, but she still has a way to go. This break from therapy's premature. Yet, I daren't try to dissuade her from her decision lest I repeat her domineering husband's behavior. We worked on her sense of agency, so what am I worrying about? She's exercising it. But, I'll miss her.*

A year later, Rosita was back. "You haven't changed," she exclaimed.

"What does it mean to you that I'm the same?" I wanted to mine some meaning.

"I need your constancy; there are so many changes in my life. I gained a lot, and I don't want to lose my self again." She sounded mature and went on. "I was scared that I'd become dependent on you if I stayed too long," she explained.

"With your history I can understand that. What made you change your mind and trust me again not to dominate you?" I wanted to hear her take on this.

"I feel stronger and I realize my fears were unfounded. Not everyone wants to overpower me and take me over. You're not my father or Enrique. Claude respects my autonomy and separateness, but we have other issues. He wants more children, and I can't give him that, nor do I want to." She asserted boldly.

"So, you're in the prime of your life and not in the pocket of a man." I felt proud of her.

Rosita is in ongoing therapy with me. She loves Claude, and despite differences, with him she enjoys a more equal power relationship. So, things between them have a good running start. The finish is yet to be determined.

I mentioned earlier in the book that rarely do wives end up with their lovers. But, that is variable, as everything else is. There are no absolutes, and it all depends on the situation and the people involved. In Rosita's case, her marriage was seriously out of kilter. Enrique's machismo and his dominating, violent behavior had eroded her self-esteem. Submissive dependency that kept her tied to Enrique was part of the legacy of generations of hapless wives. At midlife, Rosita was suffering the empty nest syndrome, which Enrique did not fill. Claude, her lover, did. So her personal and cultural history along with marital troubles interpenetrated her core self to influence her desire for an extramarital affair.

In the above two stories you met daring wives with differing cultural and family backgrounds. Farrah, a feminist, was more in touch with her autonomy than Rosita, a traditional wife. Different motivations related to aging, family history, personality, and styles of relating prompted them to take younger lovers. In doing so, they unwittingly both defied the double discrimination of ageism and sexism in our society. Older women with younger lovers seem to be making their mark in our current society. I hope that signifies a diminution of the double standard in sexuality and ageism.

In the following chapter, meet other daring wives struggling with a common phenomenon in our society—remarriage and stepfamilies.

# 8

# Remarriages and Regrets

## OUT OF STEP WITH STEPFAMILIES

*When I meet a man I ask myself, "Is this the man I want my children to spend their weekends with?"*

—Rita Rudner

## ATTACHMENT BONDS

Remarriages and stepfamilies in America are estimated at 15–20 million, with increasing numbers every year.[1] The problems that arise in remarriage differ from those of nuclear families. One of the goals of remarriage is blending the families. Unfortunately, the Brady Bunch rarely is the reality. Ex-spouses get in the way, as do stepchildren and financial stresses. Ties to former families, with strong attachments, may create wedges between the remarried spouses. Old baggage is carried over to the new marriages, presenting stumbling blocks that impede intimacy in the remarriage.

A central stumbling block in remarriage is the attachment bond to a former spouse. No matter the hostility and hateful feelings toward her ex-husband or her conscious wishes, the attachment bond of a remarried wife may continue on an unconscious level.[2] She may experience the separation as a loss and suffer from separation distress.

The chief source of anxiety, distress, sadness, and depression is separation from an intimate person.[3] The relationship between a wife and husband is certainly an intimate attachment, so that separation can be a wrenching innermost loss, much as a child may have suffered when losing a parent.

Intimate attachments are the hub around which a person's life revolves from early childhood to old age.[4] Separation is a lifelong struggle from womb to tomb,[5] and separating from an ex-husband is one of these struggles.

In the majority of cases the attachment is overcome within a year, but of course, not in all.[6] The continued attachment to an ex-spouse interferes with developing a satisfying relationship with the new spouse.[7] So the old tie, no matter how hostile or loving, creates a wedge in the remarried couple.

In the following story, meet a wife whose continued attachment to her ex-husband played havoc in the remarriage. Her struggle to separate from her ex-husband was exacerbated by earlier unresolved traumatic loss.

### Hanging On for Dear Life

Hannah and Jorge were in marital therapy to work on their new remarriage. This was the second time around for both. Jorge, a widower, had lost his wife five years earlier. His first marriage was a happy one, and he reported a loving, close attachment to his late wife Marissa. She died of cancer, and he stood by her to the bitter end, tending to her with undying devotion. The romance and sexual desire of the early years were non-existent in the last four years of her illness. Nevertheless, Jorge maintained the memories of a stable love that bolstered him to mourn and move on. His prior positive marital experience provided him expectations that he would experience yet another good marriage. So Jorge entered into the marriage with Hannah with high hopes. All was well and good, but the ghost of his late wife haunted the remarriage.

The attachment bond between Hannah and her former husband Ben drastically differed from Jorge's attachment to his late wife. A combustible relationship replete with cycles of passionate fighting, making up, and making out, Hannah and Ben's attachment bond was truly chaotic. Despite the fierce fighting, their fiery lovemaking made the frictional marriage worth hanging onto for twelve years. Another consideration was their two children. Their last fight, however, was over the top. No amount of lovemaking could repair the damage wrought. In an adrenaline fit of rage, Hannah wrenched Ben's computer from its connections and smashed it against the wall. Ben wailed, "You've shattered my entire life." He filed for divorce the next day.

Despite the hostile divorce proceedings, Hannah and Ben continued to enjoy an occasional torrid love tryst. When Hannah and Jorge remarried, Hannah silently vowed to relinquish her sexual liaisons with Ben. Vows, however, are only as valid as the person's resolve. Alas, resolve was not one of Hannah's strong points, particularly when it came to overcoming losses. There she was at a loss.

When Hannah was three, she suffered a central, traumatic loss. Tragically, her mother died in a car accident. Shocked and unable to assimilate the trauma and loss, Hannah adapted by denying her mother's death for many years. She pretended her mother was out on an errand and would soon return.

Devastated by his wife's sudden death, Hannah's father sunk into a deep depression. With the best intention to protect Hannah from his grief, he sent her to live with her grandparents. The well-intended grandparents did everything they could to distract little Hannah—everything but help her to mourn. Indeed, good intentions pave the road to hell, and Hannah was alone in her horrific hell of loneliness, fear, and sadness. Not only had her mother abandoned her, her father had done so also. The specter of abandonment met with terror, and she suffered from separation anxieties her entire adult life.

No matter the tumultuous relationships, Hannah hung onto old boyfriends even after they abused her. Once again, she denied the realities of the terrible relationships lest she face yet another dreaded abandonment. She managed to choose men with whom a real relationship of romance and stability was not likely. Her old beaus were too wild or too tame, too bad or too good, too arrogant or too meek. With Jorge she found the Goldilocks effect—he was just right!

You would think this Prince Charming would augur well for our Cinderella. With Hannah's history of attachment and traumatic loss, a loving relationship with passionate sexual desire, comfort, security, and stability was terrorizing. Real intimacy with love and desire posed the specter of becoming emotionally dependent and vulnerable to Jorge. For most of us the idea of dependency may present us with a stumbling block, but for Hannah, dependency presented her with a gargantuan mountain—abandonment and loss. Jorge was too much to lose. If she lost him, she feared she would not recover. So, unconsciously, she adopted self-protective measures to keep her safe. The distance in the marriage made dependency less likely. She did not have to go very far to maintain distance in the marriage, not any further than her former husband Ben.

"Jorge's so jealous. I don't get it. I have to talk to Ben. He's the father of my children, and he owes me money," Hannah pouted in a whiny, little-girl voice. Blonde, tight, curly hair framed a pretty round face. In true baby doll fashion, her large, innocent blue eyes opened wide, while her full lower lip protruded seductively. Her skinny frame added to her naive appearance.

"What bothers me isn't that you talk to him. It's how often you talk to him," Jorge complained. The small hands with which Jorge gesticulated seemed out of place with his rotund body. His pleading, warm brown eyes spoke of sadness.

"How do I talk to him?" Hannah looked up innocently at Jorge.

"You put on that sugary, sweet, seductive voice of yours. That's how." Jorge sounded anything but sweet or sugary. Infuriated, his warm eyes grew stone cold.

"Jorge, how do you feel now?" I asked Jorge to gauge his feeling state.

"I don't like what she's doing. I give her everything she wants. So why is she spending so much time with him?" He skirted the subject and focused on Hannah.

"Hannah, how do you feel now?" I inquired of her.

She was clearly angry. "I feel angry. I'm nice to Ben because he owes me money. And like I said, I need to talk to him about our kids."

I floated a trial balloon. "It seems Ben's a wedge between you two."

"It's not just Ben that's a wedge. What about Marissa, your serene, saintly dead wife? You keep comparing me to her. Just because I'm emotional, passionate, and alive doesn't make me a flake or a floozy. You knew what I was like when you married me." Jorge cringed at Hannah's feisty retort.

"I love you, babe, but I can't take your outbursts." Tears filled Jorge's eyes.

"I hate when you call me 'babe.' I'm no babe. I'm a well-respected professor of human sexuality. The problem's that you're not sexual; you're a prude and a wimp. I don't respect you and I don't desire you sexually." Her knockout blow sent him to the ropes. Her brief brush with naiveté gave way to brass knuckles.

"Hannah, darling, you scare me. Doc, can you see how she scares me? That's how she talks to me. When we married we had sex twice daily; now I don't desire her sexually. She's pushed me away. She's such a bitch." Well, well. Jorge's coming out of his corner and slinging back.

"It's hard to desire each other sexually when you're both out to destroy each other. Romance and desire go hand in hand with respect and trust. I think there are some problems here with respect and trust," I suggested.

"How can I trust her? Do you know she's begun to have dinner dates with Ben? What do you make of that?" Jorge asked my opinion.

"Mostly, what do you make of it, Jorge?" I placed the question back where it belonged.

"I think she's holding on to him, and until she lets go, we can't have a good relationship." Right on!

"What do you think, Hannah?" I asked her.

She got defensive. "What about Marissa? It's not like he's not holding on to her."

"But I don't date her," he defended himself.

"How can you date her? She's dead," Hannah struck back.

"Guys, we're not in court. I'm not the judge, and you don't have to defend yourselves. What's more important: who's to blame or getting along?" I now broached a cardinal area of marital relationships.

"Getting along is more important." Resounding mutuality at last!

"It sounds like neither of you have relinquished the attachment to your former spouses, which we have to work on. Your style of fighting gets vicious, so we'll have to work on that also," I proposed.

I saw the couple together for a few more sessions, before Hannah called to ask for some individual sessions with me. She sounded desperate, and Jorge was concerned about her recent disorganized, frantic behavior. He would see me individually as well. I agreed to this temporary arrangement as I, too, was concerned about Hannah's panicky state. It seemed there was something beyond the marital relationship that was plaguing Hannah. I soon found out what that something was. It was Ben.

"Dr. Fran, I don't want to stay so attached to Ben, but I can't help myself. It's gotten bad lately. I still obsess about him, wondering who he's sleeping with. I call him often and go by his apartment at night." She tossed her tied-around-the-shoulder sweater back and sighed loudly.

"So you're stalking him," I commented.

"That's not all I'm doing. Promise me you won't tell Jorge. I'm sleeping with Ben." She searched me for a reaction.

I outlined another cardinal feature of intimacy. "I don't think it's my place to tell Jorge. But when you're ready to engage in a real intimate relationship with Jorge you'll tell him yourself. Intimacy entails openness and trust."

"I don't want to hurt Jorge. I love him; it's just that I can't give Ben up. We have this strong sexual attraction to each other." She broke down into soft sobs.

"Tell me more about this attraction with Ben. Are you attracted to Jorge?" I was curious about the distinction she made.

"It's not the same. It's comfortable and safe with Ben. I have history with him. Jorge's a good lover; it's not that. I don't know what's with me." Her dark blue eyes pleaded with me for some answers.

I countered her explanation. "It's interesting that you call sex with Ben comfortable and safe, when all you did was fight. Your relationship with him was hardly safe—more like dangerous."

"I guess so. I don't get it." She was bewildered.

"With your history of attachment and tragic loss, I can see where you may fear intimate attachment. Intimacy is dangerous for you because you can become dependent on Jorge, and he can abandon you like your mother did. So you protect yourself from dependency by placing wedges between him and you. Ben is one of these wedges, and Marissa is another. The constant fighting is another way that you two degrade romance and sexual desire. Perhaps that's what went on in your previous marriage," I interpreted.

"I see a pattern, all right. I fall in love, and then I set up wedges. I also know I can't let go of Ben. I feel like I'd die without him. I've never been good at separations." Hannah's tears rolled down her cheeks.

"So you're hanging on for dear life." I empathized with her.

"It's crazy, but in Ben's arms, I feel close to my mother. He's gentle, and he caresses me with a soft touch and kisses." She stared off into space.

I joined her. "It's not so crazy. The attachment to Ben is similar to what you imagine it was to your mother. He breathes life into her dead body. That's awesome. I guess that's hard to beat."

"Jorge's passionate and sexy, but I don't feel the same. Ben knows what to do to please me, but Jorge doesn't." She compared the two again.

I offered her some agency. "Perhaps you could tell Jorge what you desire. He's new to you and he's not a mind reader."

"That's funny. I'm a professor of human sexuality, so you'd think I'd know that." She laughed at herself. How refreshing!

I commiserated with her. "It's hard to be objective about yourself when emotions get in the way."

"Talking about my mother's always emotional," she agreed.

"Of course, you loved and lost, and you fear future losses, so you protect yourself," I suggested.

"It's a lot to process. I have to think about it all." She shook her head.

In the following sessions, we worked on Hannah's separation anxieties stemming from her childhood. She began to see how her fears of abandonment kept her hanging on to a failed marriage.

Although the divorce from Ben was her idea, somehow Hannah felt she could not live without Ben. Despite the high-conflict, defunct marriage with Ben, Hannah held on. Fearing Ben would leave her, Hannah had beaten him to the punch and divorced him. This way she thought she would avoid abandonment. Nevertheless, the dissolution of a marriage is a loss, no matter who initiates it. Now she was obsessed with whether Ben would abandon her for another woman. So her sexual affair with Ben was partly to keep him from leaving her.

The other reason for her affair with Ben was to avoid real intimacy with Jorge. Jorge unwittingly collaborated in this construction of distance. His attachment to his late wife was still strong, and he made it known. While he could not have a sexual relationship with his dead wife, he did continue an emotional one. The widow's syndrome of idealizing a late husband applies to widowers as well. Jorge idealized his late wife.

In therapy, Jorge examined this so-called "perfect" relationship with Marissa only to find it had not been so perfect. Marissa was not an angel, nor was Hannah a devil. In time, he admitted that devils had more fun, anyhow.

Marissa had been a complaining, whining, childlike woman, dependent on Jorge for everything. Even when she was healthy, Jorge shopped, cooked, and worked full-time while Marissa stayed in bed until noon. Jorge revealed that he resented how she leaned on him. When she took ill, Jorge cared for her more out of obligation than love. So, he had split his relationships into polarities of good and bad, good Marissa and bad Hannah.

Jorge began to see how he unwittingly created distance with Hannah. In time, he began to appreciate her candor and to respect her independence and autonomy. The recognition of the degree of Hannah's insecurity and fear of loss and abandonment proved to be an awakening for Jorge. He, too, feared dependency, as he might lose Hannah. His parents' marriage had ended in divorce, and he lost his father, who dropped out of his life. So they had a lot in common.

Their common bond was a starter, with empathy and trust to follow. Finally, Hannah ended her affair with Ben, but Jorge had already discovered it. Suspecting an affair, Jorge had checked Hannah's cell phone and read a revealing message. Furious, he confronted her and demanded the truth. Hannah was forthcoming and begged forgiveness. The marital work had moved along well enough so that the relationship could survive this rupture. They are now working on repairing the tear, and on healing each other from old, and not so old, hurts.

In the above story, the couple unwittingly constructed blocks to intimacy in their remarriage. Both suffered from previous losses, so that relinquishing the attachment to former spouses was experienced as yet another central loss. Fear of intimacy in the new marriage stemmed from fear of losing a beloved figure, so self-protective mechanisms against dependency were unwittingly employed.

In the next story, meet a couple where a different type of attachment set up wedges in the remarriage. Attachment to adult children from a former marriage can become problematic in the remarriage. When the adult step-children and father align against the new wife, the triangle is headed for trouble; and trouble can be as close as another adult stepchild.

### Stepping Out with a Stepchild

Celeste and Steve were married for five years. This was the second marriage for Celeste and the third for Steve. Six months ago they decided they needed some help and came in to see me for marital therapy. The work needed was not proceeding well; I often thought I wanted the marriage more than they did. When I broached the subject they assured me they loved each other and wanted things to work out. Words are often belied by actions. They seemed stuck in being right, without empathy for each other.

Their conflicts centered on the divisive role played by Steve's children in their remarriage. Steve was sixteen years older than Celeste, but they looked good together. Celeste's buxom body, draped in rainbow-colored flowing robes; long, steel-gray wavy hair; and strong, pronounced facial features made for a striking mature woman. With his piercing dark eyes, bald head, and slim frame in dapper attire, Steve was the perfect complement to his blushing bride.

Steve had an adult son, Owen, from his first marriage, and three adult children, Lucy, Sally, and Peter, from his second. They were scattered in suburban towns close to Celeste and Steve. Owen, Steve's son from his first wife, lived in a trendy urban area not too far from Celeste and Steve. Eric, Celeste's young adult son from her first marriage, was away at graduate school. Eric had made a successful transition into young adulthood and become his own person and a supportive, loving son.

Steve's children lived closer to him than Celeste's child did to her. The physical proximity paralleled the emotional proximity. With the exception of Owen, Steve's children's paths to separation and individuation were blocked. They were still enmeshed with their father, and regarded Celeste as an unwelcome intrusion. No matter that they were married with children of their own—they still had not made the separation from their father. They were dependent on him financially and emotionally, much like their mother, Leah.

Leah, Steve's ex-wife, suffered from chronic debilitating anxiety, abject dependency, jealousy, and insecurity. Over Leah's pleadings, Steve had initiated the divorce six years prior to marrying Celeste. Leah, however, did not let go of the attachment, and called Steve incessantly. His children did so also. Although Steve had divorced his wife, emotionally the hostile bond remained. We stay as attached in hate as we do in love.

Celeste's stepchildren treated her with varying degrees of disdain. Lucy, the older child, had been Steve's surrogate wife, as Leah was too distressed to attend to his emotional needs. Lucy resented Celeste's arrival and was jealous of her relationship with her father. Sally, the middle child, was the flighty rebellious daughter whom her father constantly reined in. Despite her remarriage to a responsible man, Sally still called her father in desperation to get her out of scrapes with the law. John, the youngest child, had married a materialistic wife, who feared that Celeste would rob them of their inheritance. To some degree, Lucy and Sally also saw Celeste as an interloper who would abscond with their inheritance. They conjectured that Celeste, who was sixteen years younger than their father, would outlive him and get all his money.

Owen was the only stepchild with whom Celeste had a friendly relation-ship. As we all know, friendships can sometimes become more than just friendships. They can become amorous.

Celeste's protestations about her stepchildren met with deaf ears by her husband Steve. He blamed Celeste and defended his children. She fought back ferociously, insulting him and his children. Steve retaliated by insulting her. So the fighting increased and the intimacy decreased. Steve punished Celeste by withholding sex from her. She punished him in yet another way.

Owen was the only one around to sympathize with Celeste's plight. So, Celeste had a handsome young shoulder to cry on. That was not all she had with Owen. Celeste and Owen had a lot in common age-wise and interest-wise. Celeste was only four years older than Owen, and they both liked the same music, movies, and books. They were both successful lawyers in related fields. He practiced corporate law, and Celeste practiced family law. They also both loved to dance. Steve did not dance and so when the three were at a party, Celeste and Owen danced together and Steve sat out. Celeste and Owen were often mistaken as a fun-loving married couple, with an obliging father looking on.

The fights between Celeste and Steve escalated, and the word *divorce* en-tered these fights, placing further distance between them. They were in deep trouble, more than I could imagine when Celeste called me.

"Dr. Fran, I have to see you alone. This is big, and Steve can't know. He'd kill me if he knew." The urgency struck a chord of alarm.

*Steve's anything but violent. He's much more passive than Celeste. This has to be something really big. Shall I gratify her wish? Or is it to gratify my curiosity? I think I'll go for it.*

The next day, a flustered Celeste bounded into my office. Her tangled hair and wrinkled dress were so unlike her. Her keys dropped to the floor, but she did not bother to pick them up. Dispensing with greetings, Celeste got right to the point.

"I'm having an affair with Owen, Steve's son." She did not blink an eyelash.

"And?" I asked.

"And he's terrific." She explained her motivation for the affair. "Owen and I are really getting it on. Not only is he sensitive and a great listener, he's on my side. Steve's not; he's on his kids' side. Owen is the only one in my corner. I feel so alienated from the rest of the family."

"So, he's your support system in this marriage. Are there any other reasons for the affair?" I wanted her to think about it.

"Lots of reasons; Owen is young, sexy, and so good in bed. With him, I forget all the problems in the marriage." She stared out the window wistfully.

"So you escape reality with Owen," I remarked.

"So, what's wrong with that? It's better than drugs or alcohol," she retorted.

"You've got a point. But when the party's over, reality sets in. And you're frightened of Steve's reaction. How do you feel about the fact that you're having an affair with his son?" I tried to bring some reason into the dialogue.

"Steve deserves it; he's so insensitive to my feelings. And he won't make love to me. How do you think that feels?" she shouted out in defiance. Spotting the keys on the floor, she picked them up and held on tightly.

I was blunt. "So your affair with Steve's son is about getting back at him—taking revenge."

"Maybe, but my affair with Owen is empowering me. I've felt helpless in trying to reach Steve, yet I didn't want another failure. So, I stayed in the marriage, ranted and raved, but Steve doesn't hear me. He's a wimp. We've been in therapy for six months and Steve's still blaming me. I don't think he'll ever change and give me what I want." Her ire was mounting as she jingled her keys.

"Aside from a healthier relationship with his children and more sex, what else do you want?" I wondered what else Owen had awakened in her.

"I want a younger man, a more flexible man, and a man with less baggage. I want to come first in his life, not last. I'm free sexually with Owen, and I feel like I find myself with him. I lose myself with Steve." More relaxed, she relinquished the keys to her handbag.

"So, Owen awakened some real desires in you," I noted.

"That's the good thing about this love, but the bad thing is Owen and I could never be together out in the open. I don't like secret loves, but I can't let it out. I'd never hurt Steve." She had obviously given some deep thought to her situation.

"I can understand your dilemma." I felt empathy for her.

"I've decided I don't want to work on the marriage any more. I'm sorry I married Steve. We both have too much baggage. I want a divorce." Her old threats had given way to resolve.

Celeste did in fact file for divorce, and she and Steve continued to see me for separation issues. She never told Steve about her affair with Owen, but he knew she did not have both feet in the marriage. Neither did Steve. With his attachment to his children and his ex-wife and his rigidity, he constructed obstacles in their path. Celeste retaliated with his oldest son.

Neither partner had parents to provide a paradigm of a loving couple. A child must see parents fight, show aggression, and resolve conflict. This way, the child gets the message that aggression is not dangerous, and that love can be greater than hate.

Steve's father was an alcoholic with a violent temper, so all Steve heard was aggression, without resolve. Hate overtook love in his parents' marriage, but they stayed together for the children. Steve always feared confrontation with his father, who would lose it with him rather than listen to him. Steve's fear of confrontation, stemming from his childhood, paralyzed him with his children. He could not imagine that if he asserted himself with them, that they would still love him.

Celeste's family constellation did not provide her with a loving spousal unit either. Her mother, a tough, demanding woman, dominated her meek husband, Celeste's father. Her mother wanted her husband to provide her with more financial security and sexual satisfaction. Celeste's ineffectual father suffered from Parkinson's disease and was unable to satisfy his wife. In some ways, Celeste repeated this pattern in her marriage to Steve. Incapacity stemming from fear has something in common with incapacity stemming from Parkinson's. Celeste also married a man who would not satisfy his wife's desires, and like her mother, she felt deprived, resentful, and angry.

In the above story, the remarriage did not work, and Celeste and Steve divorced. Celeste remained in therapy, and Steve bowed out. One of Celeste's goals is to avoid repeating the same patterns of relating. The extramarital affair acted as a catalyst to awaken her inner desires. She knows that if she does not resolve her inner issues, she will only bring them to the next relationship. She does desire another man in her life, a strong, protective man who can be there for her. She is beginning to gain confidence that she can be there for a man in an empathic way and deal with his shortcomings in a better way than she did with Steve. Lately, she has more compassion for Steve. We are working on gaining more compassion for her.

In both stories illustrated above, we saw how old patterns of relating got in the way of resolving new problems posed by remarriage. Rather than a fresh start, the remarriages were besieged with carryover baggage. Regretting the remarriages, daring wives reached out for understanding, recognition, and love elsewhere. In one case, the marriage had enough of a foundation to sustain the blemish of infidelity. But in the other it did not; instead, the marriage acted to empower the wife so that she could leave the marriage and seek renewal within herself.

Remarriage and stepfamilies on the increase are signs of the times, as are same-sex erotic relationships. In the following chapter we will examine how daring wives—married to men—act on their desires for women lovers.

# 9

# Same-Sex Affairs

## WIVES WITH WOMEN LOVERS

*There came a time when the risk to remain tight in the bud was more painful than the risk to blossom.*
—Anais Nin

*What is straight? A line can be straight, or a street, but the human heart, oh, no, it's curved like a road through mountains.*
—Tennessee Williams[1]

## MULTIPLE MEANINGS

What is the effect on marriage of wives' affairs with other women? Does it mean they are unfaithful? What about the significance of sexual orientation for a wife's sense of self? In our current post-modern times of multi-layered experience, a woman's sexual attractions, identities, and behaviors are also multi-layered, influenced by social and cultural constructions as well as inner strivings, developmental experiences, and personal history. The meaning and significance of a wife's extramarital affair with a woman is a unique experience with a private meaning that differs for each wife. In this chapter I will explore some of these multiple meanings of wives' affairs with women.

Recent empirical evidence documents that women's sexuality is flexible, fluid, plastic, and may change over time.[2] Childhood indicators of sexual orientation do not necessarily indicate a woman's later sexual orientation.[3] For some women, sexual orientation may well be an emergent phenomenon, rather than an early-appearing trait.[4]

While one woman may have always known she had sexual desires for a woman, another woman's same-sex orientation may have gradually unfolded

during childhood and adolescence. Yet another woman's same-sex orientation may emerge abruptly at a later point in her lifetime.[5] It may even
emerge during marriage to a man.

In comparison to men, women's sex drive is more malleable in response
to sociocultural and situational factors.[6] Some women identify themselves
as lesbian or bisexual in political protest of hegemonic patriarchy in heterosexual relationships. For other women, same-sex desires may be hampered by
cultural condemnation; hence, they are unaware of or reluctant to express
their authentic desires.[7] Given our culture of greater tolerance of same-sex
orientation, other wives may feel emboldened to seek fulfillment of their
authentic desires.

The state of the marriage—a situational factor—can also influence a
wife's expression of her same-sex desire. A modern wife desires mutual
power, recognition, and attunement in the marital relationship. If her husband fails to fulfill these desires—and a woman friend does—a wife may be
surprised by her emerging sexual feelings toward her friend. An unusually
close friendship may unexpectedly give rise to sexual desire.[8]

A wife may feel confused about her identity and what her affair with a
woman means for her marriage. She may think this is only a phase. Research[9]
reveals that one quarter of young women engaged in sexual activity with
other women relinquished their activity, but not their sexual attraction. They
did not describe their experience as a phase, but rather that they changed
the way they interpreted or acted on their attractions.

Sexual identity often comes into question when a wife has an extramarital
affair with a woman. While women may have multiple sexual selves that
are flexible and fluid, they usually still seek a cohesive self.[10] Without a
cohesive sense of self, a wife may feel conflicted and fragmented. In this
case, clarity of her sexual identity is crucial for a cohesive self. Then there
are women who feel otherwise. They do not need labels to feel intact. Many
heterosexual wives engaging in affairs with other women do not identify themselves as bisexual or lesbian. They simply feel that their authentic sexual desires
cannot be met in exclusive heterosexual relationships. Still other wives may
experience their female bodies and heterosexual identity as ill-fitting. If not
for bisexuality, they could not feel sexual at all.[11]

Initially, some wives may not question their sexual identity, especially if
their husbands approve of their affairs with women. A husband still wields
a great deal of power in a wife's choices. He may request that his wife and
he engage in swinging—she has sex with a woman while he watches or
participates. Research[12] indicates that when wives had no prior sexual attractions to other women, after engaging in swinging with another woman,
many continued to have sex with both men and women. The swinging

environment and a wife's desire for fulfillment of sexual desires were other factors. Notably, however, the strongest influence was her husband's wishes.

In my clinical experience, I have worked with wives who married, had children, and engaged in affairs with other women during marriage. Some identified themselves as lesbian; after much deliberation, they ended the marriages to resume satisfying long-term relationships with their women lovers. I have also worked with wives whose same-sex extramarital affairs gave rise to turmoil for them and their husbands. Then again, I have read about wives whose continued engagement in sexual behavior with women during the marriage did not affect the marriage. In my experience, I have rarely found the last one of these three scenarios. The open marriages of the sixties and seventies do not appear to work today.

In the following story, I share a case that I found particularly interesting in light of our more open and tolerant society. I have found that discrimination and prejudice about same-sex orientation persist. Hence, sexual desire may go underground before marriage, only to suddenly surface during marriage.

### A False Front of Femininity

Diana's therapy centered on mounting anxieties that impacted her marriage, her young children, and her feelings of well-being. Obsessed with cleanliness, domestic duties, and motherhood, Diana despaired that her life ran her; and it did. A slave to her obsessions, she shortchanged the marriage and her children's development.

A tall, slender woman, Diana's tresses draped gracefully down her back. Try as she might to hold them back, strands of hair fell onto her face, which met with Diana's distress. A perfectionist, she had to have every hair in place. Unfortunately, her unruly mane had its own mind. A haircut was not an option; it would curtail her femininity. Her husband Chuck also wanted a feminine wife. Short, flared skirts or long, flowing dresses were always discreet and modest. A sweet floral scent wafted through the air as Diana sauntered over to the coach. Her southern accent completed the desired aura of the perfect mother and genteel, feminine woman.

To the naked eye, Diana could be seen as nice, too nice. Somehow, I perceived her appearance as contrived and deceptive. As Shakespeare put it, "The lady doth protest too much." A seething cauldron of anxieties, fears, and uncertainties lay just beneath the smooth, unruffled surface.

Driven perfectionist behavior precluded enjoyment of her children. Diana's expectations of perfection cast their critical eye on the children. She constantly corrected their speech, deportment, and academic performance. In our current competitive culture, many parents push their children to be perfect; so her behavior was, in part, culturally inspired. Her children, however, resenting their mother's overbearing demands, turned to their father for acceptance. So, Diana, the southern belle, became the bad cop and Chuck, the tough businessman, the good cop.

Anxieties about the chores ahead obscured Diana's ability to take pleasure in the moment. Physically present with her children, her mind wandered elsewhere—so many duties awaited her. Despite affectionate exchanges, the children sensed her distance, which did not bode well for their self-esteem. Diana's children's development was compromised, and they struck out in defiance. Diana entered therapy partly to learn how to cope with her out-of-control children. Another reason was her marital problems.

With attention to every minute detail, Diana began her ritual cleaning, cooking, shopping, and perfect parenting early in the day. PTA meetings, cooking, and parenting classes often stretched into evening hours. By 9 p.m., Diana felt exhausted and not in any shape to entertain romance or sex with her husband. The rare sexual encounters—by appointment only—took last place in Diana's priorities.

Diana told me she had sex with Chuck mainly to "get it over with," and that sex was never a big thing for her. Lately, the couple's sex life had dwindled to once every few months. Enraged, Chuck struck out at Diana, shouting, "You're a cold, frigid bitch." He felt insignificant to Diana, that he came last after the house and the children.

Although she suspected that Chuck was having an affair, Diana refused to confront him. Much to my surprise, she indicated that it did not matter that much to her. What mattered to her was maintaining the stability of the marriage at all costs. Under no circumstances would she risk rocking the marital apple cart.

After eight months in therapy, Diana began to entertain the idea that preoccupation with her children, motherhood, and domesticity were employed to ward off some deeper underlying anxieties. We were working on uncovering the meaning of these perplexing anxieties, when Diana exploded with an "a ha" moment of discovery.

"Doctor Fran, do you think I'm a lesbian in hiding?" She looked frantic.

"What makes you think so?" I returned her question with another question.

*How uncanny! I was hoping to probe the meaning of her hyperfemininity and her preoccupation with perfect motherhood and parenting—the mark of femininity. She's opened the door, possibly.*

"I bumped into Kim a few weeks ago. She's an old high school friend that I lost touch with. We'd been close friends as kids, but in our senior year she and I took separate paths. Kim came out as a lesbian and got involved with a lesbian culture where I didn't feel comfortable. Well, we got to talking and I unloaded my frustrations with my husband. Chuck thinks I have an easy job and doesn't understand my responsibilities and my fatigue. While Kim doesn't have children, she really understood me." Diana was on a roll.

I joined her. "It must be comforting to be validated by someone who isn't even a parent."

"It was more than comforting. It was warm and loving. So we made a date to meet again for a cocktail at her apartment in the city. Kim's a high-powered executive for an international moving company. Her apartment is perfectly furnished, in excellent taste. Nothing's out of place, and it's so serene." Her southern drawl sang Kim's praises.

"No children or husband to mess things," I remarked.

"I realize that. While I'd never give up my kids for an uncluttered home, I do envy her peace. I feel like I have none." Her long, flowered skirt drooped.

"What do you think her peace is related to?" I was curious to hear Diana's views.

"She's certain of her lesbian sexual identity. I was sure I was heterosexual until now. But after I tell you what happened, you'll see why I don't know what I am." Her eyes filled with tears that she stoically held back.

"So you're questioning your sexual identity. I see despair," I observed.

"I'm confused, and feel like I'm falling apart." Diana's eyes peered out at me through long, dark lashes.

"Let's examine what happened and try to find some meaning to it," I offered.

"In many ways, Kim is my ideal woman. I wish I was more like her. She's smart, successful, independent, and she doesn't answer to anyone." Diana listed Kim's culturally defined masculine traits.

*So she really admires the masculine sides of women. Her hyperfemininity may be a front to hide her masculine traits. It looks like she's disavowed her masculine traits. Perhaps she's experiencing them vicariously through Kim.*

"Perhaps these traits that you admire in Kim are the very ones you have disowned," I interpreted.

"I don't think so. I don't think I'm at all masculine. I'm feminine, but so is Kim. She's cuddly, loving, and gentle. She's attuned to me, not like my husband." She lauded Kim's feminine qualities.

"As a lesbian Kim is in touch with her masculine and feminine traits. In your preoccupation with femininity and motherhood, you made room for only feminine qualities. Perhaps, unconsciously, you fear that masculine traits equate with a lesbian or a bisexual orientation," I interpreted.

"I'm terrified that I'm a lesbian, so maybe what you're suggesting figures. You see, I'm having a sexual affair with Kim." Diana sighed in relief and continued. "Would you believe she didn't even initiate it? I did." She looked for my response. Clearly she desired attunement with me.

"I believe it. What's your sexual experience with Kim like?" I wanted her to explore the meaning of her sexual experience.

"Lovemaking with Kim's soft, gentle, and tender, along with romance and great passion. I go into another world with her. I can't get enough of her. It's nothing like with Chuck. Sex with him is obligatory; with Kim it's a compelling desire." She stared off in space.

"So, sex with Kim is sublime." I validated her.

Diana was examining herself. "It is, but I still love Chuck. Unfortunately, I'm not in love with him. I don't know if I ever was."

"Why'd you marry him?" I asked.

"I married Chuck for many reasons. He was marriage material and I wanted to please my traditional family and to raise a traditional family of my own. I can't think of what would happen to Chuck if he knew what I was doing." She shuddered.

"What do you think would happen if Chuck found out?" I asked.

"He'd think I was unfaithful and he'd be hurt. I don't want to hurt him. Do you think I'm unfaithful? It's not like I'm having an affair with another man." She made a distinction, but still wanted my opinion.

I explained my thoughts on infidelity. "I would think that if you and Chuck had a contract of trust and honesty, this secret affair could be seen as an act of infidelity."

"I guess so, and Chuck would feel betrayed and humiliated," she reflected sadly.

"What about your family?" I asked.

"Forget it. They'd disown me if they knew. I was raised to be a heterosexual, faithful wife. An affair with a woman was unheard of. And I went along with their narrow views—until now." She was looking for connections.

"So, you fell under their sway." I continued to reflect her thoughts.

"I never had much of a mind of my own. Kim is helping me get in touch with it. We're in love, but she's not pressuring me." She looked pleased.

"That's helpful. How do you feel about being in love with Kim?" I queried.

"Wonderful! But, there's more to it than that. Now that I'm aware of my sexual desires and love for Kim, I'm besieged with confusion and doubts about myself and my marriage. I'm torn; I love two people, a man and a woman. But, I'm in love with only Kim. And she's a woman. It's all very disturbing. I want to have a mind of my own once and for all." She shook her head emphatically.

"To have a mind of your own, you cannot be enslaved by judgments of others. The straitjacket of others' judgment constrains your freedom to express your real self, your authentic sexual desires, and your sexual identity. So perhaps we can work on freeing your authentic self, so you can arrive at a better place from which to decide about your marriage," I interpreted.

In our continued work together, Diana revealed that as a child she kissed another girl, and they showed each other their private parts. She trembled as she recounted her stimulating sex play. Diana and her little friend continued to have sex play until her mother caught them. Her mother pulled Diana's panties down, spanked her with a spoon, and sent her to bed without supper. She then was forced to confess her sins to the priest. The worst punishment was that she was forbidden to ever see her friend again. At the tender age of six years old, Diana had already suffered shame and guilt inflicted upon her by the judgment of others. Despite her attraction to other little girls, Diana did not dare to act on her feelings.

In adolescence, Diana continued to be attracted to other girls, but dismissed these feelings as shamefully wrong. She went to a commuter college, and although girls experimented sexually with other girls, she resisted the temptation. In adulthood, any time an attraction to a woman darted though her mind, she dismissed it as nonsense—she was a full-fledged feminine woman. With feminine clothes, her tall, slender, small-breasted body looked like that of many a heterosexual woman.

The façade Diana created was almost foolproof. She fooled herself, her husband, her family, and to some extent me. Lurking under the false front, an unfulfilled woman strove to free herself. By repressing her inner strivings and donning a mask of motherhood with a false front of femininity, Diana created a conventional, stable life. Unshackling herself from her chains of conventionality and judgment unnerved her. She feared the freedom that change and the unknown presented.

I perceived Diana as a strong, intelligent woman with incredible resolve. The construction of a feminine front to deflect from her sexual orientation anxieties was uncanny. We worked on mobilizing her strength and ingenuity to help her examine her authentic sexual and romantic desires.

Diana's appearance slowly showed subtle changes. Flowing skirts gave way to soft slacks; ruffled off-the-shoulder blouses to smartly tailored shirts; and high spiked heels to attractive lower-heeled shoes. She even got a haircut that flattered rather than detracted from her fine features. Did she still look feminine? I would say yes, in a more natural, unpretentious way.

Diana and Kim continued to see each other, and their love grew. Kim's apartment, well located in the city and close to theater, restaurants, and concert halls, proved to be a perfect location for their clandestine relationship. It was so easy to tell Chuck she was meeting a friend in the city to go to some event or other. It was not as though she lied; she was indeed meeting a friend. Diana rationalized that she was not really lying to Chuck about her relationship with Kim. She was simply not telling him the whole truth. Of course, in marriage, omitting to tell the truth is still breaking a trust.

Gaining further insight, Diana got in touch with her guilt about betraying Chuck. But, she also desired to live in the open with Kim. How do others solve guilt pangs along with discordant desires to fulfill their inner selves? They may confront their husbands directly with the truth, or they may not. Our plucky lass chose still another way to deal with her dilemma.

Seeing as Chuck was working late, Diana took the opportunity to invite Kim to her house, ostensibly to meet her children. Kim and the children hit it off immediately. Diana felt closer to Kim than ever. Not only were they lovers, but Diana could also share in her love of the children with Kim. After the children were fast asleep, the warm and cozy feeling led to passionate erotic feelings between Diana and Kim. Enraptured with each other, time stopped for them. Time did not, however, stop for Chuck. After his late meeting he came home to discover his wife in bed with another woman.

At an unconscious level, Diana's impetuous lovemaking with Kim was not so impetuous. Diana knew she would have to disclose her affair for her peace of mind and for Chuck's sake. Claiming she did not want to hurt him, Diana did not tell him directly. At an unconscious level, her brazen behavior with Kim in the marital bed was aimed at bringing the affair out in the open. It did just that.

Chuck's initial shock was followed by humiliation and rage. Despite Diana's efforts to placate him, she did not compromise her own desires. Telling Chuck she was in love with Kim met with a storm of pent-up emotions. As much as he loved Diana, Chuck was unwilling to share her with another woman. After the storm had passed, Chuck offered to forgive Diana if she would end her affair with Kim.

Diana did not end the relationship with Kim. After much consternation, Diana ended the relationship with Chuck. She is freeing herself from others' judgments and identifying herself as a lesbian. After researching the effects on children of living with two moms—indications are favorable—Diana, Kim, and the two children moved in together. The children now have a mom, a stepmom, and a dad.

In the above story, we met a wife who constructed a false front of femininity to deflect anxieties about her sexual orientation. So, personal considerations influenced her traditional lifestyle, as did generations of conventional "feminine" women in her cultural history. The camouflage was worn for protection from societal "family values" that discriminated against lesbian relationships. In this case, neither the marriage nor the individual was flawed, so they were not the motivators for Diana's choice of a same-sex affair. Rather, Diana's decision to engage in a same-sex affair was predicated on her inner strivings and her authentic sexual desire and orientation.

In the next story, meet a wife who was, to some degree, always aware of her attraction to women. She engaged in same-sex behavior before her marriage. So after she married, she did not consider her affair with another woman an act of infidelity. She was with a woman and not another man. An act of infidelity, however, pertains to the breaking of a trust, which is gender-free.

### Shifting Sexuality

"I can't accept what she's doing. She's cheating on me with a woman. How could she? What kind of a slut is she?" Nick's ruggedly handsome face contorted in rage.

"See how he talks to me. Why does he have to shout at me and call me names?" Courtney's stalwart stature gave way to tears as she pleaded for my acknowledgment.

"You deserve it; look at what you're doing to our marriage." Nick defended himself, stretching out his long legs.

"You're vile, always blaming me." Tears welled up in Courtney's eyes.

I tried to break into their hostile exchange. "How're you feeling, Courtney?"

"I'm scared. When he shouts at me, I get scared. I can't stand it," Courtney explained.

"Did you know you scare your wife?" I asked Nick.

"I don't know what she's talking about. I've never hit her. This is bullshit." Nick's explosion resounded into the waiting room.

"I see you two have a problem in hearing the other person's perspective. Neither of you listen to the other one," I suggested.

"All I want is for Nick to treat me with respect." Courtney continued to press her point.

"Look who's talking about respect. That's a joke. Do you call that respect, sneaking around behind my back with a lesbian? It's bad enough she's cheating, but with a lesbian! What is my wife, a lesbian?" Nick bellowed.

"And what if I'm a lesbian?" Courtney retorted defiantly. She sat up straight, ready and raring to go.

"It's disgusting. I don't want to be married to a dyke." He pounded his fist on the table in front of him.

"Guess what? I'm not so sure I want to be married to you. You've got this thing about anyone who's not heterosexual. You pretend you're liberal. But underneath you hate gay men, lesbian women, and bisexual people. I don't know for sure what I am, but I want to explore it," Courtney fired back, mimicking his fist pounding.

"It sounds like Courtney needs time to explore her sexuality." I turned to Nick, but he sat stone-faced, arms crossed on his chest, without responding.

"I need time to figure things out. I don't know if I'm lesbian, bisexual, or heterosexual. It doesn't much matter to me. All I know is I can't take Nick's degrading attitude." Once again, she did a Nick, with arms crossed on her chest. Was she trying to best him at his game?

Courtney's rage obviated any empathy for Nick. His fury gave rise to heated prejudice and blocked any understanding of Courtney's feelings. Neither could see how their anger destroyed empathic or loving feelings. Rather than work on getting along, they were out to stonewall each other.

"I'm out of here. It's her problem, not mine. Doc, straighten her out and then we'll talk. I'm not coming back." Nick stormed out of the room, and Courtney burst into tears.

"I don't blame him. I'm so screwed up." She was feeling sorry for herself.

"What's screwing you up so much?" I queried.

"A lot of things are screwing me up, but mainly my sexual orientation. I never gave it a thought. I always felt that I was straight and it was okay to have sex with men and women. But, I care about the marriage," she explained.

"It's interesting that you used the word *straight*. It suggests that a lesbian or bisexual orientation is crooked," I offered.

"I guess I have my own prejudice and fears of not being heterosexual or 'straight.'" She got it and continued. "I never felt crooked till now." Courtney looked sad.

"So, you were comfortable having sex with men and with women. Did you ever question your sexual orientation before?" I asked.

"I was curious, but it didn't consume me. Don't most heterosexual women also enjoy women sexually every now and then?" Her eyes opened wide in a naive stare.

"Some do; it depends on your attitude and environment," I suggested.

"Well, in college most of the girls with boyfriends also had sex with other girls. I tried it and liked it. It was no big deal," she explained nonchalantly.

"Hmm," I remarked, looking for more from her.

"Some girls at college came out as lesbians, some as bisexuals. For a while, I thought I was a lesbian, and then I thought I was bisexual. I guess my sexual identity keeps shifting. I've always liked women, but not in the same way as men." Courtney was distinguishing between her sexual desires somewhat.

I began to explore the meaning of her sexual desires. "How do your sexual desires for women and men differ?"

"It's different with women. It's a novelty, exciting. But, I like the smell and feel of a man. I feel protected by a man. There's nothing like a man," Courtney responded vigorously.

"Do you feel that way about Nick?" I asked.

"I did, but not anymore." Her flushed face almost matched her flame-red hair.

"When did your feelings for Nick change?" I asked.

"It's been a while now. He's so possessive and controlling. He calls me ten times a day to check on me. Nick tells me he doesn't trust my judgment; that he's worried I'd get into trouble or have a car accident. He's afraid I'll make it with another man. He doesn't let me wear a bikini on the beach, or a short skirt to go shopping. Is that crazy or what?" Her verve waned.

"I guess it's whatever you make of it," I suggested.

"All I know is I hate his arrogance. He thinks he knows everything and I'm a dummy. He keeps saying I can't take care of myself. That's so not true. I've always been independent and strong," she complained.

"Did you realize how possessive Nick was when you married him?" I was curious.

"No, I just thought he was protective. That's one of the things I loved about him," she reflected.

"The qualities that we fall in love with often become our nemeses. Do you think you provoke him at all?" I inquired.

"Sure, I do my own thing, and he doesn't like it. I get together with my friends on Friday nights and he has a fit. He doesn't understand that I need other people in my life. I have to feel like a separate person, but Nick wants us always to be together." She was getting to the core of their problems.

"It sounds like an impasse about distance and proximity," I interpreted.

"I need more distance. Nick doesn't recognize my needs at all, only his," Courtney complained.

"What do you think his needs are?" I was curious to see if she understood him.

Her complaints continued. "His needs have to do with sex. The kids wake me up at six and we go all day. By the time I get the kids off to sleep and clean up, I'm exhausted, but he still wants sex. He doesn't understand me."

I reflected her desires. "So you want to be understood and to have your needs recognized by Nick."

"It'll never happen with Nick. But I do feel understood and recognized by Trish. Her husband is macho also. We confide in each other, and I feel comforted by her." Courtney clarified some of the meaning of her affair.

"You're getting something important from Trish that you're not getting from Nick. It sounds like the affair is not so much about excitement and novelty, but about comfort and attunement," I interpreted.

Courtney was examining herself in greater depth. "It started out as exciting, but there's more to it than that."

"What exactly are your feelings toward Trish?" I asked.

"She's a great friend, a real close friend. Sex with her is okay. But there's something missing. It's a feeling I can't explain. I'm not in love with her." Her response was well measured.

"What about your feelings toward Nick?" I inquired.

"I'm confused there; I really don't know. I want the marriage, but I don't know how I feel about him. Please help me." Her stoic veneer stripped away and revealed a vulnerable little girl.

As a tall, statuesque redhead, Courtney's large fleshy frame, translucent skin, and deep-set eyes, offset by angular, small features, reminded me of a cross between a robust, sensual Rubens woman and a delicate, slender Modigliani portrait.

In our subsequent work, Courtney got in touch with her feelings toward Nick. While she complained that he lacked empathy for her, she also lacked empathy for him. What we hate in someone else, we hate in ourselves. So Courtney projected her own lack of empathy onto Nick. He enacted the projection for her.

As commendable as her need for separateness was, it went awry in her marriage. Fearing dependence on Nick, Courtney marched to her own tune. Reluctantly, she revealed that she did get into car accidents, and was also quite forgetful. Unwittingly, she sought Nick's protection. Nick had his own issues about possessiveness. Separateness meant abandonment—a childhood legacy. He enacted these fears in the marriage with Courtney. They each played out roles that maintained a polarization of distance and proximity. The notion of flexibility and fluid space between the couple was yet to be tackled.

Courtney's childhood revealed a tough, no-nonsense mother and lenient but absent father. Her mother preached stoicism, self-sufficiency, and independence. Many a scraped knee or throbbing shin was passed off as "It's nothing to cry about. If you don't stop I'll give you something to cry about." Warmth and empathy were not among her mother's strong points. Her father's tender and loving qualities were tantalizing indeed. However, he rarely saw little Courtney, as he worked late. Neither was he available to protect Courtney from her mother's harsh discipline.

Part vulnerable child, part stalwart woman, Courtney learned to protect herself from hurts. She projected her disowned desire for protection onto Nick. Gladly, Nick enacted the role of protective father; however, he overdid it. She also disavowed her need for empathy, recognition, and understanding, and sought her needs from Nick. But empathy and recognition beget empathy and recognition. Courtney's supplies were short in these areas.

Deprived of a nurturing parental figure, Courtney lacked a role model for nurturance and soothing. Her parenting skills were more like those of a drill sergeant than an attuned mother. The children gave her a hard time. Much to her chagrin, their oppositional behavior consumed her. For a woman who desired separateness, Courtney's disciplinary measures served to keep her fused with her children. Trish shared her feelings and commiserated with her. Courtney, however, was not in love with her.

Over time, Courtney began to see the meaning of the affair for her sense of self, her sexual orientation, and the significance of it for her marriage. Her affair—partly a friendship that had become eroticized—also maintained distance from Nick.

Courtney's parents' marriage had ended in divorce, leaving an embittered mother and a depressed father. Hence, real love and intimacy with Nick threatened her. Closeness meant dependence on Nick, which she dreaded. He could reject her much like her father did to her mother. Courtney did not want to become an embittered, lonely old woman.

The affair with Trish was safe, which of course is paradoxical. Extramarital affairs are thought to be dangerous. But are they really? At a deeper level Courtney recognized she was not in love with Trish. Should Trish leave, it would not be as devastating to her as it would should Nick leave her. The father of her children, Nick represented marriage, stability, and comfort. As to sexual desire, she recalled passionate lovemaking with Nick prior to the onslaught of aggressive hurts.

In essence, the dangerous affair was safe—a contradiction in terms, no less. But living with paradox, contradictions, ambiguity, and uncertainty is living life. Courtney and I probed the multiple layers and ambiguities of her shifting sexuality, the same-sex affair, and her flagging marriage. She ended the affair with Trish in order to see whether she could repair her marriage with Nick.

In marital therapy, Courtney, Nick, and I are working on mutual recognition, empathy, uncertainty, and ambiguity. An open, honest relationship with trust is beginning to emerge. The issue of sexual identity is taking on greater nuance. Despite her attraction to both genders, Courtney decided to curb her behavior with women and focus on Nick. She revealed that she was still attracted to women, but would not act on it. Nick feels less threatened now that she gave up her lover. He is working on acceptance of her continued attraction to women.

Fears of abandonment, dependency, and loss set the table for the sabotage of romance and love. Both partners brought a lot of ingredients to this table. They are beginning to see how they avoided intimacy by their self-protective measures. Courtney's distance and Nick's possessiveness served to keep intimacy at bay.

Courtney is now more comfortable with showing her love and caring. Nick is better able to understand her feelings without feeling threatened. Instead of dominating and possessing her, he is more open to hearing her objections; and Courtney is more open to hearing his. Also Courtney's candid discussion of her shifting sexual identity has laid the groundwork for a more honest, transparent, and intimate relationship.

Initially, Nick felt threatened by Courtney's shifting sexual identities. If she could shift sexually, could she shift partners and leave him? He is grappling with the concept that nothing in life is certain. We live in the tension between paradoxes of the known and unknown, light and dark, right and wrong, love and hate, and life and death. Rather than dreading the unknown, he and Courtney are opening up the possibility of enjoying the excitement of uncertainty. In the new, more open relationship, Nick feels safer to admit to his own same-sex attractions. He now feels freer to bond with his male friends.

In the above two stories, we saw how multiple layers of meaning and uncertainty contributed to same-sex affairs. We got firsthand accounts of how judgment of one's sexuality kills love, whereas understanding enlivens love. We also saw that women's sexual orientation is flexible and can change over time. Culture, personal history, inner strivings, and marital problems are intertwined with women's sexual identity.

The significance of sexual orientation also differs from woman to woman. For some women, confusion about sexual identity is tantamount to chaos and disorganization, whereas for others, sexual identity is a trait like any other. Rather than dualisms of right or wrong, good or bad, heterosexual or homosexual, women seek authentic sexual desire in a variety of ways. Marriage, however, places constraints on finding one's authentic self. In marriage as in life, and in therapy, we live in a paradox of freedom and boundaries.

In the following chapter, I will explore how the quest for an authentic sexual self in the form of variations of sexuality may not be consistent with boundaries of marriage. The desire for variation in sexuality is most often stigmatized by pejorative terms like *perversion*. Hence, rather than risk stigma and shame, a daring wife seeking fulfillment with variations of sexuality might do so in secret.

# 10

# Sex Goes Awry

## VARIATIONS ON A THEME

*One may not reach the dawn save by the path of the night.*
—Germaine Greer

## A SIREN'S SONG

In high-conflict marital relationships or when hostility silently simmers, sex goes by the wayside. When at war with an adversary, sex is often the last thing on your mind. Patients in my practice report that problems in their sex lives are not about the quality of sex, but the quantity. Suffering in silence or fighting to the death kills sexual desire for most wives, and sexual encounters become fewer and farther apart in the marriage.

For some wives, however, infrequent sex is not necessarily in response to marital discord. They may have their own unique sexual agenda. The sexuality of wives is hardly uniform; sexuality has various faces. In this chapter you will read about two of these variations of sexuality.

Sex in synchrony—a symphonic blending of two bodies, souls, and minds—is such that you lose yourself in your partner, only to find your true self. The height of intensity is when both partners are satisfied in the sex act, not necessarily simultaneously, but at some point. Some wives, however, do not achieve this intimate, sublime experience. No matter the quality or quantity of sex, they remain hungry for more. It is as though they are sexually insatiable.

Perhaps you remember the word *nymphomania*, a derogatory term reserved for women. No such derogatory term exists for men with excessive sexual desires. Quite the contrary, men with excessive sexual desires are regarded as virile and manly. More recently, we have come to recognize that both men and women may be sexually insatiable and hunger for more and more sex. Often their insatiable sexual hunger is related to deep-rooted psychological factors. Toxic early childhood relations can influence their hunger in adulthood.

Insatiable sexual hunger is not really a desire—an act of will—but rather a desperate need, a compulsion that is experienced as a craving. The need is pursued relentlessly like a drug. Although sexual addicts are enslaved to sex, it is far from being their goal. Rather, the pursuit of sex is in service of a different goal; sex is used to dispel feelings of inadequacy, depression, anxiety, anger, guilt, or other feelings that are unbearable.[1] Like an alcoholic or drug addict, the sexual addict relentlessly seeks satisfaction from an external source to palliate an internal pain. The sex act is not borne out of love, but performs the function of a drug. Of no consequence other than to provide the sex addict with a fix, the sex object is indispensable.

Joyce McDougall, a neo-Freudian psychoanalyst, gives us an in-depth look at sexual addiction. She writes that the genesis of sexual addiction lies in early childhood, when the early fusion state of the caregiver-infant bond persists for an extended time. This may happen if the caregiver suffers from unbearable psychic pain and uses the infant to palliate her. The caregiver is then dependent on the infant, and the infant is deprived of a soothing mother to comfort her distress or to calm her stimulation. Without the identification of a "good-enough mother"[2] who contains psychological pain or over-excitement, the infant does not develop her own internal resources for dealing with psychic pain.[3]

The growth of the capacity to be alone is hindered, and the young child constantly seeks the mother whenever she feels threatening psychic distress. As an adolescent or adult, she is unable to self-soothe in times of psychic tension. So, she seeks a solution in the external world as she did in infancy with mother. Sex or other addictive substances are transitory fixes; they provide instant gratification of somatic or bodily coping mechanisms, rather than enduring psychological ones.

Fixes provide a state of ecstasy, calm, well-being—nirvana. Alas, fixes provide only temporary relief. The shot of nirvana during the sex act lasts only as long as the magic of the sex act wears off, rendering the hungry addict even more empty, depleted, and fragmented. To quell these painful, disintegrating feelings, she is compelled to resume her pursuit for her next fix.

Rather than desiring a sexual partner, the sex addict craves the sexual object—her fix. She is constantly seeking to repair early deprivations and to palliate depression, anxiety, and self-esteem blows, particularly when these feelings are related to frightening adult love relationships.[4] What could be more frightening than frictional marital love relationships?

Women exploiting men as fixes to repair old hurts and fears of disintegration do not exactly tip their hand. If they did, they would not be successful in getting their needs met. Men—their sex objects—do not know these women are merely using them as tension-reducing devices. Like alcoholics and drug addicts, sexual addicts find uncanny, crafty ways to get their fixes. One of the successful ways female sexual addicts seduce men is to adopt guises of sex sirens, complete with seductive moods, moans, and moves. In order to get her fix, the siren lavishes her sex objects with everything they desire: romance, flattery, and fun—all self-serving. Indeed, she is good, very good.

A combination of Marilyn Monroe and Madonna, sex sirens are irresistible. How many men can resist a wily wife who happens to be a sex siren? I would say, not many. Little does he know what he is getting into; her appeal is unparalleled. In real siren fashion, she has honed her skills of seducing men to their destruction. Duped, hapless men fall in love with her, only to be dumped when they no longer satisfy her.

In the following story, meet a modern-day sex siren who uses men as sex objects to palliate her psychic pain. You will gain insight into some of the vulnerabilities of an insatiable sex addict.

### Serena's Serenade in Blue

Serena and Wilbert were in marital therapy to work on a crisis centered on emotional and sexual incompatibility. A sultry beauty, Serena's midnight-blue eyes, tanned skin, and breathy, velvet voice resounded with sensuality. Long black tresses and skimpy clothes set off her shapely body. In snake-like fashion, she slithered her way to the couch. There she stretched out seductively and peered out at me through dark-fringed eyelashes. Her waif-like "please love me" pleading look belied her frank in-your-face sexiness.

When enraged, Serena's breathy voice lost its innocence, and the velvet quality gave way to guttural outpourings. The rage centered on her husband Wilbert. She complained bitterly that Wilbert assumed a superior attitude by lecturing to her in a judgmental and moralizing tone. By placing the blame onto Wilbert, Serena let herself off the hook. Never having been in therapy, and with a tendency to act and not think, Serena did not see her role in provoking Wilbert; and provoke she did, in inimitable style.

A seductive mover and shaker, the circles Serena moved and shook things up in entailed many a sexual rendezvous. In the early stages of the marriage, sensitive, scholarly Wilbert was thrilled with Serena's sexual openness. A writer and college professor, Wilbert maintained a low profile. His well-trimmed beard, dark spectacles, and tweed, patch-elbow jackets spoke of erudition. In his fantasy world, Wilbert dreamed of a harem of sirens who would arouse him. With Serena he had a harem all in one woman. She was his dream come true!

It was not that Wilbert did not enjoy sex before he met Serena, but she was by far his best lover. Sensual, tantalizing, uninhibited, Serena was his sex siren par excellence! Who could ask for anything more? Initially, her insatiable sexual needs flattered his sense of masculinity. While she leaned rather heavily on him for help with problems related to her family and friends, her helplessness only heightened the Sir Galahad in him. In rescuing her, he felt even more powerful. At the outset of the marriage, her constant chatter, sexual needs, and endearing dependence were sweet music to his ears.

The honeymoon lasted three years, when Serena was transformed from a beautiful dream to a grotesque nightmare. Priding himself on satisfying his wife sexually, Wilbert could no longer keep up with her insatiable sexual needs. Her melodious voice had become a cacophony of discordant sounds, sights, and feelings. Feeling inadequate, he silently withdrew from her. Wilbert's withdrawal catapulted Serena into a panic. She felt rejected, dead inside, anxious, and fragmented.

A cabaret singer, Serena's lively repertoire was sprinkled with the blues. Lately the occasional became the habitual. All she could sing were the blues. Accompanied by a male jazz trio, Serena found more than a willing partner to dull her pain. If a sex siren fails to seduce her own husband, she surely feels like a flop. Only another fresh eager husband, like her piano player, could help her feel like a hit. Sure enough, he did. Together they made beautiful music.

Serena worked and played with her pianist Greg nightly. During the day, they met for additional sexual liaisons. Alas, sometimes even good things come to an end. Wilbert discovered Serena's sexual liaisons with Greg, only to feel more inadequate, betrayed, and humiliated. His self-esteem had plummeted to an all-time low. Wilbert's rage response was an attempt to ward off this devastating blow to his self-esteem. In a fit of rage, he threatened to divorce Serena. His threats brought them into therapy with me. Serena had never been in therapy before, whereas Wilbert had been in extensive analysis.

"What did he expect? He asked for it. He's cold, critical, and sexually uptight. He's got all kinds of excuses for not making love to me. He's too tired, too stressed, too busy, and too 'I don't know what.' If he doesn't want me, what am I supposed to do? Lock it up?" Serena's strident song was tinged with sadness.

"You hear how she talks to me. She's having the affair, not me. Doesn't she have any shame, guilt, or remorse?" Wilbert, the know-it-all professor, looked helplessly lost.

"Why should I feel guilty? You're depriving me of a healthy sex life. You pushed me into Greg's arms. It's your fault, not mine," she shot back, baring her teeth.

"She wants sex five times a day. We're not kids anymore; we're in our fifties. Doc, she's a nymphomaniac." He was striking back where it hurt.

"A nymphomaniac?" she countered. "You're just undersexed. You knew that I had a healthy sexual appetite when you married me. You're just making excuses again."

"You were different then; you were romantic, loving, and caring. Now all you want is that I should do you. I'm still asleep when you turn me over and sit on me. I don't think you want me; you just want my penis. It's like you need my penis to plug you up. I don't want to be used like a tampon." The previous analysis coupled with the writer in him was flourishing in full force. Wilbert, a fiction writer of romance, intrigue, and adventure, had found his match. Serena provided him with an intriguing adventure, all right, but she no longer provided him with romance.

"What do you make of Wilbert's metaphor of a tampon?" I asked Serena.

"I don't know what he's talking about. I didn't change; I'm the same as I've always been. He changed; he doesn't want me anymore. He says that I'm the problem, but he's the problem, not me." Serena's dark blue eyes welled up.

"I'm the problem? You've got nothing but problems. You're suffocating me with all your problems and your insatiable sexual needs. You're always blue, down in the dumps, and demanding my attention. When your mother died, you obsessed about it forever. My mother's got Alzheimer's and I've lost her too, but I don't dump on you. Then your kids from your first marriage didn't talk to you, and that's all I heard. You consume all the air. I'm choking; there's no room for me." He waxed articulate and self-aware, but showed little emotion. It was as though he were relating a story from his book.

"It sounds like you're feeling suffocated." I clarified Wilbert's feelings.

"Yeah, like I'll lose myself in her womb and her problems, and I'll disappear." Wilbert's eloquence was dazzling. Again, no emotion. Wilbert spoke the words without the melody.

"Serena, how do you feel when you hear Wilbert?" I was curious how his words affected her.

"He's articulate. After all, he expresses himself for a living. I'm more emotional; I speak from my heart; he's more from his head." She was no slouch either.

"So you recognize your complementary relational styles. It seems you have different emotional, cognitive, and sexual styles that you're unable to reconcile," I suggested.

"You bet. She's cheating, I'm not." Self-righteous Wilbert was tooting his horn.

"You're cheating me of what I need. It's your fault that I have Greg. He fills my needs; you don't. He listens to me, and he makes love to me. You don't do either. You have no feelings; you're a robot. Greg's a real flesh-and-blood man." She sure knew how to drive her dagger in deep.

"Sure, till you saturate him and flush him down the toilet like you did to me." He elaborated on his graphic metaphor.

"I'm leaving. I can't take him." Brows furrowed and long hair tossed back, Serena bolted out of the room in Scarlet O'Hara style. A few minutes later, fetching smile and all, she slunk back into the room.

*Wow! She's good, really good, and he's not so bad either. By vying for power, they alternate positions. They disown parts of themselves and identify with the other who enacts those parts. So despite their seeming separateness, they remain fused.*

*She tramples on his feelings, and he lords it over her. She acts and he talks. She's split off her cognitive side and he acts it out, whereas he's split off his emotional side and she acts it out. Sometimes words are stronger than actions. She gains power with her extramarital affair, dumping on his self-worth. In turn, he saves himself and gains power by taking the high road, and delegating her to the low road. Then they blame each other, without an understanding of each other. How sad. I feel for both of them. They both seem to be good people suffering bad blows to self-esteem and other painful emotions. By bashing each other, they add salt to old wounds.*

I suggested a goal. "I see that you're both busy blaming each other rather than trying to understand each other. I think you both have internal pain that you're not aware of. It's important to uncover old hurts in order to understand your misdirected efforts at finding cures."

"I don't want to be in the same room as him. Can I see you alone?" Serena implored me.

"Wilbert, how do you feel about that?" I asked.

"It would be good for her. She's never been in therapy before. I have. She doesn't know how to talk about things. In her family no one talked; everything was swept under the rug. My family was calm, cool, and collected. They communicated in a rational way. She doesn't know how to do that." His patronizing, condescending manner cut to the core.

"Serena, how do you feel about what Wilbert said?" I wanted to see if she would rise to the challenge.

"He's treating me like a stupid child. That's what he always does. He's the big know-it-all, and I'm the dumb little wife." In her direct manner, Serena got her licks in.

"Do you feel like a dumb little wife?" I asked her.

"With Wilbert I do. He demoralizes me. I know you help women to feel empowered, and I want to see you without Wilbert." She maintained her stance and desire for separateness.

"That's just fine with me. Focus on her, Doc. I don't need any more therapy. I've had plenty." Wilbert's retort, once again, placed him in the one-up position.

I agreed to work with Serena on a one-on-one basis, until they were ready to get together. At this point, Serena did not think she was in love with Wilbert any longer. She agreed to get to know herself better and then to make a decision about the marriage. While Wilbert was still in love with Serena, he also understood that the marriage would not survive unless she felt the same way.

In my work with Serena, she disclosed a history of desperately seeking sexual satisfaction that went back to adolescence with roots in childhood. She also revealed a pervasive depression, emptiness, anxiety, and fears of abandonment that threatened to fragment her fragile self. The only relief of her intolerable psychic tension lay in sexual activity.

In therapy, Serena veered from subject to subject, looking off into space, and suddenly returning with a blank stare. I wondered if she was artfully dodging me. Indeed, pursuing her, I was always following her. So, she took control of the relationship.

*This may be part of her mystique, her ineffable appeal. Or she may be fearful of letting go of control and so she needs to be in control of me. Then again, she may just be so fragmented internally. Perhaps it's not an either or, but it's all of these that I'm experiencing with Serena. She's a complex woman, as most interesting women are.*

The genesis of her inner turmoil lay in early childhood. Through sexual satisfaction, she valiantly sought a cure for her damaged self. Often a child has an absent father and a present mother. Her mother Charlene was present, in an intrusive, clinging, suffocating way, and her father Harry was absent in a tantalizing, distant way. His frequent travels took him to exotic places that were kept under wraps. Serena thought he lived a double life.

When her father returned home, he was a regular husband, albeit an inattentive and critical one. Serena was his little darling. Holding her on his lap, he stroked her and told her she was his favorite girl. On his secret trips, Serena imagined him as a dashing CIA agent with several lovelies in his bed—a real-life James Bond! She dreamed about being his top girl, and he colluded with the wishes. So, the oedipal conflict with a seductive, absent father raged on unresolved to take shape in her sexual exploits later on. She could not seduce her father sexually, but she sure learned how to seduce substitute fathers.

Charlene, Serena's mother, remained loyal to her husband, adoring him and longing for him in his absence. A lonely, depressed wife, Charlene suffered in silence. She found solace in her only child, little Serena. In motherhood, Charlene felt whole, alive, and worthwhile. Charlene and her mother, Serena's grandmother, had an inordinately close relationship and Charlene replicated the same relationship with her daughter, Serena. Just as Charlene had worshipped her mother, Serena worshipped her mother—an intergenerational transmission of fused mother-daughter bonds.

Feeling depleted and missing a husband, Charlene turned all her attentions to Serena. Unwittingly, Charlene used Serena to palliate her pain. By using Serena as a soothing object, Charlene stifled Serena's growth. As an extension of her mother, Serena's true self was subverted into a false self—in compliance with her mother's needs and not her own authentic needs.[5]

Instead of internalizing a soothing maternal figure, Serena internalized an intrusive, overpowering one who threatened her developing self. Infants need a good-enough mother,[6] in whose presence they can be alone to develop their own internal resources for coping with psychic tension. Little Serena was deprived of such a maternal representation. In the wake of intense stress, depression, anxiety, or excessive stimulation, Serena felt overwhelmed and fragmented.

Before Serena could cry, her mother cheered her up; before she could fall, her mother picked her up; and before she could show anger, her mother hushed her. With her overprotective parenting, Serena did not develop a sense of self-mastery or a way to cope with intense emotions. Not able to rely on herself, Serena desperately clung to her mother.

A steady twosome, Serena and her mother ate together, slept in the same bed, and palled around together. At a young age, Serena accompanied her mother to adult romance movies and concerts, much like a beau. Serena remembered being her mother's shadow, and the terrible time she had separating from her to go to school. Indeed, Serena never learned to be alone. As a child, the thought of being alone terrorized her, and she began to masturbate profusely to calm her terror.

During adolescence, Serena discovered the joys of sex with boys, which far surpassed those of masturbation.

"I sat in the back of the bus, with three guys on the way to the football game. They each took turns getting me off, and then I did them. We hid behind a blanket so no one saw us. I had lots of guys after me." She seemed pleased with herself.

"So, you put out for the boys and you were popular," I suggested.

"You sound judgmental, just like Wilbert. I needed them. I craved sex back then. I still do. It's how I feel alive and vibrant." Without shame or embarrassment, Serena brazenly disclosed some of her secret self.

*I was judgmental. What was I thinking of? Serena's not a promiscuous tramp, putting out for boys; she's a desperate little girl seeking a solution to her pain.*

"I value your frank disclosure, but I'm not perfect. I goofed and I'm sorry I hurt your feelings." My disclosure exposed my fallibility. I hoped our bond was strong enough to withstand the empathic failure, and it would allow her space for her fallibility.

"I feel bad that I struck out at you. It's not your fault." She was quick to protect me.

I made connections. "I notice that you came to my rescue quickly, and protected me at your expense. Do you recall early experiences where you protected your mother?"

"Mom cried a lot, and I comforted her. Sometimes, she was too tired to cook or clean, so I did it for her. I remember she spilled some hot coffee on me, and started to shriek. I had a third-degree burn, but I had to calm her down. She was so anxious." Tears streamed down her face as she recalled her poignant childhood.

"So you were the little mother and little husband to your mother. Who was there for you?" Her sadness penetrated my every fiber. Tears filled my eyes, and I averted her glance. Quickly, I recovered and looked back at her.

"I see you're moved. Thanks so much. It's so good to know that I can have an impact on you." Serena was amazing!

"The roles were reversed with your mother and you. And you were hurt badly. It seems you're seeking someone to heal you," I interpreted.

"I'm in perpetual state of needing someone to heal me. It's like there's a gaping wound that doesn't mend. Sex is the best medicine," she explained. I was taken aback by her articulate self-awareness. So, without Wilbert, her strengths emerge.

"I understand. Does it matter much who the doctor is who administers your medicine?" I probed further.

"I never thought of it that way. But come to think of it, I've had a lot of doctors, mostly interns, not too experienced. Before Greg there was the UPS guy Phil. He delivered more than my parcels. I invited him into the house for a cup of coffee, and before you knew it we were making it on the kitchen floor. My back was sore, but my soul soared. The high lasted about four hours, and then I felt ashamed of myself, hating myself. Phil wasn't my type: short, chubby, and boring. I like more serious, strong, exciting types. Nevertheless, I found myself reaching into my purse for his phone number. This affair lasted four months. He was devastated when I told him it was over." Serena stayed right on track.

"I can imagine." I could.

"Well, after Phil there was Sal, the produce guy. He's a stunning hot Italian with dark curly hair and a buff body. He may not have been much to talk to, but he sure was good at other things." She shot me a "just between us" look and winked mischievously.

"I think you're teasing me." I laughed. She joined me, and we both enjoyed the levity that softened the underlying sorrow and pain.

"It wasn't only sex that he was good at. Sal was a super produce guy. I can never tell if a melon's ripe, but he was an expert picker. While he examined the fruits and vegetables, he looked me over. I could tell he was dying to examine me further. I got that old ache back and we made a date for later that day." She was candid, all right. Her stories were seductive, but there was a similarity—a pattern.

"So you were the pick of the crop. Was he?" I asked.

"Not exactly. He was firm on the surface, but mushy inside, like an overripe fruit. He fell in love with me, wanted me to leave my husband and live with him. That was out of the question, so I had to end it. He was destroyed for a long while and kept calling me. I felt bad for him, but I knew it wouldn't work," she explained.

"It sounds like you're so fearful of being alone, so fearful of falling apart that you're constantly seeking someone to fill you in. Like a drug, sex is your fix; and like a fix, the effects wear off quickly and you feel worse than before. So, you feel compelled to find yet another fix," I interpreted.

"I get it. You've explained how this happened with my lousy childhood. And I've thought about it. So, how can I change?" Her blue eyes beseeched me.

*She's ready and raring to go. She sure is a mover and shaker—a truly daring wife.*

"When we use external devices like drugs, alcohol, or sex, the effects are transitory. By developing internal psychological coping mechanisms, the effects can be lasting. You have made considerable strides, and I'm hopeful you can do it. It took considerable strength and ingenuity to come up with your sex solution to pain and tension reduction. So, we'll work together to change your direction." I offered some interpretation and an honest appraisal. Indeed, while Serena's sex solution was misguided, it showed her survivor instincts.

In continued work, we focused on Serena's assets other than her sexual prowess. Slowly her power base moved from seducing men to their destruction, to taking control of her internal states. Serena learned to be alone in my presence, where I listened, did not intervene, and allowed her to save herself. She feared going down a long tunnel to her demise. I gently guided her down the hole, and she felt supported. To her surprise, rather than the Terminator, she met with Peter Pan.

Her marriage with Wilbert needed a lot of work. As Serena progressed, Wilbert felt more confident in doing some marital work. His arrogance did not help her to overcome her feelings of inadequacy and deprivation. Serena seemed to have more compassion with Wilbert and decided she wanted to try to work on the marriage. Wilbert agreed. They have a lot of repair to make within themselves and between themselves.

In the above story you met a tragic waif-wanton woman—a sex siren. Just under the surface of her seductive wiles lay a lonely, deprived, damaged little girl. She used sex as her fix to ward off intense fear of disintegration. An early poignant childhood, a culture of sexual media messages, and a condescending husband all figured into the picture. Yet, Serena was daring in many ways. Not only did she dare to defy the double standard with extramarital affairs, Serena dared to examine her painful past and try to change her present in order to pave the way for a brighter future. Serena was plucky, all right. How many of us can match her moxie?

In the above section you read about one variant of sexuality in which you saw how the fair sex can also be fallible. Soon you will encounter another daring wife, engaged in yet another variation of sexuality. You will learn more about the darker aspects of some of the fair sex. Before you embark on this treacherous leg of the journey, I will offer you some thoughts that will ease the way.

## SURRENDER AND SUBMISSION

*If you surrender to the air, you can ride it.*
—Toni Morrison

*When love rules, there is no will to power, and where power predominates, love is lacking. The one is the shadow of the other.*
—Carl Gustav Jung[7]

As we have seen in the historical review at the beginning of the book, women's sexuality is profoundly influenced by culture. It also emerges from within childhood patterns of relating that get played out in adult erotic relationships and from internal strivings. For some wives, mutual sexual arousal is the most intimate, sublime experience imaginable.[8] They are able to surrender themselves to the other and lose themselves in the experience, only to expand their selves and find their true, authentic selves.[9,10]

Sex is highly personal and differs for all of us. We never really know what another person's subjective experience is really like.[11] A wife can tell if her husband reached orgasm, but he does not know for sure if she has. She can fake it. In the past, wives who did not reach orgasm were considered frigid—physically defective. In order to avoid shame and stigma, wives faked orgasm. Some still do. With the exception of medications or illness, orgasm is psychological, not physical. Orgasm involves surrender.

Surrender has multiple layers of meaning for wives. Not all wives feel free to surrender sexually with husbands. The free expression of women's sexuality has been hampered by societal influences. Women's sexuality has been threatening to men for years. Men are still haunted by the old historical theme of sexually voracious female predators. Women have been branded as dangerous, insatiable vampires cannibalizing men.[12] In the above poignant story, Serena was one of these hapless women. In direct contrast, in the nineteenth century, women were denigrated as sexless, without sexual desire.[13]

It seems women cannot win. They have been perceived as either too hot or too cold. Hence, women may deny their sexual desires or inhibit their free abandon to sexual surrender. Indeed, they may not want to want.[14] They may fear that tender, vulnerable feelings arising from surrender with husbands will be trampled. Trusting themselves in the presence of an intimate partner is an anathema. Protecting themselves by refraining from surrender to erotic union, they miss out on the transcendent, sublime, oceanic experience.

It is mainly fear that holds people back from sexual surrender and love. Fear kills love.[15] To arrive at the expansive moment of surrender, wives must first unshackle themselves from the constraints of fear. But, often that is easier said than done. Early noxious experience may prohibit trust in erotic relating.

Other psychological factors also inhibit surrender and authentic expression of desires. Surrender of one's self with another who can frustrate, tease, discard, reject, or gratify is exciting to some, and terrifying to others.[16] Traumatic childhood experience may rear its ugly head to intrude on sexual passion and inhibit surrender.

Surrender also involves relinquishing self-control. Letting go of self-control may arouse the terror of loss of one's hold on reality, disintegration by inner forces, or inability to defend against dangerous external forces.[17] For others, however, it may be the ultimate transcendent experience. In an early toxic environment, it may have been dangerous to let one's guard down, so self-control was a crucial form of protection.

Surrender is often confused with submission. In the West, surrender means defeat, to surrender your arms. In the East, surrender means transcendence, liberation. Surrender entails an expansion of the self—freeing the self.[18] In surrender there is only the ecstasy of the moment, without impingement from painful past experience. Tragic childhood experience distorts the true self into a false self of defensive barriers that block energy and growth.[19] The goal in therapy is to unshackle ourselves from our childhood bonds and false selves in order to release the true self that creates new experience. With insight, we can let go of defensive barriers to surrender to our true, authentic selves. Surrender is in service of growth.

Submission is a perversion of surrender. Submission means you lose yourself in the power of the master and become enslaved to him. If he controls you, you are collapsed into him, and you cease to exist. If you control him, he is collapsed into you, and he ceases to exist.[20] So, submission is self-negating, whereas surrender is self-affirming. The dialectic of domination and submission underlies the slave–master relationship, whereas in surrender there is no such dialectic. The erotic union that entails surrender is a mutual power relationship of sharing experience.

The erotic union is found in the paradox of difference and sameness, distance and merger, and recognition of each other as unique, yet united by similar feelings.[21] By sharing in an ultimate pleasure, you expand yourself, rather than collapse yourself into another. Not everyone, however, can live with paradox, and so surrender in sex can become distorted.

It is not difficult to see how sex in marriage may go awry. Surrender with a husband may be dangerous, so a wife may seek surrender elsewhere. She may fear surrendering to a husband and losing control. To feel in control she may want him to submit to her. Should he refuse to play this game of domination and submission, she may find other willing partners, as her earlier sisters did.

Domination and submission, the basis of sadomasochism, were popularized in the eighteenth and nineteenth centuries by writers like Marquis de Sade and Leopold Ritter von Sacher-Masoch.[22] Masochistic men sought female flagellates to whip them, and some brothels specialized in sadomasochism. That was then, and this is now. Femme fatales still dominate and flagellate men. In the following case study, meet a wife who dared to practice her art of domination with men outside of her marriage. You could easily view her as femme fatale, but there is more to the story than meets the eye.

### Eve's Ghostly Garden of Evils

It was one of those dull, late winter days, with trees unclad and sun still low in the sky. A drizzling rain went on and on. But like the weather, life is not certain. Out of the blue, events can change everything in an instant. If we are lucky, exciting new devilish experience comes our way. If we surrender to the moment, the experience will stretch our horizons. Such was my growth experience with Eve. I learned a lot from her, and she said she learned from me. It all began with a phone call.

"I have to make an appointment with you," a disembodied voice whispered over the telephone wires.

"Have to?" My curiosity was aroused.

"Yeah, I'm on probation and the cops say I have to be in therapy." Her dull emotions matched the day.

"And how do you feel about embarking on a therapeutic journey?" I asked.

"Well, I might as well. I've embarked on a lot of journeys, so why not this one?" Her words were compelling. I am always fascinated by daring women. Was she one of them?

We made an appointment, and she arrived right on time. This was a good sign. Light brown hair tied back in a ponytail, little to no makeup, and loosely fitting slacks in an attempt to disguise her pear-shaped body, Eve looked like a regular suburban housewife on the way to grocery shop. I soon found out she was anything but a regular housewife.

"My life's a mess. The police caught me in a motel with a guy, and my husband wants to divorce me." No eye contact, no expression of desperation.

*A ha! I remember the scandalous story of a suburban housewife in a hot-bed motel with paid male customers. Who could forget it? A salacious woman in our sleepy, staid suburb! She sure doesn't look too spicy! What gives?*

"How did this all come about?" I asked.

In a dispassionate monotone voice, she began to tell her tale. "My husband's a control freak. Ryan is on a power trip with me."

"How does he do that?" I inquired.

"He controls the money, how I walk, and how I talk. I have to ask him for money every day. He yells that I spend too much. As you can see I'm not wearing expensive clothes, handbags, jewelry, or anything. I wear clothes from the Gap. You know what he wears? He wears Armani clothes. He tells me I waddle like a duck; well, he struts like a peacock. You won't believe this, but he calls me a fat piece of crap. Sure, I've gained a few pounds, but he's no oil painting, with his beer belly and gold chains." The words tumbled out without any expression. It was as though she were talking about someone else, not herself or her detested husband.

I went for some emotions. "So, your husband humiliates and dominates you. How do you feel about that?"

"I'm used to it. It doesn't bother me," she replied coolly.

"Doesn't bother you? How do you manage that?" I was incredulous.

"I shut him out. I turn my switch off," she explained in the same flat voice.

"Do you ever turn your switch back on?" She sure was a mystery.

She responded, and I spotted a spark. "Sure I do. That's where the motel and the guys come in. I get turned on with them. There I'm myself. My husband complains that I'm frigid."

"Do you think you're frigid?" I asked.

"I can't orgasm with my husband, but I can reach orgasm by masturbation and by other ways," she taunted me.

"What other ways?" I had to hear this.

"The cops don't know and my husband doesn't know, so I have to be sure this is confidential." Eve was not ready to trust me.

I explained the parameters of the privacy laws. "Everything is confidential unless you are at harm of hurting yourself or someone else or in the event of child abuse. Then I have to break confidentiality."

She shrugged off my remarked. "I do hurt men, but they ask for it. Anyhow, what I do isn't life-threatening."

*She's tantalizing me and she's whetted my prurient interest. Wow!*

"I'm a dominatrix. What I do's something like what you do. It's an art. I know you spend a lot of time studying your art and I do, too," she explained.

*As analysts we've been compared to a lot of things: a dentist maybe, but never a dominatrix. Does she think I will dominate her, whip her, or humiliate her? What am I thinking? I'm clearly out of my league. I've read about femme fatales and sadomasochism, but I've never met a real-life dominatrix!*

"Do you think I'll punish you?" I asked.

"No, but I may punish you. You may judge me, like the last therapist. He warned me that I was headed for Hell. I told him to go to Hell. I can be blunt." Her tepid temperature shot up a couple of degrees.

*Do I see a fleeting feeling? I wonder how she learned to disconnect from her feeling.*

"I see. Try me," I challenged her.

"Well, better still. Here's a picture. They say a picture's worth a thousand words, and so I can save some money here." Her sense of humor was at play. Reaching into her handbag, she pulled out a photo.

"Wow! I wouldn't have recognized you. That's quite a pose!" I was stunned. The transformation from an average suburban housewife to an imperious dominatrix whipping a subservient man was a sight to behold! The photo showed brilliant, long auburn hair that flowed down her red satin robe trimmed in black fur. The open robe revealed high leather boots, a black leather thong, flaring hips, and pointed breast plates.

In the photo, Eve peered icily through glistening green eyes at a little bald man. Blindfolded, on his knees, he appeared to be pleading with her. In her left hand, she wielded a long, tapered whip, reserving her right hand for even more torture. On the table I could see whips studded with needlepoints and nails. The smile on her face was one of triumph.

"You seem to feel triumphant," I remarked.

"Sure I do. He's such a loser. All men are. Get this. See this sap. I tie him up, hold up the whip, and sashay around the room. Then he gets on his hands and knees like a puppy dog. He begs me to whip him, to spit on him, to piss on him. The more I punish and humiliate him, the more he wants." The refrigerator look in the picture was back. I suppressed a shudder.

*She gets turned on by just telling me about it. I'm feeling dizzy and disoriented. Am I turned on? Like her masochistic customer, I'm dying to hear more of her disturbing, but titillating story. As a professional, I have a responsibility to society, so I have to toe the line. I must find out how far she goes. She may mortally wound these men. I may be looking at a cruel Cleopatra who served her nightly lovers up on deathbeds. Wow!*

"Do you ever maim or mutilate these men?" I asked.

"Not on your life. I'm a professional, not an amateur. They don't know when to stop, but I do. I don't go in for blood sports, death scenes, or any perversions. If my husband knew what I did, he'd call me a pervert, but I'm not. I have savoir-faire. I torture them only to a point. Then I take off their mask and let them see me masturbate. They beg me to untie them, but I don't let them touch me. They masturbate themselves, and we never have intercourse. So, it's not like this is adultery. I don't have sex with these masochistic guys. I give them what they want, and I get what I want." She was explicit. I was relieved that she did not harm the men.

"And what exactly do you want?" I asked.

"I don't know. I know I hate their weakness," she responded quickly.

"Perhaps at an unconscious level you want them to be strong and stop you, but they don't. They do not survive you, they collapse into you," I interpreted.

The preeminent feminist and psychoanalyst Jessica Benjamin[23] has written cogent work on sadomasochism. The sadistic dominatrix usurps the power and inflicts pain, all the while wishing that the masochist will not crumble or retaliate. She seeks someone who can withstand her attack and survive it. Her search, however, is prejudged by her childhood disappointment with a caregiver who did not survive her. Her masochistic customers do not survive her, either. They usually just collapse into her, crumble, and cease to exist.

The sadist's unconscious wish is that the masochist will withstand her attack. In this way she has a real person outside of herself, rather than a non-person who has been swallowed up by her. She can then recognize him as a separate individual, and she is not alone. In early childhood, she was unable to achieve this separateness with her caregiver. In adult erotic union she keeps repeating this sadomasochistic pattern of relating. Unconsciously she wishes to finally get it right by fixing the damaged caregiver so she can be there for her child. Then the child can have a true self and surrender freely.[24]

In our continued work together, the ghosts that haunted Eve began to reveal themselves. Her ghosts were anything but friendly; they were fiendish. Eve remembered herself as an angry child with violent temper tantrums. Her mother, a depressed alcoholic, simply collapsed into tears when her daughter lost her temper. She was ineffective in setting limits or meting out punishment for Eve. As she grew older, Eve's rage knew no bounds. With impunity, she abused her mother mercilessly. She even struck her mother, but the only response she got was that her mother cried, drank some more, and collapsed on the floor.

Eve's parents stayed together in a loveless marriage. Her mother drank, did not work, and cared for her children minimally. After school, Eve often came home to a filthy home with her mother in bed. Her mother tried to sober up, but she did not quite make it. Eyes bloodshot and empty, her mother stared off into space. So, Eve never really knew a "good-enough mother."[25] Eve's rage was directed partly at her mother, and to a greater part at her father.

Our work revealed a tragic and traumatic history of incest. By her father's abuse of power, he betrayed Eve's body and murdered her soul. Her fragile mother was so out of it that she did not see, or want to see, what was going on. When little Eve tried to enlist her support, her mother told her not to lie, as lying was a sin. So helpless, hapless Eve had no one to whom she could turn.

At age ten, Eve lost her innocence to her cruel, sadistic father. Not only did he penetrate her vaginally, he did so anally. She blocked out the excruciating pain by disconnecting from the moment, and taking control of her mind—the only thing she could control. She explained that her mind left her body to go up to a corner in the ceiling. Looking down on herself, she saw a little girl safe in the arms of her mother. Later in adult erotic union, she feared surrendering to self-control, as she might be violated again. Her fear of surrender played out on the marriage. Surrender with her husband Ryan signaled abject subjugation, much like she suffered at the hands of her father. Ryan's controlling ways did not help matters any.

When young children experience events that are too horrific to assimilate, they make accommodations. Eve's accommodation was to dissociate all feelings from the ghastly moment. Her dissociated state, a valiant effort to survive the cruel abuse, was the training ground for her later tendency to disconnect her feelings from her thoughts.

Infants enter the world with the assumptions of a benign world with good-enough caretakers; a fair world with a sense of meaning, where good things happen to good people. All of these assumptions are shattered when a trusted parent sexually abuses a child. She loses trust in others; engages in impaired relationships; and suffers depression, anxiety, and a host of posttraumatic symptoms.[26] Eve was plagued with recurrent nightmares and intrusive thoughts and suffered from distrust, depression, and anxiety. Mostly, she loathed herself and viewed herself as damaged goods. Dependent on the powerful parent, the powerless child must preserve the image of the parent as the good one and blame herself instead.

In her dominatrix role, powerless little Eve identified with her powerful father—the aggressor. In dispensing punishment to the masochistic men, she adopted her father's brutally abusive stance. She could not stop her sadistic father, and the masochistic men did not stop her. Eve was repeating an old sordid script, unconsciously wishing to finally get it right.

The intense work has been excruciatingly painful for both of us. Unearthing evil ghosts traumatized her. I explained that our goal was to transform those fearful ghosts to non-threatening ancestors with whom she could live and grow.

Often, Eve stormed out in tears. I saw this as a breakthrough. She seemed to feel safe enough to express feelings in my presence. When she was verbally abusive, I set limits that met with hollering and further insulting. With great difficulty, I stayed firm.

Once she told me that she wanted to string me up by my fallopian tubes. This one got to me, and I suddenly feared she was going off the deep end. I consulted a colleague who helped me to gather myself and tell Eve, in no uncertain terms, that I could not work with her if I felt endangered, and that she would have to cool it. She did cool it. She apologized for scaring me. Eve was beginning to see me as a separate person with my own needs and desires.

There are still many starts and stops, but progress is slowly being made. Eve's husband Ryan has also survived the shock of discovering just what Eve was up to at the motels. As she predicted, he did call her a pervert, but as he became aware of her tragic childhood and his role in perpetuating the dynamic, he felt compassion for her. Ryan is now a part of her team and is interested in learning about a shared power relationship with mutual trust, respect, love, and romance. So is Eve. She hopes that in time, she will surrender with Ryan and not fear being attacked. Eve is striving for growth and transformation.

In the above story I worked with a femme fatale whose tragic childhood warped her sexuality. Her sadistic father betrayed her, as did her fragile mother. Deprived of a good-enough mother or father, she searched for her authentic self in misguided ways that women have in the past.

I have worked with numerous incest survivors and children of alcoholic parents. Working with a dominatrix was a first. Through this experience, Eve and I are listening, learning, and moving toward growth. I am indebted to her and to all the daring wives who shared their inner lives with me.

In the above two cases, I examined the poignant inner lives of wives who engaged in variations of sexual expression. One was a sexual addict, and the other was a dominatrix. These are only two examples of the panoply of sexual proclivities and practices. If you notice, I use the term *variations* and not *perversions*. *Variations* does not place value judgments on human sexuality. As such, it inspires our curiosity and expands our horizons. *Perversions* is a pejorative term that places a straitjacket of prejudice and discrimination that constrains understanding and diminishes our world.

# 11

# Conclusion

## IMPLICATIONS FOR MARRIAGE AND AMERICAN SOCIETY

*You must be the change you want to see in the world.*
—Mahatma Gandhi

Sacred marital vows are spoken by millions of Americans every day. They are also broken every day. While not all American couples follow these painful paths, many do. Husbands and wives engage in extramarital affairs, hurt each other, divorce, and disrupt the security of young children's lives. Nevertheless, hopeful Americans continue to marry every day. You may wonder, why marry? Is it blind faith, naiveté, hubris, or hope? Perhaps it is an amalgam of all of these. Most important, over the centuries Americans have married because sex and love within the sanctity of marriage have been central for happiness and fulfillment. Of course, other reasons may enter the picture. No matter the infidelities and vicissitudes, I have no doubt marriage will continue to be vital for meaningful lives. Not in the same form, but marriage will reshape itself, only to reshape itself again and again.

Women's infidelity—enacted over the centuries—will also reshape itself again and again. It has in the past and will continue to do so in the future. In the fourteenth century, the game of courtly love set the stage for noble, older wives to play around with younger male troubadours of a lower station. Some of these wives entered into arranged marriages with older men they did not love. So the affairs were an escape from loveless marriages. Most wives, however, played this game as a frivolous dalliance that was the fashion of the day. Whereas older wives with younger lovers are part of the American scene today, most modern wives are decidedly not noble, frivolous, or dilettantes. Struggling with existential angst related to aging or discordant marriages, some daring wives try to renew themselves with younger lovers. Others simply feel more compatible with younger men.

The reaction by society has also changed. Fourteenth-century daring wives were neither condemned, nor did they come to a bad end like their nineteenth-century sisters. In our current society, we do not pin red letters on wives who engage in extramarital affairs, nor do unfaithful wives kill themselves. But harsh arbitrary judgments, castigations, and even punitive measures persist.

Despite the sexually repressive social mores of the nineteenth century, wives engaged in extramarital affairs. Often they defied their oppressive husbands, lives, and the draconian double standard. The dam of repressed feelings finally overflowed in the twentieth century under the leadership of the women's liberation movement. Feminism raised women's consciousness and awakened their sexual desires.

Inspired by the sociopolitical sexual revolution, some wives had extramarital affairs merely to experience their raw, unfettered sexuality. Research reports[1, 2] and my clinical experience indicate that wives today—not withstanding the myriad of personal factors—act on their desires for extramarital affairs mainly in response to marital dissatisfaction and not merely to express their sexuality.

Given the robust research and clinical evidence, it follows that reshaping marriage is the key to reshaping women's infidelity. As women's infidelity reshapes itself, it will in turn affect marriage and society. It is a continuous loop, with no beginning or end. I have aspired to demonstrate how history, culture, and insight into psychological problems are constantly interpenetrating to shape and reshape women's infidelity, marriage, and society.

I have also tried to show the role that our current climate plays in married life, and the discontents that influence women to engage in extramarital affairs. One pervasive societal influence that gives rise to changing problems in marriage is the changing economic conditions. The high cost of living has transported scores of wives, raising children, off to the workplace. Marriages are unduly stressed by wives' dual roles of homemaker and career.

Husbands are working long and laborious hours to keep up with their costly lifestyles, and are not emotionally available to wives. Stay-at-home wives, stuck in drab, humdrum, thankless lives of domesticity miss the colorful, exciting careers they left behind. They also resent their husbands, whose work brings them excitement and acknowledgment. Feeling dismissed or ignored by husbands, wives seek affirmation in extramarital affairs.

Another recent societal phenomenon that places stress and strain on marriage is that of remarriage and stepfamilies. With 50 percent of marriages ending in divorce, stepfamilies and remarriages compose a great part of the American landscape. Remarriages bring novel problems. Unwilling to loosen prior ties, partners carry over old baggage that impacts remarriages. Prolonged attachments to former spouses or problems incurred by stepchildren interfere with romance and intimacy in the remarriage. Resisting an unencumbered, sexy lover on the scene is difficult indeed.

Same-sex affairs, a sign of the times, have implications for marriage and American society. If ever there were a poster child for intolerance, prejudice, and discrimination, the double whammy of wives engaging in extramarital affairs with other women might well be it. Harsh prejudicial judgment of wives' sexual orientations has done nothing to strengthen marriage and society. Rather, intolerance and discrimination have brought humiliation, alienation, and persecution to innocent people whose sexual orientations differ from the heterosexual status quo. Since the individual is a microcosm of a societal macrocosm, our view of wives with same-sex affairs is directly related to our view of diversity in American society.

In a similar vein, I have examined variations in sexuality expressed by some wives. With a history of male domination and female submission, some wives today fear submission, and encounter problems in sexual surrender with husbands. You met two wives who desired variants of erotic enactments in which their husbands refused to participate. Stepping outside of the marriage, they found numerous eager lovers to participate in variations of sex.

One wife chose to transform herself into a dominatrix and torture willing masochistic partners. Another wife used men as objects, similar to drugs, to fill an insatiable hunger. When you first encountered these women, you may have experienced disbelief, disgust, or moral indignation. Then again, you may have experienced fascination. Initially, you may have regarded them as perverts. How about after you learned about their tragic childhood experiences? How did you feel after reading about their horrific histories that stirred the pot to boiling, indelibly scalding them and deforming their sexuality?

I will bet that by gaining insight into their traumatic pasts, you viewed these women's stories of sexual variations as tragic and poignant rather than sordid and perverse. Instead of a rush to judgment about others engaged in sexual practices that differ from one's preferences, insight to individual situations and psyches brings empathy. Therein lies hope for tolerance of diversity and a united—rather than divided—society.

Many of the overarching problems in marriage parallel those of society, as do solutions. Greater harmony in marital relationships can be training grounds for greater harmony in sociopolitical relationships. Mutual recognition, understanding, empathy, power, respect, and reciprocity have reverberated throughout the text. Not only does a shortage of awareness and skewed power relations bring strife to the private sector, it also brings strife to the public sphere. Disenfranchised people of diverse races, colors, ethnicities, religions, and sexual orientations are its victims. Oh, if only we could understand each others' plight in both marriage and in society!

Male domination and female submission are a loud bell that has echoed through the ages. Transformed by sociopolitical forces, wives were rendered into submissive, passive, powerless, delicate creatures—objects to others. The second wave of feminism has awakened women's sense of agency, power, strength, and subjectivity. Yet, too often one foot remains stuck in the past.

Women compose over half the population of American society, presenting an urgent cry for them to show their stuff. Women's capacity for nuance and flexibility helps them to access and exercise their multiple sides. Tough and also tender, competitive and also cooperative, loving and also firm, good girls and also bad girls, we are subjects of our desires and also objects to others. Embracing both sides of the coin, we can create a space for dialogue. In the process, marriage and society have much to gain.

Lessons learned from marriage can transcend the individual to help society. In both marriage and society, it takes neither free abandon to willful acts nor tight, rigid, constraints, but both—a dialect between acting impulsively on a whim and paralytic restraint. This type of dialectic is just one of the ways that facilitate reshape and change in marriage and society.

Reshaping marriage and American society begins with you and me. Each of us is an individual whose actions affect not only marriage, but also American society. I am hopeful that change can be made in marriage and also in society.

We all want meaningful and fulfilling lives, yet infidelity and psychic pain persist. Just as there is no one reason for infidelity, personal suffering, or sociopolitical suffering, there is no one solution. I have outlined just a few of the myriad emotional states—wild ecstasies, dark despair, heart-rending dilemmas, and optimistic solutions—experienced by wives. My hope is that you will resonate with these daring wives and be inspired to make fresh choices and changes. I believe if women will it, we can do it. Women have always created change and will continue to do so.

Feminism has raised our self-awareness and introduced us to our agency, autonomy, will, and ability to make choices. It takes a daring wife to choose an extramarital affair, but it takes an even more daring wife to choose to confront herself, gain insight, and work through her personal and marital problems. Armed with knowledge, daring wives acquire the tools to make choices. It also takes courage to change. Over the millennia, from birthing to tackling the patriarchal hierarchy, women have demonstrated courage.

In researching the subject matter of this book, I have plunged into multiple disciplines of psychoanalysis, sociopolitical history, philosophy, pop culture, and feminism. I have also plumbed the depths of the inner worlds of my patients and of myself in case studies.

The wives in the case studies illustrate the vast individual differences within groups and subgroups. So, wives who have extramarital affairs compared to wives who do not, are not two discrete groups, but lie along a continuum of disavowal, denial, dreaming, desiring, and acting. Each wife within the two groups is unique and diverse. Likewise the women in the subgroups of wives—stay-at-home wives, working wives, younger wives, older wives, remarried wives, those engaged in same-sex affairs, and those in variations of sexuality—all differ from each other, not only across subgroups, but within subgroups.

Each woman's unique self has been influenced by her own personal history and cultural experiences. Just as we cannot view a group of wives through a distorted lens of prejudgment, we cannot view a group of people in society through a distorted lens of prejudgment. If we fail to see the differences, the nuance, and the complexities in people of diverse colors, races, religions, ethnicities, and sexual orientations and regard them as alike, we fail to uphold American values.

Along the way I grew more and more aware of the implications of women's infidelity for marriage, American society, and our future. Once a wife gains insight into the conscious and unconscious meaning and significance of her extramarital affair, she can make informed conscious choices about her behavior. But first she must feel safe to explore herself, learn, and articulate her issues.

Arbitrary judgment with essential absolute truths does not facilitate an arena of safety for women to articulate their desires. Instead, arbitrary judgment is the handmaiden of prejudice, discrimination, and bigotry that impedes human progress. For marriage and society to grow stronger, they must be open to nonjudgmental attitudes that facilitate insight by listening, learning, and understanding meanings. Historically, judgment and artificial values did not help, but instead harmed marriage and society. If we can withhold judgment on wives who engage in extramarital affairs, they will feel safe to make choices that facilitate honest and open marital relationships.

The concept of choice is a complex one. In the book, I have discussed the idea of an individual, true self. In order to make choices, we need authentic selves. Nevertheless, I have also reiterated the postmodern concept of cultural construction of our selves. Taken at face value, an individual self is not in concert with postmodern theory that posits socially constructed, multiple, and fluid selves.[3] If our selves are strictly socially constructed, the spirit, the soul, individual agency, will, accountability, and/or desire to change are lost.[4] I do not believe we are either socially constructed or endowed with inherent core selves—we are both. Not only are we constructed by historical, social, and childhood forces, but with insight, we can also access our true selves.

The true self with will and agency feels free to makes choices and assume responsibility for consequences. The paradox of having a self that makes choices and a self that is socially constructed and embedded in culture is only one of the paradoxes I have shown in intimate relationships. Expressing our authentic selves and our real desires while taking into consideration the feelings and welfare of our husbands is a seeming contradiction. Surrender to our inner strivings within the constraints of marriage is a necessary tension of intimate relating.

Intimacy is found in the tension between the self and the other, novelty and familiarity, sex and love. Paradox is rife with ambiguity and uncertainty. In the bedroom and in politics, paradox, uncertainty, and ambiguity threaten our sense of safety and security. Living with uncertainty and contradictions is not easy.

In our post-9/11 era, ominous clouds of uncertainty, insecurity, and danger hover overhead. Just yesterday, an Internet headline read, "Survey: 70% Risk of WMD Attack within Decades." Alarming! Oh, how comforting it would be to have certainty and security for our children and ourselves. We can, but the price may be rigid ideologies of blind faith in right and wrong, good and evil, rulebooks with dos and don'ts. I believe that would be a far greater danger than living with uncertainly and insecurity. By constructing polarities of right and wrong, white and black, good and bad, powerful and powerless, and demonizing unfaithful wives and deifying faithful wives, we risk destroying the very foundations on which American society is based.

Opposites imply that one is better than the other. The dualities of heterosexual/homosexual, right/wrong, good/bad, love/hate, and white/black hardly describe women's sexual experience or their desires for extramarital affairs. Neither do they describe societal experience. Rigid dualities place a higher value on one side, while they devalue the other side—the breeding ground of intolerance, prejudice, and bigotry.[5]

Open, flexible dialogue affords us the opportunity to better understand multiplicity and individual differences within groups. The process is saturated with ambiguity, nuance, complexity, and diverse attitudes, feelings, and behaviors. Nevertheless, it is only through open dialogue that can we aspire to the basic rights laid down by our founding fathers—life, liberty, and the pursuit of happiness.

My focus on the psychology of personal and interpersonal marital relations has been mainly in the foreground, with society in the background.

Their positions, however, constantly reverse themselves. In the same way that the "personal is political," our sociopolitical climate is personal.

The sociopolitical zeitgeist resonates with slogans like "moral values." So, just what is meant by "moral values"? I hope they are not more of the artificial, rigid ones of yesteryear that endangered wives' physical and psychological welfare. I am all for moral values that encourage a safe haven for wives. I am talking about open-minded, informed moral values, so that the double standard is a thing of the past and wives' sexuality is not devalued as excessive—threatening men—or as frigid and sexless—displeasing men. A society in which wives are finally respected as equal to men in power, autonomy, and sexual desire is more of what I call moral values.

How about "family values"? Prejudicial attitudes against people with gay, lesbian, bisexual, or transgender orientations have nothing to do with family values. Casting harsh prejudicial judgments on wives who engage in extramarital affairs and winking at husbands who do the same is harmful. I hardly think the double standard or prejudice strengthens marriages, families, or American society.

I believe family values entail a lot of things, but prejudice is not one of them. Teaching our children tolerance and inviting their curiosity to learn about diversity is consistent with family values. Children who learn about people who differ from them in sexual orientation, race, color, ethnicity, or religion expand their horizons. The children are the future, and hope for marriage and American society lies in their hands. It is up to us to provide them with a firm foundation of tolerance so they can forge new paths to progress.

In writing this book—whose initial intention was for you to gain insight into women who stray—I too have strayed intellectually. My wanderings led me to multiple side trails that intersect with the central topic. The triad of the individual, marriage, and sociopolitical paths constantly inter-penetrates. Within these paths, numerous trajectories—mutuality, recognition, tolerance, diversity, reciprocity, surrender, romance, real love, authentic sexual desire, marital constraints—entwine with each other. These intertwined paths form a complex maze of ambiguity, uncertainty, and paradox. Shucks. Just when you were looking for conclusions with definite truths! But there is no conclusion with a final truth.[6] There is no end to learning, understanding, theorizing, and hoping—only more of them.

I realize that my thoughts for marriage, families, and American society are utopian. Despite the seemingly insurmountable hurdles that I struggle with, I continue to imagine change. I hope I have inspired you to imagine change in yourselves, your relationships, your marriage, and your world.

Creative acts begin in the mind, in the imagination. In reality, paradox, contradictions, ambiguity, and uncertainty prevail and flood imagination. The renewal of marriage in the wake of its breakdown is part of an ongoing process of paradox, uncertainty, and ambiguity. That does not mean to give up on imagining, or to relinquish the goals of individual, marital, and societal change, but to muster courage, continue the process, and accept the inevitable pitfalls.[7]

# Notes

## INTRODUCTION

1. http://www.brainyquote.com/quotes/authors/r/robert_orben.html.
2. http://www.quotationspage.com/quote.html.
3. Harry Stack Sullivan. (1953). *The Interpersonal Theory of Psychoanalysis*. New York: W.W. Norton, p. 32.

## CHAPTER ONE

1. Carl Gustav Jung. (1992). *Psychology of the Unconscious*. Bollingen Foundation. (Original work published 1917)
2. Leo Tolstoy. (2000). *Anna Karenina*. New York: Random House, Modern Library Paperback Edition. (Original work published 1877)
3. Gustave Flaubert. (1989). *Madame Bovary*. New York: Bantam Books. (Original work published 1857)
4. Erica Jong. (1973). *Fear of Flying*. New York: Holt, Reinhart, and Winston.
5. Linda Wolfe. (1975). *Playing Around: Women and Extramarital Sex*. New York: William Morrow.
6. Melanie Klein. (1975). *Envy and Gratitude and Other Works*. New York: Delacorte Press. (Original work published 1946–1963)
7. Shere Hite. (1976). *The Hite Report: A Nationwide Study of Female Sexuality*. New York: Macmillan.
8. Shere Hite. (1989). *Women and Love: The New Hite Report*. New York: Random House Value Publishing.
9. J. A. Davis & T. W. Smith. (1996). *General Social Surveys, 1972–1996: Cumulative Codebook*. Chicago: National Opinion Research Center.
10. Bonnie Eaker Weil. (1994). *The Forgivable Sin*. Fern Park, FL: Hastings House Book Publishers.
11. Peggy Vaughan. (2003). *The Monogamy Myth*. New York: Newmarket Press.
12. Carol Botwin. (1994). *Tempted Women*. New York: William Morrow, p. 14.

13. Alfred Kinsey, et al. (1953). *Sexual Behavior in the Human Female*. Philadelphia: W. B. Saunders.

14. Carol Botwin. (1994). *Tempted Women*. New York: William Morrow.

15. A. Greeley. (1994). Marital infidelity. *Society, 31*, 9–13.

16. M. W. Weiderman. (1997). Extramarital sex: Prevalence and correlates in a national survey. *Journal of Sex Research, 34*, 167–174.

17. R. G. Parker. (1997). The influence of sexual infidelity, verbal intimacy, and gender upon primary appraisal processes in romantic jealousy. *Women's Studies in Communication, 20*, 1–24.

18. J. A. Davis & T. W. Smith. (1996). *General Social Surveys, 1972–1996: Cumulative Codebook*. Chicago: National Opinion Research Center.

19. D. C. Atkins, N. S. Jacobson, & D. H. Baucom. (2001). Understanding Infidelity: Correlates in a national random sample. *Journal of Family Psychology, 15*, 735–749.

20. J. A. Davis & T. W. Smith. (1996). *General Social Surveys, 1972–1996: Cumulative Codebook*. Chicago: National Opinion Research Center.

21. D. C. Atkins, N. S. Jacobson, & D. H. Baucom. (2001). Understanding infidelity: Correlates in a national random sample. *Journal of Family Psychology, 15*, 735–749.

22. M. W. Weiderman. (1997). Extramarital sex: Prevalence and correlates in a national survey. *Journal of Sex Research, 34*, 167–174.

23. P. England & I. Brown. (1992). Trends in women's economic status. *Sociological Perspectives, 35*, 17–51.

24. D. C. Atkins, N. S. Jacobson, & D. H. Baucom. (2001). Understanding Infidelity: Correlates in a national random sample. *Journal of Family Psychology, 15*, 735–749.

25. Carol Botwin. (1994). *Tempted Women*. New York: William Morrow.

26. D. C. Atkins, N. S. Jacobson, & D. H. Baucom. (2001). Understanding infidelity: Correlates in a national random sample. *Journal of Family Psychology, 15*, 735–749.

27. M. W. Weiderman, & E. R. Algier. (1996). Expectations and attributions regarding extramarital sex among young married individuals. *Journal of Psychology and Human Sexuality, 8*, 21–23.

28. D. C. Atkins, N. S. Jacobson, & D. H. Baucom (2001). Understanding infidelity: Correlates in a national random sample. *Journal of Family Psychology, 15*, 735–749.

29. P. Blumstein & P. Schwartz. (1983). *American Couples: Money, Work, and Sex*. New York: William Morrow.

30. S. P. Glass & T. L. Wright. (1988). Clinical implications of research on extramarital involvement. In R. Brown & J. Field, eds., *Treatment of Sexual Problems in Individual and Couples Therapy*. New York: P.M.A. Publishing, pp. 301–346.

31. J. A. Davis & T. W. Smith. (1996). *General Social Surveys, 1972–1996: Cumulative Codebook*. Chicago: National Opinion Research Center.

## CHAPTER TWO

1. George Santayana. (1981). *Life of Reason*. New York: Scribner. (Original work published 1901)

2. Reay Tannahill. (1992). *Sex in History*. London: Scarborough House Publishers.

3. Ibid.

4. Ibid.

5. J. D'Emilio & E. B. Freedman. (1997). *Intimate Matters: A History of Sexuality in America*. Chicago: University of Chicago Press.

6. Reay Tannahill. (1992). *Sex in History*. London: Scarborough House Publishers.

7. J. L. Goldenberg, T. Pyszczynski, S. K. McCoy, J. Greenbert, & S. Solom. (2002). The anxiety-buffering function of close relationships, evidence that relationship commitment acts as a terror management mechanism. *Journal of Personality and Social Psychology, 82*(4), 527–542.

8. T. Pyszczynski, J. Greenberg, & S. Solomon. (1999). A dual-process model of defense against conscious and unconscious death-related thoughts: An extension of terror management theory. *Psychological Bulletin, 106,* 835–845.

9. Reay Tannahill. (1992). *Sex in History*. London: Scarborough House Publishers.

10. Linda Wolfe. (1975). *Playing Around: Women and Extramarital Sex*. New York: William Morrow.

11. Ibid.

12. Reay Tannahill. (1992). *Sex in History*. London: Scarborough House Publishers.

13. Ibid.

14. Linda Wolfe. (1975). *Playing Around: Women and Extramarital Sex*. New York: William Morrow.

15. J. D'Emilio & E. B. Freedman. (1997). *Intimate Matters: A History of Sexuality in America*. Chicago: University of Chicago Press.

16. Reay Tannahill. (1992). *Sex in History*. London: Scarborough House Publishers.

17. Ibid.

18. Ibid.

19. Linda Wolfe. (1975). *Playing Around: Women and Extramarital Sex*. New York: William Morrow.

20. Reay Tannahill. (1992). *Sex in History*. London: Scarborough House Publishers.

21. Ibid.

22. Linda Wolfe. (1975). *Playing Around: Women and Extramarital Sex*. New York: William Morrow.

23. J. D'Emilio & E. B. Freedman. (1997). *Intimate Matters: A History of Sexuality in America*. Chicago: University of Chicago Press.

24. Reay Tannahill. (1992). *Sex in History*. London: Scarborough House Publishers.

25. Ibid.

26. Ibid.

27. Ibid.

28. J. D'Emilio & E. B. Freedman. (1997). *Intimate Matters: A History of Sexuality in America*. Chicago: University of Chicago Press.

29. Alexis de Tocqueville. (1938). Fortnight in the Wilderness. In G. W. Pierson, *Tocqueville and Beaumont in America*. New York: Oxford University Press.

30. D. H. Lawrence. (1964). *Studies in Classic American Literature*. New York: Viking.

31. Hamlin Garland. (1892). *Other Main Traveled Roads*. New York: Harper.

32. G. J. Barker-Benfield. (2000). *The Horrors of the Half-Known Life: Male Attitudes toward Women and Sexuality in the Nineteenth-Century America*. New York: Routledge.

33. John Todd. (1867). *Serpents in the Doves Nest*. Boston: Lee and Shephard.

34. G. J. Barker-Benfield. (2000). *The Horrors of the Half-Known Life: Male Attitudes toward Women and Sexuality in the Nineteenth-Century America*. New York: Routledge.

35. Ibid.

36. Seale Harris. (1950). *Woman's Surgeon*. New York: Macmillan.

37. G. J. Barker-Benfield. (2000). *The Horrors of the Half-Known Life: Male Attitudes toward Women and Sexuality in the Nineteenth-Century America*. New York: Routledge.

38. Ibid.

39. Seale Harris. (1950). *Woman's Surgeon*. New York: Macmillan.

40. Jeffrey Moussaieff Masson. (1986). *A Dark Science: Women's Sexuality and Psychiatry in the Nineteenth Century*. Translated from works originally published 1880–1900 in French and German. New York: The Noonday Press, Farrar, Straus, and Giroux.

41. G. J. Barker-Benfield. (2000). *The Horrors of the Half-Known Life: Male Attitudes toward Women and Sexuality in the Nineteenth-Century America*. New York: Routledge.

42. Rachel P. Maines. (1999). *The Technology of Orgasm: Hysteria, the Vibrator, and Women's Sexual Satisfaction*. Baltimore, MD: Johns Hopkins University Press.

43. J. D'Emilio, & E. B. Freedman. (1997). *Intimate Matters: A History of Sexuality in America*. Chicago: University of Chicago Press.

44. Peter Gay. (1995). *The Naked Heart: The Bourgeois Experience, Victoria to Freud*. New York: W.W. Norton, p. 343n.

45. J. D'Emilio & E. B. Freedman. (1997). *Intimate Matters: A History of Sexuality in America*. Chicago: University of Chicago Press.

46. Ibid.

47. Sigmund Freud. (1965). New introductory lectures: Female sexuality, femininity. In J. Strachey (Ed., trans.), *The Standard Edition of the Complete Works of Sigmund Freud, Vol. 22* (pp. 112–135). London: Hogarth Press. (Original work published 1932)

48. Sigmund Freud. (1965). Three essays on sexuality: Infantile sexuality. In J. Strachey (Ed., trans.), *The Standard Edition of the Complete Works of Sigmund Freud, Vol. 7* (p. 195). London: Hogarth Press. (Original work published 1901–1905)

49. Sigmund Freud. (1965). Dissolution of the Oedipus complex: Some psychical consequences of the anatomical distinction between the sexes, female sexuality, femininity in new introductory lectures. In J. Strachey (Ed., trans.), *The Standard Edition of the Complete Works of Sigmund Freud, Vol. 22* (pp. 112–135). London: Hogarth Press. (Original work published 1932)

50. Ibid.

51. Ethan Viney. (1996). *Dancing to Different Tunes: Sexuality and Its Misconceptions*. Belfast: The Blackstaff Press.

52. Havelock Ellis. (2001). *Studies in the Psychology of Sex: Analysis of the Sexual Impulse, Love and Pain, the Sexual Impulse in Women*. Honolulu, HI: University Press of the Pacific. (Original work published 1906)

53. Havelock Ellis. (2001). The sexual impulse in women. In *Studies in the Psychology of Sex*. Honolulu, HI: University Press of the Pacific, p. 179. (Original work published 1906)

54. Angus McLaren. (1999). *Twentieth-Century Sexuality: A History*. Malden, MA: Blackwell Publishers.

55. Peter Gay. (1995). *The Naked Heart: The Bourgeois Experience, Victoria to Freud*. New York: W.W. Norton.

56. Nathaniel Hawthorne. (1981). *The Scarlet Letter*. New York: Bantam Dell. (Original work published 1850)

57. Gustave Flaubert. (1989). *Madame Bovary*. New York: Bantam Books. (Original work published 1857)

58. Leo Tolstoy. (2000). *Anna Karenina*. New York: Modern Library Paperback Edition, Random House. (Original work published 1877)

59. Kate Chopin. (1976). *The Awakening and Selected Stories of Kate Chopin*. New York: Signet Classics. (Original work published 1899)

## CHAPTER THREE

1. J. D'Emilio & E. B. Freedman. (1997). *Intimate Matters: A History of Sexuality in America*. Chicago: University of Chicago Press.

2. Frederick Lewis Allen. (1931). *Only Yesterday: An Informal History of the Nineteen Twenties*. New York: Harper & Brothers.

3. D. H. Lawrence. (1983). *Lady Chatterley's Lover*. Cutchogue, NY: Buccaneer Books. (Original work published 1928)

4. Reay Tannahill. (1992). *Sex in History*. London: Scarborough House Publishers.

5. Jeanine Bassinger. (1993). *A Woman's View: How Hollywood Spoke to Women 1930–1960*. New York: Alfred A. Knopf.

6. Ibid.

7. Ibid.

8. Graham Greene. (1991). *The End of the Affair*. New York: Penguin Books. (Original work published 1951)

9. David Halberstam. (1993). *The Fifties*. New York: Random House.

10. Ibid.

11. Ibid.

12. Ibid.

13. Ibid.

14. Ibid.

15. Ibid.

16. Grace Metalious. (1991). *Peyton Place*. Boston: Northeastern University Press. (Original work published 1956)

17. David Halberstam. (1993). *The Fifties*. New York: Random House.

18. Alfred Kinsey, et al. (1953). *Sexual Behavior in the Human Female*. Philadelphia: W.B. Saunders.

19. David Halberstam. (1993). *The Fifties*. New York: Random House.

20. Betty Friedan. (1991). *The Feminine Mystique*. New York: W.W. Norton. (Original work published 1963)

21. W. H. Masters & V. W. Johnson. (1996). *Human Sexual Response*. New York: Little, Brown.

22. Ethan Viney. (1996). *Dancing to Different Tunes: Sexuality and Its Misconceptions*. Belfast: The Blackstaff Press.

23. Kate Millet. (1970). *Sexual Politics*. New York: Virago Press.

24. Shulamith Firestone. (1970). *The Dialectic of Sex*. New York: William Morrow.

25. Karen Horney. (1933). The denial of the vagina. *The International Journal of Psychoanalysis, 14*.

26. Clara Thompson. (1943). Penis envy. *Psychiatry, 6*.

27. Clara Thompson. (1950). Some effects of the derogatory attitude towards female sexuality. *Psychiatry, 13*.

28. Simone de Beauvoir. (1972). *The Second Sex*. New York: Penguin Books. (Original work published 1949)

29. Melanie Klein. (1975). *Envy and Gratitude and Other Works*. New York: Delacourte Press. (Original work published 1946–1964)

30. J. D'Emilio & E. B. Freedman. (1997). *Intimate Matters: A History of Sexuality in America*. Chicago: University of Chicago Press.

31. Ibid.

32. Reay Tannahill. (1992). *Sex in History*. London: Scarborough House Publishers.

33. Jennifer Baumgardner & Amy Richards. (2000). *Manifesta: Young Women, Feminism, and the Future*. New York: Farrar, Straus, and Giroux.

34. Ibid.

35. Ibid.

36. Ibid.

37. Ibid.

38. Elizabeth Wurtzel. (1998). *Bitch: In Praise of Difficult Women*. New York: Doubleday.

39. Jennifer Baumgardner & Amy Richards. (2000). *Manifesta: Young Women, Feminism, and the Future*. New York: Farrar, Straus, and Giroux.

## CHAPTER FOUR

1. Frank Pittman. (1989). *Private Lies: Infidelity and Betrayal of Intimacy*. New York: W.W. Norton.

2. Jessica Benjamin. (1998). *Bonds of Love: Psychoanalysis, Feminism, and the Problem of Domination*. New York: Pantheon Books.

3. Karen J. Maroda. (2004). A relational perspective on women and power. *Psychoanalytic Psychology, 21*(3), 428–435.

4. Jessica Benjamin. (1998). *Bonds of Love: Psychoanalysis, Feminism, and the Problem of Domination*. New York: Pantheon Books.

5. Ibid.

6. Stephen A. Mitchell. (2002). *Can Love Last? The Fate of Romance over Time*. New York: W.W. Norton.

7. Ibid.

8. D. C. Atkins, N. S. Jacobson, & D. H. Baucom. (2001). Understanding infidelity: Correlates in a national random sample. *Journal of Family Psychology, 15*, 735–749.

9. M. W. Weiderman & E. R. Algier. (1996). Expectations and attributions regarding extramarital sex among young married individuals. *Journal of Psychology and Human Sexuality, 8*, 21–23.

10. Muriel Dimen. (2003). *Sexuality, Intimacy, Power*. Hillside, NJ: Analytic Press.

11. Ibid.

12. Ibid.

## CHAPTER FIVE

1. Karen J. Maroda. (2004). A relational perspective on women and power. *Psychoanalytic Psychology, 21*(3), 428–435.

2. Ibid.

3. Ibid.

4. Ibid.

5. Jennifer Baumgardner & Amy Richards. (2000). *Manifesta: Young Women, Feminism, and the Future*. New York: Farrar, Straus, and Giroux.

6. Jody Messler Davies. (2003). Falling in love with love: Oedipal and postoedipal manifestations of idealization, mourning, and erotic masochism. *Psychoanalytic Dialogues, 13*(1), 11.

7. Stephen A. Mitchell. (2002). *Can Love Last? The Fate of Romance over Time*. New York: W.W. Norton.

8. Ibid.

## CHAPTER SIX

1. Toni Morrison. (1987). *Beloved*. New York: Knopf.

2. Jennifer Baumgardner & Amy Richards. (2000). *Manifesta: Young Women, Feminism, and the Future*. New York: Farrar, Straus, and Giroux.

3. Karen J. Maroda. (2004). A relational perspective on women and power. *Psychoanalytic Psychology, 21*(3), 428–435.

4. Reay Tannahill. (1992). *Sex in History*. London: Scarborough House Publishers.

5. Jennifer Baumgardner & Amy Richards. (2000). *Manifesta: Young Women, Feminism, and the Future*. New York: Farrar, Straus, and Giroux.

6. Ibid.

## CHAPTER SEVEN

1. Sheryl A. Kingsberg. (2002). The impact of aging on sexual function in women and their partners. *Archives of Sexual Behavior, 31*(5), 431–437.

2. Lois W. Banner. (1992). *In Full Flower: Aging Women, Power, and Sexuality*. New York: Knopf.

3. Ibid.

4. Sheryl A. Kingsberg. (2002). The impact of aging on sexual function in women and their partners. *Archives of Sexual Behavior, 31*(5), 431–437.

5. Lois W. Banner. (1992). *In Full Flower: Aging Women, Power, and Sexuality*. New York: Knopf.

6. Frances Cohen Praver. (2004). *Crossroads at Midlife: Your Aging Parents, Your Emotions, and Your Self*. Westport, CT: Praeger.

7. Ibid.

8. Lois W. Banner. (1992). *In Full Flower: Aging Women, Power, and Sexuality*. New York: Knopf.

9. Frances Cohen Praver. (2004). *Crossroads at Midlife: Your Aging Parents, Your Emotions, and Your Self*. Westport, CT: Praeger.

10. Ibid.

## CHAPTER EIGHT

1. James H. Bray. (2001). Therapy with stepfamilies: A developmental systems approach. In Susan H. McDanile, Don-David Lusterman, et al., eds., *Casebook for Integrating Family Therapy: An Ecosystemic Approach* (pp. 127–140). Washington, DC: American Psychological Association.

2. Bram P. Buunk & Wim Mutsaers. (1999). The nature of the relationship between remarried individuals and former spouses and its impact on marital satisfaction. *Journal of Family Psychology, 13*(2), 165–174.

3. John Bowlby. (1973a). *Attachment and Loss, Vol. 2: Separation: Anxiety and Anger*. New York: Basic Books.

4. John Bowlby. (1980). *Attachment and Loss, Vol. 3: Loss, Sadness and Depression*. New York: Basic Books.

5. Margaret S. Mahler, Fred Pine, & A. Bergman. (1975). *The Psychological Birth of the Human Infant*. New York: Basic Books.

6. J. Goldsmith. (1980). Relationship between former spouses: Descriptive findings. *Journal of Divorce, 14*, 1–19.

7. Bram P. Buunk & Wim Mutsaers. (1999). The nature of the relationship between remarried individuals and former spouses and its impact on marital satisfaction. *Journal of Family Psychology, 13*(2), 165–174.

## CHAPTER NINE

1. Tennessee Williams. (1947). *A Streetcar Named Desire.*
2. R. F. Baumeister. (2000). Gender differences in erotic plasticity: The female sex drive as socially flexible and responsive. *Psychological Bulletin, 126,* 347–374.
3. Lisa M. Diamond. (1998). Development of sexual orientation among adolescent and young adult women. *Developmental Psychology, 34*(5), 1085–1095.
4. Lisa M. Diamond. (2000). Sexual identity, attractions, and behavior among young sexual minority women over a 2-year period. *Developmental psychology, 36*(2), 241–250.
5. Lisa M. Diamond. (1998). Development of sexual orientation among adolescent and young adult women. *Developmental Psychology, 34*(5), 1085–1095.
6. R. F. Baumeister. (2000). Gender differences in erotic plasticity: The female sex drive as socially flexible and responsive. *Psychological Bulletin, 126,* 347–374.
7. Lisa M. Diamond. (1998). Development of sexual orientation among adolescent and young adult women. *Developmental Psychology, 34*(5), 1085–1095.
8. Lisa M. Diamond. (2003). Was it a phase? Young women's relinquishment of lesbian/bisexual identities over a 5-year period. *Journal of Personality and Social Psychology, 84*(2), 352–364.
9. Ibid.
10. Michelle C. Jacobo. (2001). Revolutions in psychoanalytic theory of lesbian development: Dora to dykes and back again. *Psychoanalytic Psychology, 18*(4), 667–683.
11. Diane Elise. (2000). Women and desire: Why women may not want to want. *Studies in Gender and Sexuality, 1*(2), 125–146.
12. Joan K. Dixon. (1984). The commencement of bisexual activity in swinging married women over age thirty. *Journal of Sex Research, 20*(1), 71–90.

## CHAPTER TEN

1. Joyce McDougall. (1995). *The Many Faces of Eros.* New York: W.W. Norton.
2. D. W. Winnicott. (1971). Mirror role of mother and family in child development. In *Playing and Reality.* London: Tavistock.
3. Joyce McDougall. (1995). *The Many Faces of Eros.* New York: W.W. Norton.
4. Ibid.
5. D. W. Winnicott. (1965). *The Maturational Processes and the Facilitating Environment.* New York: International Universities Press.
6. D. W. Winnicott. (1971). Mirror role of mother and family in child development. In *Playing and Reality.* London: Tavistock.
7. Carl Gustav Jung. (1992). *Psychology of the Unconscious.* Bollingen Foundation. (Original work published 1917)
8. Stephen A. Mitchell. (2002). *Can Love Last? The Fate of Romance over Time.* New York: W.W. Norton.
9. Jessica Benjamin. (1988). *Bonds of Love.* New York: Pantheon Books.
10. Emmanuel Ghent. (1990). Masochism, submission, surrender. *Contemporary Psychoanalysis, 26*(1).

11. Stephen A. Mitchell. (2002). *Can Love Last? The Fate of Romance over Time*. New York: W.W. Norton.

12. Braum Dijkstra. (1996). *Evil Sisters: The Threat of Female Sexuality and the Cult of Manhood*. New York: Knopf.

13. Reay Tannahill. (1992). *Sex in History*. London: Scarborough House Publishers.

14. Diane Elise. (2000). Women and desire: Why women may not want to want. *Studies in Gender and Sexuality, 1*(2), 125–146.

15. Emmanuel Ghent. (1990). Masochism, submission, surrender. *Contemporary Psychoanalysis, 26*(1).

16. Stephen A. Mitchell. (2002). *Can Love Last? The Fate of Romance over Time*. New York: W.W. Norton.

17. Ibid.

18. Emmanuel Ghent. (1990). Masochism, submission, surrender. *Contemporary Psychoanalysis, 26*(1).

19. D. W. Winnicott. (1965). Ego distortion in terms of true and false self (pp. 140–152). In *The Maturational Process and the Facilitating Environment*. Madison, CT: International Universities Press.

20. Jessica Benjamin. (1988). *Bonds of Love*. New York: Pantheon Books.

21. Ibid.

22. Reay Tannahill. *Sex in History*. London: Scarborough House Publishers.

23. Jessica Benjamin. (1988). *Bonds of Love*. New York: Pantheon Books.

24. Emmanuel Ghent. (1990). Masochism, submission, surrender. *Contemporary Psychoanalysis, 26*(1).

25. D. W. Winnicott. (1965). *The Maturational Process and the Facilitating Environment*. Madison, CT: International Universities Press.

26. Frances Praver. (1995). Validation of a child measure for post traumatic stress responses to interpersonal abuse (Doctoral dissertation, St. John's University).

## CHAPTER ELEVEN

1. D. C. Atkins, N. S. Jacobson, & D. H. Baucom. (2001). Understanding infidelity: Correlates in a national random sample. *Journal of Family Psychology, 15*, 735–749.

2. M. W. Weiderman & E. R. Algier. (1996). Expectations and attributions regarding extramarital sex among young married individuals. *Journal of Psychology and Human Sexuality, 8*, 21–23.

3. David Schwartz. (2004). Extreme normality: Preface and performance. *Psychoanalytic Dialogues, 14*(6), 835–858.

4. Cleonie White. (2004). Culture, influence, and the "I-ness" of me. *Psychoanalytic Dialogues, 14*(4), 653–691.

5. Muriel Dimen. (2003). *Sexuality, Intimacy, Power*. Hillside, NJ: Analytic Press.

6. Ibid.

7. Jessica Benjamin. (1988). *Bonds of Love*. New York: Pantheon Books.

# Index

## About the Author

FRANCES COHEN PRAVER is a clinical psychologist and psychoanalyst specializing in women's issues, couples therapy, and trauma. The author of *Crossroads at Midlife*, she has appeared on *Good Morning America* and *WNBC Weekend in New York*, and has been quoted in the *New York Times* regarding women's infidelity.